Astrological Timing of
CRITICAL ILLNESS

Early Warning Patterns in the Horoscope

This breakthrough text—its riveting focus upon early-warning patterns of critical illness in the horoscope—is essential for every astrologer…

Master astrologer Noel Tyl has found the way to appreciate the "accumulated developmental deficit" from birth throughout the aging process and to anticipate critical illness. Using the predisposition of the natal horoscope and then Solar Arcs and Transits to measure development, Tyl has defined a process of detection for a host of critical illnesses, including breast, prostate, and other cancers; heart disease; diabetes; and more—even suicide. When your clients heed your insights and warnings and seek medical consultation and treatment, astrology will have served humankind more powerfully than ever before. This early detection of potentially life-threatening disease can lead to better chances for survival, cure, or even prevention.

Tyl painstakingly researched more than seventy cases to test his patterning discoveries! Your analytical skill will be alerted, tested, and sharpened through these very same cases, which include notables such as Carl Sagan (bone cancer), Betty Ford (breast cancer), Larry King (heart attack), Norman Schwarzkopf (prostate cancer), and Mike Wallace (manic depression), and many, many others.

About the Author

Noel Tyl is one of the foremost astrologers in the world. His twenty textbooks have led the teaching of astrologers for two generations, he is counsel to individuals and corporations, and he is a busy lecturer throughout the United States and Europe.

He is a graduate of Harvard University in Social Relations (Psychology, Sociology, and Anthropology). He also founded and edited *Astrology Now* magazine.

Noel wrote *Prediction in Astrology* (Llewellyn Publications, 1991), a master volume of technique and practice with Solar Arcs, and edited Books 9 through 16 of the Llewellyn's New World Astrology Series: *How to Use Vocational Astrology, How to Personalize the Outer Planets, How to Manage the Astrology of Crisis, Exploring Consciousness in the Horoscope, Astrology's Special Measurements, Sexuality in the Horoscope, Communicating the Horoscope,* and *Astrology Looks at History.* In 1994, his master opus, *Synthesis and Counseling in Astrology—The Professional Manual* (almost 1,000 pages of analytical technique in practice), was published, and *Astrology of the Famed* appeared in 1996, followed in 1997 by *Predictions for a New Millennium.* Noel lives in the Phoenix, Arizona area.

To Write to the Author

If you wish to contact the author or would like more information about this book, please write to the author in care of Llewellyn Worldwide, and we will forward your request. Both the author and publisher appreciate hearing from you and learning of your enjoyment of this book and how it has helped you. Llewellyn Worldwide cannot guarantee that every letter written to the author can be answered, but all will be forwarded. Please write to:

Llewellyn Worldwide Ltd.
P.O. Box 64383, Dept. K738–2
St. Paul, MN 55164-0383, U.S.A.

Please enclose a self-addressed, stamped envelope for reply or $1.00 to cover costs. If outside the U.S.A., enclose international postal reply coupon.

Astrological Timing of
CRITICAL ILLNESS

Early Warning Patterns in the Horoscope

Noel Tyl

1998
Llewellyn Publications
St. Paul, Minnesota, 55165–0383

FIRST EDITION
First Printing, 1998

Cover design by Tom Grewe
Cover art by Boris Starosta, Charlottesville, VA
Editing and interior design by Connie Hill

Library of Congress Cataloging-in-Publication Data
Tyl, Noel, 1936–
    Astrological timing of critical illness : early warning patterns in the horoscope/ by Noel Tyl. — 1st ed.
        p.   cm. --
    Includes bibliographical references and index.
    ISBN 1–56718–738–2 (pbk.)
    1. Astrology and health.   I. Title.
BF1729.H9T85   1998   98-11787
133.5'861—dc21   CIP

Llewellyn Publications
A Division of Llewellyn Worldwide, Ltd.
P.O. Box 64383, Dept. 738-2
St. Paul, Minnesota 55164-0383, U.S.A.

Printed in the U.S.A.

That which can be foreseen
can be prevented.

—Dr. Charles H. Mayo

Recent Books by the Author

Prediction in Astrology (1991)

Synthesis and Counseling in Astrology—The Professional Manual (1994)

Astrology of the Famed (1996)

Predictions for a New Millennium (1997)

Llewellyn's New World Astrology Series, edited by the Author:

How to Use Vocational Astrology

How to Personalize the Outer Planets

How to Manage the Astrology of Crisis

Exploring Consciousness in the Horoscope

Astrology's Special Measurements

Sexuality in the Horoscope

Communicating the Horoscope

Astrology Looks at History

Contents

Horoscope Examples   xi
Preface   xiii
Foreword by Mitchell E. Gibson, Doctor of Psychiatry   xvii
Introduction by Jeffrey Wolf Green, Astrologer   xxi

1. **Astrological Symbolism
   and Our Vulnerabilities to Critical Illness**   1
   An Orientation to Body Weakness   8
   The Fire Family   16
   The Air Family   21
   The Water Family   39
   The Earth Family   50
       Skin Cancer—Melanoma   53
   Aspect Routings   58
   Dual Rulerships   60
       Synthesis Guidelines   61
       Simplifying Structures   62
   Aging   69

2. **Early Warning Patterns in the Horoscope**   75
   The Dark World of Cancer   75

       Solar Arc Review   79
       Prostate Cancer   81
       Testicular Cancer   101
       Colon Cancer   109
         Initial Review of Early Warning Patterning   115
       General Infections   116
       Stomach Cancer   123
       Bone Cancer   123
       Kidney Cancer   129
       Pancreatic Cancer   133
         The Dynamics of Early Warning   140
       Thyroid Cancer   142

Breast Cancer   145
    Solarscope Review   165
Sinus Cancer   167
    Final Review of Early Warning Patterning   170
Life and Sensibility Centers   171
    The Heart   171
    The Heart and Extended Illnesses   191
    The Brain: Stroke   200
    Suicide   223

3. Client Interaction: Making Creative Connections
    and Delivering the Message   245
Accumulated Developmental Deficit   245
    Creative Connections   254
The Search for Meaning   263
Communication of Warning   268
    Consultation Syntax   269
    Cursory Diagnostics   270
    Review of the Past   270
    Disclaimer   271
    Key phrases   273
        Inquiry about death   277
With Whom to Communicate.   279
    Ethical Concerns   285
Medicine and Astrology: How Close Are We?   288
A Post Script   292
    Working Together   292

Bibliography   293
Index   297

Horoscope Examples (Private Cases not listed)

Agnew, Spiro	48
Brynner, Yul	196, 198
Buchwald, Art	35
Crenna, Richard	143
Cunanan, Andrew Phillip	241, 242
Denning, Hazel	67
Dylan, Bob	177
Ford, Betty	147, 148
Garland, Judy	25, 234
Gauquelin, Michel	237
Green, Jeffrey	261
Hamilton, Scott	103
Helfgott, David	222
Hemingway, Ernest	231
Hepburn, Audrey	110, 112
Hitler, Adolph	239
Jacobs, Jayj	180
Kaps, Ed	87
Keith, Brian	235
King, Larry	182
Levant, Oscar	218
March, Marion	209, 211
Mastroianni, Marcello	135, 137, 138
McEvers, Joan	202
MiXXe, AdZe	105
Monroe, Marilyn	228
Negus, Joan	131
Roosevelt, Franklin D.	205, 207
Roosevelt, Theodore.	28
Rostenkowski, Daniel D.	96
Sagan, Carl	126
Schwarzenegger, Arnold	51
Schwarzkopf, Norman	76, 78, 83
Tyl, Noel	57
Wallace, Mike	37

Additionally: 34 horoscopes of private cases.

Data for all example horoscopes are drawn from personal records provided by private clients or from established archives (principally the Lois Rodden DataBank and *Internationales Horoskope Lexikon*. Freiburg, Germany). Any suspect data of celebrities was cleared with Lois Rodden. To the best of my ability, the data presented here is of highest accuracy, with the source-of-data established in practically every case. Where there are exceptions, discussion accompanies the text. For those horoscopes that are untimed, Solarscopes are used with accompanying explanations.

PREFACE

The preparation of this book has been demanding: I have had to focus deeply on suffering and fear; I have had to empathize with so many dimensions of critical illness, often going to bed at night feeling too close to the "symptoms of the day." Through it all, it has been difficult not to write a book on detailed diagnosis, not to write a book about healing. While I share with you a fascination with these areas of study, I am not qualified in either of these categories to write an authoritative text.

Over the years of my practice, teaching, and writing, the astrological specialties that have developed strongly in my work are in psychodynamic analysis and developmental timing. These are the focal points of this book. At the same time, this work is also a presentation of probability: it organizes what we do know in astrology about cursory diagnosis—identifying the potentials an individual has to develop specific critical illnesses—and then anchors securely the process of measurement that can predict challenges to the physical system and the possible onset of these illnesses.

This study begins simply and grows in astrological/measurement sophistication. There are some seventy horoscopes which will exercise observation and build authority in reading planetary networks and timing patterns. The work becomes technical but, I hope, never obscure and always practical. The objective is stated many times—to the point of redundancy—that, in the face of challenge to the life system, we lead the client to medical checkup and specialized attention. This early warning, so clearly possible through astrology, saves lives.

Special Sensitivities

As we begin this study, I feel that it is important to share with you my extreme sensitivity about this book's intense focus on cases of somatic and systemic break-down, covering most common critical illnesses, on the negative body state, specifically on the dark world of cancer. This sensitivity is born of my personal wish to believe that we are invincible by nature, that we can do anything we want to do—need to do—just by applying ourselves to that objective; and that we should live long enough to do it all! Of course, in my personal expression, this is the bravura of my Leo Moon and my Capricorn Sun-Jupiter conjunction in the 7th House: I do believe in a good, dramatic God, a beneficent creative principle, and I project onto others an urgent possessiveness of life time.

I have long known that my weakness as an astrologer is that I am too positive: I believe in all others and their abilities, their hopes and their development. On the other hand, my strength as an astrologer is that I see growth and insight possible through acknowledgment of our physical struggle to live; through study of how that struggle becomes more desperate with age; and through appreciation of how that struggle is deeply connected with developmental considerations throughout our life.

Appreciation

In my effort to bring this information to astrologers and others, I have not been alone. My wife Christa Tyl von Legat has seen many special things accomplished through astrology; some of those things have been miraculous and indeed have saved lives. It was she who urged me to share what I know in this field of cursory diagnostics and early warning timing; and it is she who receives my deepest appreciation for the motivation and the support to write this study, and for her many thoughts of highest quality that touch the pages that follow.

How very much I appreciate the time and attention the extraordinary Dr. Ingrid Naiman, medical astrologer and lady of wisdom, has given to my many explorative questions and discussions.

I welcome Dr. Mitchell Gibson, Psychiatrist, openly into the world of astrology. His skills now open the door even further between our professions.

There were the many uplifting calls and discussions with my longtime friend and colleague Marion March; how I appreciate her having known about this book from its very beginning and never flagging in her enthusiasm for my work during its development.

And, Lois Rodden, who has never shown anything but support of accuracy and discovery, whose mistressry of data is graced by gentle spirit and warm friendship.

There is Ed Kaps, member of the Board of Directors of the American Foundation for Urologic Disease, who himself was one of the earliest tests and confirmations of the timing patterns (see page 87): my appreciation for his encouragement and liaison with prostate cancer support groups. There is Elsa Rector for her similar help with breast cancer research and Phoenix-area support group participation. And of course, the many private cases who gave permission for their life trauma to be presented here to help us all learn.

There are astrologers Karen Helouin and Basil Fearrington, long-time student and now professional colleague, both of whom, privy to my early findings, watched them grow and shared with me the excitement of the creative process.

There are the doctors who listened and cared as much as they could; the support groups who listened and understood more than they thought they would; the clients who heard, understood, and won. I thank them all for working with me and letting me work for them.

There are my students, those extraordinarily talented "new" professionals emerging from my rigorous Correspondence Course for Certification: their work supplied many hundreds of observations and field tests of the material presented in this study. Among those professionals, I must acknowledge especially the superb work accomplished by Barbara Banfield, Beat Scheiwiller, and Susan Vicha, all with ties to the field of medical research.

And finally, there are my living astrological colleagues who are included in these pages under not-the-best of circumstances: Jeffrey Green, Jayj Jacobs, Marion March, Joan McEvers (and Joan Negus). It is collegial rapport and mutual respect indeed that these astrologers have allowed their case of critical illness to be presented in this study and that not one of them asked to see beforehand what I would have to say. I have taken that trust and responsibility most seriously, and I thank them deeply.

—Noel Tyl
Fountain Hills, Arizona
September 1997

FOREWORD

Astrology is one of the oldest sciences known to mankind and for millennia was closely linked to the medical arts. Dozens of great scientists and scholars from antiquity such as Galen, Aristotle, Nostradamus, Bacon, and Paracelsus studied and practiced astrology. Paracelsus is credited with writing that: "any doctor (medical) without a thorough knowledge of astrology is a pseudo-medicus (sham doctor)!" Today, Western scientists have had little or no real exposure to the vast and mostly unexplored vistas of using astrological data in the diagnosis and treatment of mental and physical illness.

An exception is Carl Jung, one of the most prominent scientists of the twentieth century. Jung was a medical doctor who routinely ran astrological charts on his patients in order to gain better insight to the inner nature of their problems. These insights added to a revolution in medicine at that time, and enhanced greatly our understanding of human archetypes and how they influence health and disease.

Astrologers have made a number of attempts to integrate astrological principles into medical practice. Unfortunately, the great majority of this work has gone unheralded because of the lack of recognition or sufficient data necessary to form a coherent theory of astromedicine. This sad state of affairs is about to change.

Noel Tyl is known world-wide as one of the greatest analytic astrologers of modern times. His more than two dozen volumes of astrological research have become classics in their genre. In this newest book, *Astrological Timing of Critical Illness,* Tyl outlines a brilliant new direction for establishing useful and verifiable astrological signatures for the prediction and timing of potentially serious illnesses.

Tyl has streamlined and sharpened traditional rulership theory and presents the discovery that, inherent within the natal charts of each individual, there are *latent potentials* that are reflected by the astrological positions of the planets. In relation to the presence or absence of disease, these potentials form what he calls an "accumulated developmental deficit." Each planetary aspect that he has discovered to be related to a specific disease state has a latent propensity toward triggering illnesses when given sufficient impetus from the native's life circumstances. In other words, given enough stress over a period of time, certain planetary aspects tend to trigger specific diseases. Ironically, Noel's research echoes the most modern thinking in molecular genetics: that much of the physical manifestation of illness can be linked to a specific defect within a gene or gene complex.

Careful documentation of specific diagnoses and pathological conditions is a crucial requirement of any research protocol aiming to link planetary aspects to physical or mental illness. In this work, Noel has painstakingly researched for diagnostic accuracy more than 70 cases. This all-important aspect of the work has been only sporadically present in many astrology research efforts to date, and its presence adds a significant degree of credibility to this work.

In case after case, Noel delineates very carefully elucidated predictions concerning a host of diseases which seemingly defy all traditional medical thinking. He has been astonishingly accurate in an unbelievable number of cases; a fact that has captured the attention of a number of medical professionals. Noel shows that astrology is able to foresee serious illnesses. Through his deductions in the cases of such famous personalities as Ernest Hemingway, Carl Sagan, Norman Schwarzkopf, Audrey Hepburn, Marilyn Monroe, and Mike Wallace, he provides instructive guidelines to *anticipate in time* the onslaught of critical illness.

Does this principle hold true only for planetary aspects which pertain to physical illness or can it be extrapolated to the emotional realm as well? In my own work as a psychiatrist, I have often wondered if there were validity to the notion that some clients were destined to suffer from chronic illness while others were predetermined to be more fortunate in their recovery process. This led me to erect birth charts on nearly 2000 clients with a medley of divergent psychiatric clinical diagnoses. To my amazement, I began to see specific and unique patterns of planetary activity which were related to each diagnosis. Most of the patterns were discernible only by examining planetary positions in terms of graphical representations of right ascension and declination. I noticed that patients who suffered from chronic severe depression tended to have a Saturn/ Pluto parallel at a rate much higher than the control group. Attention deficit disorder patients tended to have a higher number of planetary eclipses and a several-fold increase in the very rare binary planetary eclipses when compared to the control group. [A planetary eclipse occurs when two planets are in conjunction and parallel to each other at the same time. A binary eclipse occurs when three planets are in conjunction and parallel to each other at the same time.] I noticed similar signature changes in the birth charts for clients who were diagnosed with chronic alcoholism and drug abuse, anxiety disorders, and schizophrenia.

My working relationship with Noel Tyl began shortly after I submitted my own research proposal to Llewellyn Publications. Publisher Carl Llewellyn Weschke quickly recognized the amazing consonance between Noel's research and mine. Working completely independently of each other, we had both come to similar research conclusions regarding a connection between certain birth aspects and human illness. We were both finishing the work at about the same time. Even more amazingly, we lived only sixteen miles apart. Carl Jung would have greatly appreciated the synchronicity.

It is appropriate that Noel Tyl, who has been called the "Dean of American Astrologers," should be the first to publish a major research title designed to bridge the gap between Western medicine and psychiatry. After reading this book, I am convinced that astrologers and medical doctors alike will never look at human illness in the same way again.

—Mitchell E. Gibson MD

Diplomate: American College of Forensic Examiners
Diplomate: American Board of Psychiatry and Neurology
Diplomate: American Board of Forensic Medicine

INTRODUCTION

I t is my distinct privilege to introduce *Astrological Timing of Critical Illness* by Noel Tyl. This book could not have been written at a better time in our human history: an accelerated nature of mutation is now occurring within the forms of life we call viruses, bacteria, and parasites. This is combined with deep levels of stress in the human condition, which occur for many reasons, stress that itself can trigger disease and illness, and arouse areas within the body that may possess genetic liabilities.

The fundamental premise of Noel Tyl's book is that properly educated and knowledgeable astrologers can play a vital, life-significant role in their relationship with other human beings: we are able to forewarn our clients of the possibility that a critical illness, disease, or problem *may manifest at specific points in time.* In so forewarning, we can guide the client to the relevant medical services before a cataclysmic physical situation occurs.

Within this premise, Tyl writes in very passionate terms about the necessity for astrologers not only to learn relevant astrological correlations with anatomy and physiology but to develop as well a unified language for those astrological correlations. One of the inherent weaknesses in the discipline of our astrology is that these astrological correlations with human phenomena are not consistent. This inconsistency also applies to anatomical and physiological correlations. Tyl argues that, until there is a unified langauge of astrological correlations, we at best have some astrologers who really know their stuff and provide valuable assistance to their clients, and, at worst, we have some astrologers who are primarily doing guesswork, leading to a fundamental disservice to their clients.

Within this frame, Tyl provides a succinct historical overview of the different astrological/medical correlations and how we can understand the affinities and differences. Essentially, Tyl states that the differences in the various correlations are not necessarily wrong; if we adjust our glasses to embrace a new perspective, we can see the interactions of various factors *that create sympathetic reactions from other factors*. It is this sympathetic reaction of various factors interacting with other factors that is the basis of the different astrological correlations, according to Tyl.

In this book, Tyl demonstrates his innate brilliance by showing us, suggesting to us, how to understand these interactive factors so that an accurate understanding of what is happening within one's physical body can occur. By appreciating these interactions, an accurate understanding of the genetic blueprint that all of us bring into life can occur: *the natal imprint of who we are*. It is vital for the astrologer to understand this natal imprint so that, as we move through life, we can understand *at what points in time* specific physical conditions, illness, disease, or any of many potential physical problems implicated in the natal imprint may manifest.

Tyl provides case history after case history in order to illustrate his ideas. The greatest strength of this book is Noel's ability to provide remarkably accurate astrological techniques that serve as timing devices, or warning signals, for the potential onslaught of critical illness. One of his strengths as an astrologer is Noel's renowned ability to predict events in the future; individually and collectively. This, of course, involves the use of various transits and progressions. More importantly, this involves a deep understanding of the various types of aspects to natal points within the horoscope. The understanding of the interactions of the various aspects occurring through transit and progression is perhaps Tyl's greatest ability. It is this ability of his to synthesize tremendous amounts of information leading to "the bottom line" or cause for any given event or manifestation that will reward you, the reader, tremendously.

When you read and absorb the vital information and knowledge in this book you will not only be doing yourself a service, but, as a practicing astrologer, you will be able in turn to bring a great gift to your clients, perhaps the greatest gift of all: health, and the *protection* of that health.

—Jeffrey Wolf Green
Boulder, Colorado

1.

ASTROLOGICAL SYMBOLISM AND OUR VULNERABILITIES TO CRITICAL ILLNESS

I n the beginning, when learning astrology, the student is presented with lists of meanings: sharply defined descriptive labels of what the Signs of the Zodiac stand for and what the planets represent. These meanings carry with them an aura of great authority, a sense of completeness—after all, these data come down to us tried and tested from times long, long ago!

We confront the fact that astrology *knows,* and, if we can learn astrology, we can know too. In those beginning stages, none of us thinks that there is any updating to do: we learn that the fixed star Algol has to do with decapitation and surely still does, but little time is spent with how, in modern times, we might lose our head in other ways, or what the symbolism could mean beyond the literal.

These meanings are most specific when we learn how the signs and the planets "control" specific parts of our body, head to toe. We see the grim engravings from the fifteenth century, flaps of skin pulled from a body to show the heart, with the Leo label and the Sun's rulership thereof, with Virgo signs swimming along the intestines, even specific references to less prominent inner organs like the spleen, giving rulership in some drawings to Saturn. Those organs *belong* to us; "the planets are within" as Paracelsus taught. Indeed, we sense a vitally important registration of astrology and, as well, we sense an unalterable state of affairs.[1]

Such meanings have always been essential to our sense of security, our need to know who we are and why we exist; our mind needs labels. Since disease is older than humankind, the earliest people had a lot of explaining to do when they began to be aware of themselves. In the beginning, the belief that emerged was that disease came not from natural causes but from *super*natural ones; that it arose from the action of unfriendly spirits, from demons. A counter-force of magic had to be created and directed *against* those supernatural forces. The lineage of the shaman and, later, in the flowering of Egyptian culture, the priest—those who ministered against illness—evolved.

The Greeks in the fifth century B.C.E. perhaps signal the turning point in the formal regard for and management of disease: disease was pursued not in the spirit world but in nature, in the workings of the body, in the earthly surroundings of men and women. It is very important that we appreciate in that time the work of Hippocrates (c. 460–c. 377 B.C.E.[2]): he was a great observer, experimenter, writer, and teacher of medicine, whose ethics and outlines of practice live today in the Hippocratic Oath taken by our doctors.

Hippocrates was the first healer to record symptoms and accumulate facts. He examined the sick carefully and recorded what he saw without any spiritual theorization. He was using principles of science in the study of disease. He developed aphorisms like, "Consumption comes on mostly from eighteen to thirty-five years of age; apoplexy (loss of consciousness from an arterial disturbance in the brain) is commonest between the ages of forty and sixty. Weariness without cause indicates disease."[3]

While Hippocrates signaled an era of realism, the Greek surmise about diseases was not yet completely correct: Aristotle thought that nerves and tendons were the same; that arteries held air instead of blood (in Greek, the

---

1 Paracelsus (Theophrastus Bombastus von Hohenheim) lived from 1493 to 1541 and is regarded broadly as one of the very greatest physicians, occultists, and alchemists of all time. From his native Switzerland, Paracelsus wandered over a great deal of Europe so that he could come to a direct personal knowledge of all things; he channeled the arts of alchemy toward the preparation of medical remedies. He adopted the name "Paracelsus" to boast of his superior position with regard to the medical lore inherited from the Greeks and Romans, specifically the work of Celsus in the first century. The formal name of Theophrastus was given to him by his father, after the first botanist, who had been a pupil of Aristotle.

2 B.C.E.: Before the Common Era.

3 Reported in Haggard, Chapter 6.

word "artery" means a passage for air); that mucous running from the nose issued from the brain. With the fall of Greece from its world power position, the earliest steps taken toward anatomical knowledge were inexplicably brought to an end in their development, to be lost for some 1,800 years.

Alexander the Great took the Greek medicine throughout the known world (c. 336–323 B.C.E.), and, in each of the far-reaching lands of his conquests, this knowledge took on the vestigial superstitions and native observations of the indigenous people: the realities of disease took on labels and explanations through reference to the planets, to colors, and to numbers. The Romans viewed medicine still in terms of religion, defining a god or goddess for nearly every symptom of disease. Through religion, occult explorations, and philosophical Arabian influence, *astrological explanation* gradually gave European medicine a new orientation.

The bridge from Hippocrates through Roman times and into European Medieval and Renaissance culture was provided by a Greek physician at the court of Roman Emperor Marcus Aurelius. The physician's name was Galen (c. 130–c. 200 C.E.), meaning "peaceful one." He was trained as a philosopher before turning to medicine and—as Paracelsus was to do 1,200 years later—he traveled widely for many years to study the human condition first hand. He studied anatomy, in the main from dissection of hogs and apes, to learn the arrangement of the internal organs. He won great acclaim for how well he treated the severe wounds incurred by gladiators. He earned his position in the Emperor's court through an impressive record of diagnostic and surgical success and his healing of prominent citizens and officials.

Galen's influence through his books was so powerful that, some 1,300 years later, when the Flemish biologist Andreas Vesalius (1514–1564), then and now regarded as the "father of anatomy," wrote the first true anatomy of the human body revealing organs never before located, Vesalius was initially discredited because things he had discovered were different from what Galen had found. When William Harvey, physician to King Charles II of England, discovered how blood circulated in the body, it was said that he was wrong because Galen had found it otherwise![4]

Galen was the first to demonstrate facts. He would cut the spinal cord in animals to show that paralysis of the legs was due to nerve injury in the back. Galen showed that the heart pumps *blood* and that the lungs draw

---

4 Haggard, Chapter 8.

in air when we breathe. Galen was the first great experimenter; he developed a diagnostic methodology.

From Arabia, a tremendously influential body of knowledge flowed into central Europe—and astrology was a preponderant current in that flow. Arabian chemists discovered such important substances as alcohol, sulfuric and nitric acids, silver nitrate, and bichloride of mercury, and this chemistry was founded on a philosophy that was astrological. There was a belief in an elixir of life which could bestow perpetual youth and cure all disease. Alchemical study flourished; dissolving gold (the Sun) so that it could be eaten or drunk would restore life.

Our astrological system of meanings with regard to the physical body issues from that Arabian-European influence.

With all this burgeoning awareness, thinkers of the seventeenth century were yet hard pressed to explain a new realm of human study: the *mental* makeup of men and women. While the early researchers were coming to grips with anatomy and nature's causal relationship with dysfunction, they were thrown back to primal instincts when they were confronted, for example, with insanity. An aberrant mental state remained the domain of evil demons, of spirits working against the religion. It took a long time for disease to be seen as invading our thoughts as well as our body. It was entirely reasonable, then, that the Moon became the label for the brain; in that lunar symbolism we could see the fleeting changeability of thoughts, the watery gushiness of the brain itself, the fearsome symbolic occurrence of eclipse equated with the attack of "lunacy."

As we focus in on the development of our specific European legacy as astrologers, we must acknowledge the parallel evolvement of the study of illness that occurred in the Far East, in China.

In the thirteenth century, China was by far the most advanced, wealthy, innovative, and powerful country in the world. The Kublai Khan (grandson of Ghengis Kahn) was the "overlord of mankind." China ruled the seas and had captured the bulk of the sea trade from the Arabs, warring in the Indian Ocean. The military outreach was some 6,000 miles westward to the Danube, to victories throughout Hungary and Poland.

All males of the Chinese society were somehow employed with civil service. The support of the Emperor was total. And, in medicine, as with Galen healing the wounds of gladiatorial battles, Chinese physicians had learned throughout a thousand years of battles how arrow wound punctures created reactions elsewhere in the body, i.e., about nerve conduits carrying the Chi (the flow of life) throughout the body.

The most important medical text vital then, and even to this day, came out of China's antiquity: the *Huang Ti Nei Ching* (called "the Yellow Emperor's Classic on Internal Medicine").[5] Legend dates this Emperor and the book to 2629–2598 B.C.E. but, in historical reality, the dating is perhaps 479-300 B.C.E., almost exactly contemporary with the Hippocratic Collection of volumes. The book is written in the form of a conversation between the Emperor Huang Ti and his prime minister. Maladies are discussed on a physiophilosophical level. The dominant form of treatment—to return a patient back to *Tao* ("The Way")—was/is acupuncture.

This Chinese study of such long and pervasive influence is based upon the yin-yang concept of opposites, on the five elements (Metal, Water, Wood, Fire, Earth), and on a maze of correlations that typically identifies ancient Chinese philosophy. For example, there are thirty-two ways listed to measure the pulse, from "sharp as a hook" to "like water dripping through the roof" or "like a sword lying flat ready to be used." It is startling to see in the following short excerpt the ancient presence of what we today call holistic thinking; it is in great part the way of our study as we study the observations of life development and body breakdown going hand in hand throughout the aging process. The Emperor speaks:

> "When the spirit is hurt, severe pains ensue; when the body is hurt, there will be swellings. Thus, in those cases where severe pains are felt first and the swellings appear later, one can say that the spirit has injured the body. And in those cases where swellings appear first and severe pains are felt later, one can say that the body has injured the spirit."
>
> Ch'i Po answered: "The utmost in the art of healing can be achieved when there is unity."
>
> The Emperor answered: "When the minds of the people are closed and wisdom is locked out they remain tied to disease. Yet their feelings and desires should be investigated and made known, their wishes and ideas should be followed; and then it becomes apparent that those who have attained spirit and energy are flourishing and prosperous, while those perish who lose their spirit and energy."
>
> Life itself is the beginning of illness.[6]

---

5 "Yellow" here has nothing to do with skin color. The color yellow stood for "centrality" (like the sun; the gold of the alchemist), and thus "majesty." (Think of the "Yellow" River, Hwang Ho, flowing 2,903 miles in Northern China.) The royal reference here is to the Emperor-author Huang Ti.

6 Majno, pp. 240–244.

It is with the beginning of life that *astrology* itself lives. As life develops—not just for the individual, but for generations, for epochs—astrology must develop as well. Our Sign and Planet and House labels that define what we know about illness are hard pressed to assimilate the anatomy we know now in greatest detail, the chemistry we know to the miracle levels of genes, the psychology we know from a century of introspection, experimentation, and discovery.

For example, we say that the Moon rules the breasts and the stomach, the gestation period, and one of the eyes, physically; the Sensorium—a catch-all reference perhaps for the soul, surely a leftover from the time past when the Moon ruled the brain—and the reigning need of the personality, psychologically; Riboflavin (vitamin B_2), Potassium...and more. The more subtle (less physical) we get in our labeling references, the less sure we are of how we should use that information—since few of us are medical doctors—and the more we contradict ourselves in our studies. Magnesium is given rulership by the Sun in some studies, by the Moon in others; Calcium is given rulership by Saturn (because of earth minerals and bones) or by the Moon (perhaps because of the association with milk, the breasts, etc.)—and how does astrology show the cooperation of Magnesium and Calcium, so vital for good physical chemistry?

And then there are the problems of astrology keeping pace *with its own development:* Dr. H. L. Cornell completed his epic research effort, *The Encyclopaedia of Medical Astrology,* just as Pluto was discovered. He gave rulership of the bowels and the alimentary canal, now given to Pluto, to the Moon.[7]

Additionally—in practically all compendia of rulerships—we have, for example, the problems of the prostate gland being ruled by the sign Scorpio (Cornell) and the spine being ruled by "the Sun, Neptune, and Leo" (a mixture of planets and a sign); the thyroid gland ruled by Mercury *and* by Taurus and Scorpio. But we actually see in our work, often enough to be startling, that a difficult placement of *Venus* corresponds to a problematic thyroid; and then a challenged Venus in Libra *can* register also as the lower back; and the *planet* Pluto certainly does rule the prostate gland, doesn't it?

---

7 The first edition of Cornell's work was published in 1933, just three years after Pluto was discovered. He wrote on page 653: "This planet will not be considered...as very little is known of it, and at present is considered by many Authorities to be a hypothetical planet. It is also doubted by some Writers as being a part of our Solar system..."

We have the concerns of natal *aspects* to or from the significator, projection of the significator by Progression or Arc; we have other planetary projections to the significator in its natal position, and the transit of the significator into new aspects, or transits to the significator made by other significators—all of which adjusts the initial meaning-symbolisms significantly.

To get all of this within our grasp, theorists continue to expound on the Moon, the Sun, and all the planets—and now, the hypothetical Uranian projections and mid-point synthesis pictures are included—somehow to capture everything, to justify and extend the authoritative presentations made in our earliest texts, to prove that the planets above *are* within us here below.

So often indeed, astrology *is* remarkably accurate with symbolisms applied to the issue of illness, as we shall see. This relevant accuracy is best appreciated in terms of a large-picture approach to intrinsic weaknesses in the body that can manifest as specific ailments. But the process of diagnosis quickly becomes dauntingly bewildering, still awkwardly out of our grasp. Medical diagnosis in astrology is at a level of development lower than the state-of-the-art levels reached in other branches of astrology, such as psychological delineation.

There are a gifted few, the doctor astrologers, who *can* grasp the interrelations between archetypal symbolism and sophisticated diagnosis to a more advanced degree. While their work continuously brings us closer to the reliability we long for, these medical astrologers themselves are still learning how archetypal symbolism and clusters of synthesis define illness presented in the horoscope (now working with illnesses never heard of just one generation ago). Medical diagnosis is still astrology's prime frontier. It is exciting to look forward someday to the tie that will almost surely be made between the nuances of astrology's harmonic measurements and genetics.

Now though, as we approach the central focus of this book, it is important for me to state that I am *not* a medical astrologer. While we will soon review a good deal of diagnostic information—which all astrologers must know and *can* learn without specialized education—this book is not a book about diagnosis or healing. Astrologers are urged to pursue Medical Astrology further with experts like Dr. Ingrid Naiman in Santa Fe, New Mexico, whose work is perhaps at the very forefront of

in this field and is shared through her Course of
oks; like Eileen Nauman of Cottonwood, Arizona,
er twenty-five years, with a highly developed nutri-
hor and originator of a "Med-Scan Technique" to
rabilities.

ges, we need to look again at the information that
helpfully in making cursory diagnosis of illness and
issuing *medical referral* to our clients; we will review the information that
has a high correlation with successful insight. And this will rest on the
specific research focus of this study: *astrology's extraordinary strength
of timing.*

As astrology seizes the birth moment, it intercepts illness from the time
before birth (including inherited disposition) and then witnesses growth
through the present that expands with the onslaught of time ahead, as
the life system works for fulfillment. This book focuses on the astrological
timing of critical illness, the early warning patterns found in the horoscope, about which we may now say there is high reliability.

An Orientation to Body Weakness

Our holistic premise about what causes illness is that illness reflects an
imbalance, a frustration of relationships with things outside the self and/
or parts of the internal system, an imbalance that has become overly tense.
When need tensions (chemical, nutritional, environmental, temperamental,
psychological, inherited) are unresolved, unfulfilled for too long, the
tension backs up within the body, defenses are overpowered, and
dysfunction occurs. Just as we see needs through the symbolizations of
the planets and developmental tension through aspect structures, we can
begin to suspect/detect *where* in the body individuals are particularly
vulnerable for the backup of tension and the breakdown of function.

It is important to appreciate the pervasiveness of life-awareness
(consciousness) within our body and its systems. Psychological disposition, for example, is not confined to one planetary symbol or to one set
of behavioral activities; it is distributed throughout the horoscope,
throughout the behaviors that create the persona.

For example, in Freudian terms each planetary symbol will have *id* content, *super ego* function, and *ego* manifestation:[8] Mercury in its sign—how we need to think in order to be efficient—will have instinctual content, socially refining filters, and characteristic manifestation; Venus in its sign—how we need to relate for optimum comfort—will have its primal content, its censorship adjustments, and its characteristic expression. Similarly, Mars defines the need to apply energy a specific way; Jupiter defines individual reward needs; Saturn, the internalization of necessary controls; Uranus, the intensification thrusts for individuation; Neptune, the illusive capacities of visualization; and Pluto, the focus of self-empowerment.

All of these concerns use a particular kind of Sun energy and all our behaviors work together to one degree of integration or another to fulfill the development-propelling, reigning need of the personality, symbolized by the Moon.[9]

Similarly, the study of vulnerability, debilitation, dysfunction, disease is not confined to the 12th House–6th House axis of the horoscope. It extends to *any* aspect of developmental tension, i.e., any planets in square, opposition, or conjunction; considering as well the semisquare and the sesquiquadrate, and, most importantly, *the quindecile*. [The quindecile (Latin for 15, i.e., aspects in 15-degree intervals, specifically in my work *the 165-degree aspect*) is seen easily as 15 degrees beyond quincunx or 15 degrees short of opposition. My research in over 400 cases has repeatedly shown the dramatic importance of the QD as *disruption, separation, upheaval, obsession*. To preserve the passion so often manifested with the QD, I arbitrarily use the Italian pronunciation, *quin-deh-chee'-lay*.][10]

Astrology knows that the predominantly focused, developmentally tense planetary placements in any individual's horoscope *refer to the parts of the body that weaken most easily under attack, duress, let down, frustration.*

---

8 Freud postulated three personality components: the id (Latin for "it"), the primitive core in every person, the domain of basic drives that seek immediate gratification, predominantly sexual in orientation; the superego (Latin for "above the I" or "Higher I,") the restraint and cautions developed in the personality through identification with the parents, the conscience, community laws; and the ego (Latin for "I"), that which emerges in development to handle transactions with the environment, locating situations to fulfill needs, specifically id-orientated needs (the Sun-Moon blend and the need structures of the planets as behavioral symbols).

9 The alliance of psychological need theory and astrological symbolism pervades all my work and is systematically developed in Tyl, *Synthesis & Counseling in Astrology—The Professional Manual*. Specific references as they apply to health matters are presented there on pages 246–268.

10 Full development of the quindecile is presented in Tyl, "Minor Measurements, Major Meanings," published in the December–January 1997–98 issue of *The Mountain Astrologer*. See also, Tyl, *Astrology of the Famed*, the Leonardo da Vinci section.

The accuracy of this reference seems to increase when the aspect configurations under analysis do indeed relate to the 12–6 axis, classically assigned to health/illness matters.

To this point in this text, our understanding is tidily organized. But in our application of this understanding, there is confusion ahead, as we have already suggested: we do not yet know if it is a Sign, Planet, Aspect, or House, singly or together that define an organ, a function, an indisposition, a threat. While astrology does have areas of study well developed with conspicuous sureness, there still is vagary, especially on the medical frontier.

For example: some medical theory suggests that Leo rules just one organ, the heart. Other theorists like Cornell—whose work was monumental in its time, and clearly as painstaking, informed, and accurate as he could accomplish almost seventy years ago—gives rulership by Leo to the heart *and* the spine, and adds some sixty lines of listings of *other* considerations. Then, with the rulership listings for Libra we also find references to the "back," specifically the lower back, *along with* the kidneys and much more, of course.

We find references to the 5th House for the heart and the spine, for athleticism and children, and so much more!

Then, we see the astrological construct for heart-difficulty extended *to all the fixed signs;* this is a "law of sympathy or reflex action" inherited with no little validity from times past. We read references to Mars "afflictions" to the Sun, that aspects of high developmental tension are concomitant measurements of heart disorder; then, we learn that *the strong Mars-Sun relationship gives vitality, a rallying force under an attack to the system;* then we know that Mars, especially square the Sun (or Moon), suggests surgery, and on and on. We face a grand swirl of knowledge seeking order. It is bewildering.

Horoscope 1, Female

Look at horoscope 1 on page 12: this thirty-five-year old woman has a powerful opposition aspect between Saturn retrograde in the 11th and the Sun in Leo in the 5th, and that axis is squared by Neptune. We can see very easily that the Sun rules the 6th, *which alerts us conspicuously to analyze the Sun-Saturn opposition (squared by Neptune) in terms of potential illness, debilitation.* Additionally, Neptune, squaring the Sun-Saturn axis, rules Pisces in the 12th; Uranus, ruler of the 12th, is unaspected (ptolemaically) and threatens to "run away with the horoscope."[11]

We see Mars, ruler of her Ascendant, square her Moon in the 6th. This is a strong energy reinforcement of her (personality's) reigning need to express her Leonine life energy (a born leader) in terms of being correct, exact, insightful, and discriminating...with a cautious deliberation, detailed preparation, knowing that the small ways can lead to the grand. As well, since the Moon rules the 4th, one arm of the parental axis, we can expect upheaval in the early home, an echo of the Saturn-retrograde phenomenon, ruling the 10th, the other arm of the parental axis.[12]

While the horoscope suggests dramatically that there are difficulties in development and that there are great power reserves to put the self forward, we are indeed *alerted to specifics of potential physical breakdown.*

This young woman did grow up in a broken but not unhappy or underprivileged home. She did well at college and, during those years, became a superb athlete. As an adult, she is an image of physical strength...but in the past few years she has begun to move obviously gingerly; her large frame is putting on weight since exercise is out of the question.

Has her heart broken down (Leo, the Sun, 5th House)? Did all the athleticism, from early swimming championships to career-closing power-lifting, extract its toll? Or has a congenitally promised breakdown occurred in her spine (Saturn for bone, Sun for spine, 5th House)? Will either condition or both be exacerbated by the transit of Uranus in Aquarius conjoining Saturn and opposing the Sun throughout 1998?

These are questions that I feel are in the purview of the non-specialist, practicing astrologer. We must know these more-often-than-not reliable frameworks of diagnosis within the confusion of all we don't know. These astrological observations are the guidelines to the questions we may ask of the client: "I am not a medical doctor, but sometimes the horoscope speaks helpfully about the weak parts of the body, especially when it is under stress, emotional, vocational, etc. Has there ever been detected by

---

11 I call Uranus, in its unaspected condition, "peregrine" (see Tyl, *Synthesis & Counseling in Astrology,* pages 155–190) and anticipate the peregrine planet to dominate the persona; in this case, an intense development of individuality and a constant declaration of that development. This lady is an executive of *computer* support services for an airline.

12 Throughout this book, when I present characterological images in analysis, they are drawn from the 144 Sun-Moon polarities and other insight discussions developed in Tyl, *Synthesis & Counseling in Astrology.*

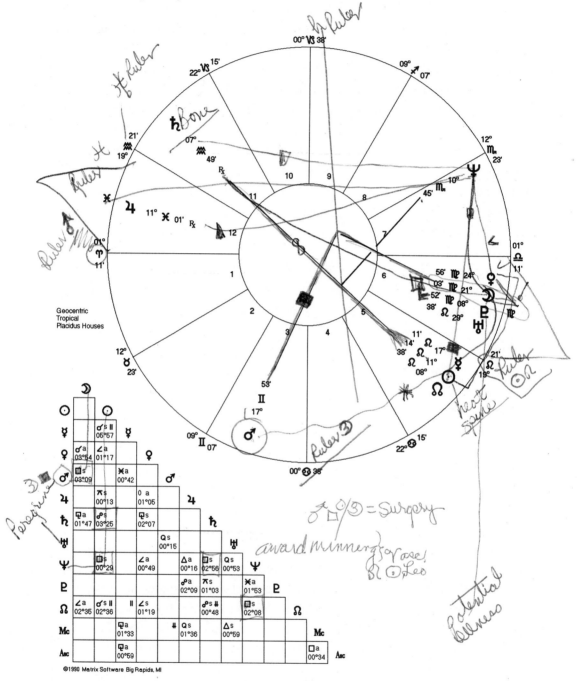

Geocentric
Tropical
Placidus Houses

©1990 Matrix Software Big Rapids, MI

Horoscope 1, Female

stethoscope or electrocardiogram a congenital heart anomaly? Is there back pain, pain in your spine?"[13]

This woman *has* developed the condition of a severely pained spine, which will someday too soon require, according to her doctors, a "total fusion." There is nothing wrong with her heart at this time in her life (mid-thirties); there seems to be no cause for alarm beyond the normal signals of diminished exercise, diet concerns (Moon in *Virgo* squared by Mars), etc., in that she does not smoke or drink. Her back problem will probably intensify and perhaps intrude further on her work situation in March, August, and December 1998.

Now, what if you and this lady were in consultation *fifteen years ago?* You would have seen a slender, powerful, streamlined, vital athlete entering the business world: "What are your plans, now, with all the competitive athletic regimen behind you?" If she suggested that she would go into power weight-lifting, think how important it would have been for you to say, "But, one moment please, there is every indication here in the horoscope that the spine is weak (perhaps congenitally); it might not respond well to the stress of weight training to such an extent. Is there some other way for you to make an award-winning individual statement [Leo Sun with an Aries Ascendant and Uranus peregrine[14]] as you already have done with swimming?"

This is the beginning of the main thrust of this book: how astrologers can use the knowledge of our craft to warn about bodily weakness and critical illness. We shall see that, while the symbolisms can be confusing for diagnosis, the timing of the onset of physical anxiety usually is not.

Indeed, there is more to this case than we are discussing, but few of us are medical doctors as well as astrologers. How complete can we presume to be in the normal practice of astrology? Going further with the medical analysis of a horoscope requires quite specialized skills; and it is then that the work approaches *healing.* Let us become proficient with *the detection of possibility* as far as we are able in order to make studied referral to medical experts. This is emphatically *not* an empty, ameliorative suggestion: we

---

13 This way of asking the client about a possible condition of illness is exactly how I have learned to do it with authority, without alarming the client unduly, preserving the possibility that I am incorrect, and yet not undermining the entire consultation, which probably has gone exceedingly well in terms of rapport and insight about other issues.

14 Peregrine is the planetary state of not making a Ptolemaic aspect within the horoscope (conjunction, square, sextile, trine, or opposition). The peregrine planet "flavors" the horoscope strongly, often 'runs away' with it. Please see Tyl, *Synthesis & Counseling in Astrology,* pages 155–190, with many case examples for all planets.

must know that it is simply astounding how few people get physical checkups until it is too late, how little most people know about their health. Astrology and astrologers *can* save lives.

Horoscope 2, Constance

Horoscope 2 shows Constance at age fifty-nine. Note that there are three focal points of high developmental tension: the Moon-Pluto conjunction in Leo; the Sun in wide conjunction with Mars, both in Leo opposed by Jupiter, with Mars squaring the Ascendant[15]; and Saturn-retrograde opposing Venus in its own sign.

Clearly this is high self-dramatization, with the Leo emphasis and with Pluto ruling the Ascendant, conjoining the Moon: everything should be tied to ego-flair, importance, pride, vanity, forceful drama...all overcompensating for early homelife difficulties linked clearly to the father figure, resulting in a crisis about being lovable, which, in turn, is played out through difficult relationships (Venus in the 11th—love received—ruling the 11th and the 7th is opposed by Saturn retrograde; Uranus squares the Sun/Moon midpoint).

What are the vulnerable weak points is this highly expressive woman's body? "I am not a medical doctor, but sometimes the horoscope speaks helpfully about the weak parts of the body, especially when it is under stress, emotional, vocational, etc. Has there ever been detected by stethoscope or electrocardiogram a congenital heart anomaly? And secondly, is there back pain, pain in your spine?"

Constance replied that she does have a heart murmur and that she has been turned down for insurance. Indeed, she also has spine problems which come to the surface "when I'm around people who 'squash' me!" Here we see clearly the Venus in Libra "affliction" significant through aspect with Saturn, through the sign Libra, and by House reference of Saturn's position. Everything suggests lower back pain.[16]

---

15 In my work, I normally keep orbs small: 6.5 degrees for the Sun and for the Moon, 5 for the other planets, and 2 for the Nodal axis and for minor aspects. I feel that the "tighter" the aspects, the fewer aspects there are to deal with, the higher the reliability of analysis. Here, note that the Mars-Jupiter opposition is just out of orb (but Jupiter is retrograde) and Jupiter *is* in clear opposition with the Sun; for me, this sharing of aspect by Jupiter brings Mars into conjunction consideration with the Sun; I see a synthesis of the three bodies. Orb is a measure of consciousness. Constance here *has made* the Sun-Mars conjunction happen in her life.

16 This is extremely common and reliable: the stress upon a planet in Libra, especially Venus, corroborating lower back pain. Indeed, with Venus involved we can also anticipate difficulty with kidneys, bladder, or thyroid gland, all under rulership of Venus.

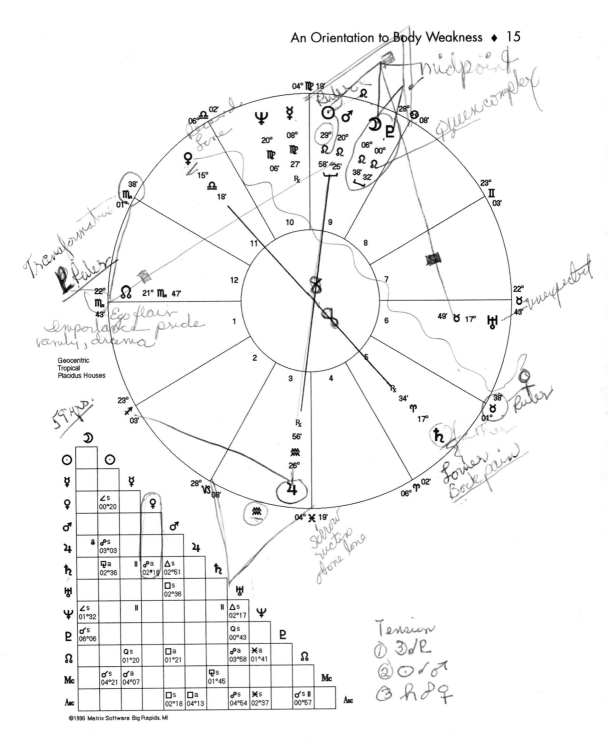

Horoscope 2, Constance

Geocentric
Tropical
Placidus Houses

@1990 Matrix Software Big Rapids, MI

Let's study the Moon-Pluto conjunction a bit further: Pluto rules the Ascendant and the Moon in Leo suggests the reigning need focus of a queen complex; we anticipate enormous ego emphasis and flair. The Moon rules the 9th, and there are four powerful planetary accentuations in the 9th House: Constance has grand study experience in spiritual matters and is also "addicted" to writing high-romance novels. The Moon and Pluto make no other Ptolemaic aspect in the horoscope, existing as a peregrine conjunction, an "island conjunction" running away with self-empowerment. She says candidly, "I feel no one loves me, but everyone thinks I'm magnificent!"

For her health profile, this conjunction links her Ascendant with the Moon, her sensorium, her reigning need-focus of being. This is a centralization of power manifestation, and Pluto also rules the 12th. Along with the Sun-Mars conjunction, and the square from Uranus to Mars, we can bring into our awareness the 5th House, ruled by Mars here, referring as well to the heart and to the spine. What we are seeing is that the heart murmur and the lower back condition *are somehow connected.* If her self-worth and intimacy anxieties had been treated (Houses 2, 11, 5, 7), *might the heart condition never have come to prominence, or the spine to acute discomfort?*

We simply do not know for sure. But this relationship between development and illness is one of the avenues of inquiry of this study, and it will be developed strongly in the pages that follow.

The Fire Family *management of Energy*

With the heart so dramatically central, with the concept of energy brought forward through the Sun, the ruler of Leo, and through Mars, the ruler of Aries, we begin to assimilate the essence of the Fire Family: *the management of energy.*

The sign Sagittarius and its ruler Jupiter complete the Fire triplicity. We can construct the image of energy born in Leo/Sun, distributed by Sagittarius/Jupiter, and applied through Aries/Mars.

The heart weighs only about one pound but manages to pump some five or more quarts of blood into the system per minute. In a single day,

---

17   The heart actually has two pumps, each with a pair of chambers (the lower is called a ventricle and the upper is called an atrium). The contractions of the muscles of these two chambers create the heart's pumping action.

that's about 2,000 gallons of blood that are pushed through the body's circulatory system! The blood provides oxygen-rich cells to the tissues to nourish them. The arteries take the blood to the tissues and the veins bring the blood back to the heart. The blood brought back is recycled through the lungs (to pick up oxygen) before it starts out once again through the heart and into the arteries.[17]

Aries classically rules the head, the arteries of the head and brain, the sinuses. Mars energy figures in functions of force, anger, danger, speed, heat, fever, the sex act, surgery. When tensions of insecurity and childhood patterns of self-worth anxiety and/or suppressed anger in life development manifest in relation to a Mars under high developmental tension in the horoscope, the focus is usually on migraine headaches.

Additionally, Mars symbolically stirs up anxiety in the part of the system signified by the planet with which it makes a strong aspect. In Case 2 (see page 15), it is obvious through the conjunction with the Sun in Leo; in Case 1 (see page 12), Mars agitates the Moon in Virgo (intensifying the cerebral, didactic, discriminating, and exacting nature of Virgo *and also* bringing strongly to the foreground concerns about diet and the intestines (Virgo, 6th House). This reference to diet is reiterated by the Saturn opposition with the Sun, the ruler of the 6th (natural House to Virgo), and with Mercury, co-ruler of the lady's 6th, brought into the opposition with Saturn by its conjunction with the Sun.

Classically, Jupiter was given rulership over the liver probably because the liver is such a large organ (weighing about four pounds; next to the skin, the largest organ of the body) and Jupiter is the biggest planet. According to Ingrid Naiman, the liver is without doubt the most important organ beyond the heart that is governed by fire, a fire sign.[18] This can feel awkward here in our discussion since Jupiter as ruler of Sagittarius can refer to the liver even if Jupiter is *not* in a fire sign. This is an important observation to which we shall return shortly.

Again, we feel the confusion that still haunts the medical astrology frontier. Naiman suggests reasonably that we can hope eventually to see body *structures* as Signs and body *functions* as Planets (this is perhaps ideal organization of thought, but the dichotomization does not yet hold up in practice as we know). Naiman's Fire orientation for the liver is focused by the liver's vital role of determining the amounts of nutrients

---

18 Naiman, *The Astrology of Healing,* page 55.

(energy) that are sent to the rest of the body; by its role in assisting (through the bile it produces) with the absorption of fats into the intestines; and the storage of glycogen (a complex carbohydrate) that is converted into sugar for release into the bloodstream when sugar in the blood is low.

In short, Naiman says, "Fire rules the internal combustion process (digestion). The energy released by biochemical and chemical processes of the body is fiery. Hormones, enzymes, coenzymes, etc. are carriers of fire, and of these, insulin is probably the most specific fiery hormone."

The Mars consideration within this Fire Family for the body's engine is clear when we understand that *the increase in body temperature* (fever, Mars) that attends the work of purification and transmutation in the body enables the body to throw off toxins and waste.

Constance, Horoscope 2, was taking an elaborate regimen of vitamins at the time of our consultation. I urged her to get a physical checkup since she was not feeling well, not up to her Leonine, Martian best. The report came back from the doctor that parasites were present in her system, rendering inefficient the digestion of all the vitamins she was taking, knocking the system off balance.

Cornell says "parasites" are ruled by the sense of Virgo (diet) and "afflictions" involving Mercury or Venus. Note in Constance's horoscope (see page 15) that she does have Venus under great stress, and Mercury is in its own sign, retrograde, and *peregrine*, i.e., running wild in her development! And central to our view here is the *Jupiter* opposition with Mars and the Sun. The potential for diet problems is eminently clear, as it is for her heart and back problems.

Additionally, Sagittarius makes reference to the hips, thighs, and the sciatic nerve that runs down the outside of the thighs from the lower back at the beltline, and, of course, to the liver, its function ruled by Jupiter.

A further note on the liver: for the past twenty years, I have asked thousands of people in private consultations and in lecture audiences—those who have *Venus and Jupiter in strong aspect with one another*—about the incidence of diabetes in their family or personal history. I suggest strongly that it is noteworthy indeed that *in excess of eighty percent* of all these people with such an aspect configuration *confirmed* such incidence of diabetes.

Here's why the Venus-Jupiter connection symbolizes diabetes: the pancreas, a long thin organ about eight inches long, located behind the stomach, produces hormones essential to the digestion of food; the hormones produced by the pancreas metabolize the food we eat. They regulate how we use glucose, a simple form of sugar (Venus) that is a major source of energy for our cells. The pancreas must function efficiently in relation to our meals, exercise, stress, and infections. Insulin is one of the hormones produced by the pancreas *when the concentration of glucose (Venus) in the blood increases.* Surplus glucose is stored by the liver (Jupiter).

Diabetes results when there is a lack of insulin supply from the pancreas: the body's cells are therefore unable to use the glucose in the bloodstream. This is a tension between Venus and Jupiter.

More than ten million Americans have diabetes mellitus (meaning, in Greek, *passing-through honey*). It is estimated that at least another five million are unaware that they have the ailment. Until the discovery of insulin in 1921, the almost inevitable result of insulin-dependent diabetes mellitus (IDDM) was death.[19]

The condition of hypoglycemia is basically an insulin reaction when the concentration of glucose in the blood falls *below* normal. When too little glucose circulates in the system, the nervous system and other cells, and they become energy-starved. This is the danger for diabetics if a meal is missed or if there is extended physical activity using up energy (or for someone *without* diabetes when drinking alcohol with minimal food intake).

"Reactive Hypoglycemia"—or so-called "borderline hypoglycemia"—manifests as an obviously nervous, irritable, disoriented reaction at some time between meals, when the level of glucose (sugar) in the blood falls close to or below the normal range. Additionally, stress and anxiety can trigger the production of adrenaline (epinephrine), just as low blood sugar does, and the body responds with symptoms that resemble hypoglycemia.

Clearly Venus and Jupiter are involved with chemical (emotional) stress, which can manifest in erratic eating behavior with a compulsion for

---

19 Mayo, pages 925–926. About one in ten people with diabetes have IDDM; the others have non-insulin-dependent diabetes mellitus (NIDDM), which is also known as adult-onset diabetes or Type II diabetes. These people have bodies that resist the effect of insulin in their bloodstream and they require more and more insulin to maintain normal amounts of glucose in the blood.

sweets. Astrology associates "sweetness" (nutritionally and characterologically) with Venus, "enthusiasm" with Jupiter. In my horoscope (page 57), I have Jupiter conjunct the Sun and Venus opposed the Moon, ruler of the Ascendant, none of them with any undue developmental tension: I have always had a "sweet tooth;" I *need* sugars often; I feel the "borderline hypoglycemic symptoms" on occasion and, with every physical checkup, I am keenly alert to the blood analysis and liver reports, particularly as they relate to sugar.

But there is confusion in our literature: the liver has been given rulership by the Moon, Venus, the sign Cancer, the sign Leo, the sign Libra, the planet Jupiter, the 4th, 5th, 6th, and/or 7th House, and more. The pancreas was not even specifically identified in function as late as in the seventeenth century. While diabetes seems consistently ruled by Venus; sugar is ruled inconsistently by Jupiter, Sun, and Venus.[20]

But let me repeat, please, that there is now sureness emerging: there is completely reliable evidence in my studies that the presence of diabetes in one's family history or in oneself is indeed keyed with high probability to the square, conjunction, opposition of Venus and Jupiter (even trine or sextile, etc.; in short, *any* contact). We will see many cases of diabetes throughout the studies in this book. Without any preselection on my part, the strong relationship between Venus and Jupiter present in the background of any chart presented in this book correlates with the incidence of diabetes every time but two (at present).

---

20 See historical listings presented in Lehman.

The Air Family

The Air Family oversees all concerns with nerves, interactions with the environment (from the air we breathe and how we breathe it, to social relationships and how we manage the personal resource exchange with others), how we communicate and how we get around in our world (locomotion, mobility). Clearly, if our *social interaction* needs are thwarted, there are reactions in the our *nervous system;* health can be undermined (Saturn stressed in Libra, for example, perhaps calling attention euphemistically to a "weak spine"); the mind can interpret the situation to points of depression—certainly one of the most prominent debilitation areas in modern life; we can have social or physical paralysis; we can have obsessively focused, clouded, or scattered thinking.

Libra rulerships include mainly the lower back, the kidneys, the bladder, the fallopian tubes. Tension structures in Libra or referring to Libra are normally highly reliable indices of lower back problems: throughout the second half of the twentieth century, lower-back problems have been one of the easiest ways for our bodies to manifest tension, because of our modern history of easier work styles, transportation conveniences, and diminished exercise; i.e., the weakness in the lower back "invites" breakdown.

As we clarify reliable astrological symbology in reference to physiological orientation and as we keep an eye on the confusions that still exist, I think we can gain some clarity and practicality when we adjust in our mind *the sense* of the word "rulership." For example, we see in our literature that a stressed Mars in Libra can refer to the spine through sign (Libra) or migraine headaches through planet (Mars; and reflex cross-reference to Aries, the sign opposite Libra), especially if Mars is in the 5th House or ruling the 5th House, and/or is related to the 12–6 axis, or is related somehow to the 8th House (!, for reference to the spine, according to the masterful William Lilly of long ago). In our sense of "rulership," we are seeking *specific, unalterable connections to make our work more reliable,* and we are bewildered and frustrated. We are looking for law, and there is none.

I want to suggest that we adjust this sense of and search for specificity: let's generalize a bit; let's identify in the horoscope strong references to concepts that say "spine," for example; and then let's inquire about *the client's reality,* learn about the manifestation of symptoms *in the individual client's life.* We then can bring our astrology to the reality being lived by the client. We can now know enough to identify weakness in the horoscope *and in the client's life experience;* we *can* anticipate attack and we can affect medical referral. Let's explore *process* instead of law.

Yes, this could be seen as a suggestion to honor *all* rulership specifications; but in terms of practicality, it is a suggestion to follow the prevailing logic and the empirical record in pace with our times now: the glyph for Libra describes the beltline area, that zone of the body, including the organs inside that area. A reference to that area through developmental tension focused in Libra and/or through Venus, its referent ruler, or *through any planet stressed within that "zone"* will lead us to ask our client about the spine, the lower back in particular.

Perhaps we should define some practical limits for our work individually: medical astrologer Eileen Nauman relates the lumbar vertebrae to Libra but concentrates as well on the kidneys in that region and the inflammations possible, for example, with Mars in Libra; she has extended her skill with highly developed nutritional insight with regard to calcium deficiency, etc.,[21] but few of us have that specialized expertise, and most of us can easily feel inadequate within all of the possibilities and confusion. We feel that astrologers should *know;* they should *not* be guessing!

I know the limits of my knowledge on this frontier in astrology. I know that I can seek out and identify strong references to what we know is relevant, say, for the lower back. I know that I can discuss what I have detected with my client, inquire about its validity, and perform my role as an astrologer by making referral to the next step, to a specialist for professional diagnosis and healing.

Aquarius rulerships include the calves and ankles and, through Uranus, the nervous *system;* high-tech therapies like X-Ray, CT Scan, and MRI. We see "tightly wired" conditions and temperamental quirks that develop into personality traits. Under pressure, there is *a sympathy of function* among manifestations of Mars, Mercury, and Uranus.

Gemini rulerships include the breath, the lungs, nerves and nervous habits; allergies; the shoulders, arms, and hands; movement; the oxygenation of the blood; stress. So often, nail-biting, leg-bouncing, fidgeting, and other nervous habits accompany a Mercury position that is under high developmental tension. The mind obviously plays an extraordinary role in directing the occurrence and endurance of Mercury-referenced illness; it is often clearly routed by Mercury and its rulership references.

---

21 Nauman, pages 23, 24, 198.

Horoscope 3, Female

Horoscope 3 (page 25) shows astrological constructs of extremely high developmental tension among Air, Fire, and Water Families. The absence of Earth articulation within the horoscope classically suggests "impracticality." According to Naiman, the symptoms of a deficiency of the Earth element are similar to *an excess of Air*. This includes absent-mindedness, anxiety or worry, brooding, creativity, difficulty being alone, giddiness, neurotic tendencies, pains, diminished libido, restlessness, chattering; hormonal imbalances, emaciation, intolerance, and lack of realism. We can note easily how clearly depicted the Mercury-orientation is in so many of these functional disturbances.[22]

The Sun-Moon blend in this horoscope brings the energy to diversify and communicate (Gemini) together with an opinionation force that is formidable (Sagittarius). For personal fulfillment, being influential will be of greatest importance; the mind and nervous system will be working overtime, as it were, to plot, plan, and outwit the environment in the drive to establish personal importance.

This drive is strongly reinforced by Pluto's position on the Ascendant, squared by Jupiter.

We easily see all this energy within a grip of suppression, keyed by the 12th House focus and the accentuation *below the horizon* (including the 12th House): we can suggest that there is lots of unfinished business in development, and all of this would be important in full analysis of the horoscope.

The dominating aspects are clearly the exact opposition between Mars and the Sun in Gemini, and the opposition between Pluto and the Moon, ruler of the Ascendant. These aspects suggest tremendous nervous tension, reactant tension (emphasis on Mutable signs), and a kind of repression (the retrogradation of Mars; i.e., the energy goes in before it goes out; there is a filter for censorship, evaluation, a controlling rein on arch opinionation; super-ego functions).

Analysis grows with further corroboration: Saturn is tightly square Mercury, dispositor of the Sun and ruler of the 12th House *and the 4th House*, one arm of the parental axis (Saturn placed in the 4th as well).

---

22 Naiman, *The Elements: Symptoms of Disease*, pages 112–114 and 122. Another clear example of this general elemental predisposition shown in horoscope 3 is the horoscope of Marilyn Monroe (see page 228).

Neptune, the ruler of the 10th, the other arm of the parental axis, is peregrine: the family concerns and tensions, the unfinished business, could dominate the life; a theatrical lifestyle (pretend world) could do the same, perhaps as an escape. Uranus at the Midheaven in the 10th squares the Mars-Sun opposition axis, suggesting high excitability, intense reflex actions, impulse, sudden events, and over-exertion, causing breakdown of efficiency and health.[23]

Three more measurement techniques should be introduced at this point of our growing study. First, the Aries Point: the Aries Point (AP) in the horoscope is conceptually and astronomically tied to *all* 0-degree points of the four Cardinal signs. It is extremely sensitive to involvement with any planet or other point or midpoint by conjunction, square, or opposition. When the Aries Point is activated in a personal horoscope, there is the potential of *conspicuous public projection* for the person in terms of the planet, point, or midpoint configurated with it. An orb of two degrees is recommended.[24]

This horoscope shows Mercury and Saturn exactly upon Aries Points, at 00 Cancer and 00 Libra, respectively. The two planets are in exact square, with Mercury ruling the 12th and placed in the 12th, and in retrograde motion. This registers not only a physical breakdown potential in terms of the nervous system (an echo of the Mars opposition to the Sun in *Gemini*) but also a potential struggle with deep depression (Mercury and Saturn contact; mind, introversion, suppressive controls; a difficulty with relationships, acknowledging Saturn's rulership of the 7th; perhaps maudlin thoughts about death, Saturn ruling the 8th, Pluto rising; and, with more synthesis details developed, a potentially suicidal frame of mind). *And,* because of the positions so dramatically set with the Aries Points, *all of this is brought forward somehow,* worn on one's sleeve, so to speak. It is projected into others' awareness. With Pluto rising, a thrust to prominence can be anticipated, and this thrust would carry with it into public view the inner turmoil we are seeing suggested through the major aspects.

The second consideration to add to our analytical arsenal are Midpoint structures, pictures of synthesis of three (or more) astrological symbols. The Midpoint Table (90-degree Sort) presented here is arranged in terms of the fourth harmonic, the relationships of the square, conjunction, or

---

23 Tyl, *Synthesis & Counseling,* Appendix: see a detailed word-image overview of all 1,014 possible midpoint and Solar Arc structures possible in the horoscope: Uranus=Sun/Mars.

24 Please see Tyl, *Synthesis & Counseling* for full development, pages 303–312.

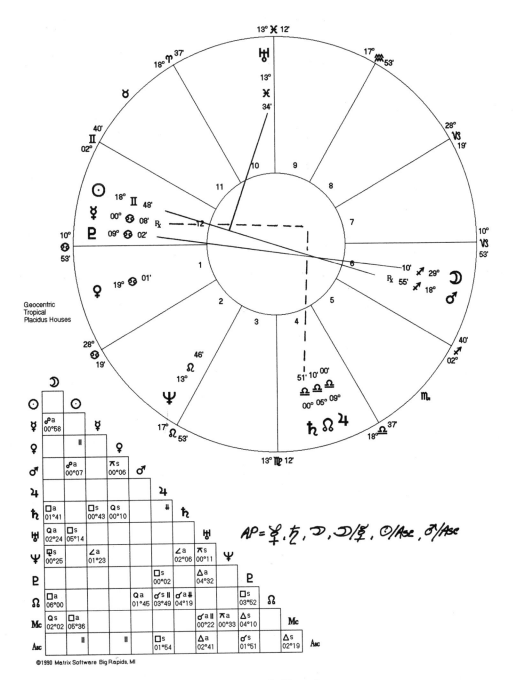

Geocentric
Tropical
Placidus Houses

AP = ☿, ♄, ☽, ☽/☿, ☉/Asc, ♂/Asc

Horoscope 3, Female

opposition. All Midpoints that occur in Cardinal signs are listed from 000 to 29 degrees 60; all that occur in Fixed Signs are listed from 30.00 to 59.60; in Mutable, from 60.00 to 89.60.

Midpoint Sort: 90° Dial											
☿	000°08'	♇/Asc	009°58'	☽/Mc	036°11'	☿/♄	045°30'	♅/♆	058°40'	♅/☊	084°22'
♄	000°51'	Asc	010°53'	☽/♅	036°22'	♀/Mc	046°07'	♀/♃	059°00'	☉/☿	084°28'
♄/☊	003°01'	♀/♇	014°02'	☿/Mc	036°40'	♀/♅	046°18'	♄/♆	067°18'	☿/♂	084°32'
☉/♀	003°55'	♀/Asc	014°57'	☿/♅	036°51'	☽/☊	047°10'	♆/☊	069°28'	♃/Mc	086°06'
♀/♂	003°58'	☉/♆	016°17'	☉/♄	039°50'	☿/☊	047°39'	♃/♆	071°23'	♃/♅	086°17'
☽/♇	004°06'	♂/♆	016°20'	♂/♄	039°53'	☽/♃	049°05'	Mc	073°12'	☉/♇	088°55'
☿/♇	004°35'	♀	019°01'	♇/Mc	041°07'	☿/♃	049°34'	♅/Mc	073°23'	♂/♇	088°59'
♃/♄	004°56'	☽/♆	021°28'	♅/♇	041°18'	♄/♇	049°57'	♅	073°34'	☽	089°10'
☽/Asc	005°02'	☿/♆	021°57'	☉/☊	041°59'	♄/Asc	050°52'	☉	078°48'	☽/☿	089°39'
☊	005°10'	♆/♇	026°24'	Mc/Asc	042°03'	♇/☊	052°06'	☉/♂	078°52'	☉/Asc	089°51'
☿/Asc	005°31'	♆/Asc	027°19'	♂/☊	042°03'	☊/Asc	053°02'	♂	078°55'	♂/Asc	089°54'
♃/☊	007°05'	☉/Mc	031°00'	♅/Asc	042°14'	♃/♇	054°01'	♄/Mc	082°02'		
♃	009°00'	♂/Mc	031°04'	♆	043°46'	♀/♄	054°56'	♄/♅	082°13'		
♇	009°02'	☉/♅	031°11'	☉/♃	043°54'	♃/Asc	054°57'	☽/☉	083°59'		
☽/♀	009°06'	♂/♅	031°15'	♂/♃	043°57'	♀/☊	057°06'	☽/♂	084°03'		
☿/♀	009°35'	♀/♆	031°23'	☽/♄	045°01'	♆/Mc	058°29'	☊/Mc	084°11'		

Clearly here, we see Mercury and Saturn at the Aries Point, 00 Cardinal signs. From the 90 degree sort of the Table, we know that Mercury and Saturn will be conjunct, square, or opposed each other. But as well, note the Moon, Moon/Mercury, Sun/Ascendant, and Mars/Ascendant positions between 89.10 and 89.54, i.e., in the last degree of Mutable signs, one degree short of 00 Cardinal. This means AP=Mercury= Saturn=Moon=Moon/Mercury=Sun/Ascendant=Mars/Ascendant.

These Midpoint pictures show us a tremendously publicly projected personality potential, *a major contrast with the inhibited 12th House,* the Mercury-Saturn tie, and the retrograded, suppressed developmental profile we have seen suggested in our analysis so far. Since the personality always fights for homogeneity, for the unity necessary for maximum efficiency in the effort to fulfill needs, contrast is trauma. There is a split here, but the Aries Point tries to mend it by bringing inner world and outer world together.

Mercury=Sun/Ascendant: "thinking about who one really is in relation to others; existential awareness and sensitivity." Mercury=Mars/Ascendant: "a sharp tongue, verbal disputes, telling someone off, intolerance."

The third additional measurement we need in our study is notation of the "oriental" planet (having to do with the eastern direction), the planet rising (in clockwise motion) just before the Sun. In this horoscope,

Uranus is oriental, and we can expect the adventurer, the chance-taker, the individualist with some eccentric behavior, the unusual. The elevated position of Uranus focuses this uniqueness in the public eye through the profession.[25]

This is the horoscope of Judy Garland, a living-legend entertainer in her time (June 10, 1922, 6:00 A.M. CST: Grand Rapids, *Minnesota*). Her adoring public lived with her through her enormous bouts of depression, medicine and alcohol abuse, chaotic relationships, suicide attempts.

Among the Midpoint pictures we can see Neptune=Sun/Jupiter and Neptune=Uranus/Ascendant. The former suggests increased sensitivity and a loss of concentrated orientation (as well as inspiration professionally here); the latter, the sharing of emotions, the registration of martyrdom that can be exploited by others.

This analysis of Garland's horoscope has been more psychodynamically detailed here in order to emphasize the Air Family's orientation to *interaction with the environment,* from the air we breath and how we use it to the relationship factors we need to define much of our identity. Garland's problems were born early on in her life, in a precocious theatrical childhood, and her nervous system, mind-set, and body reacted to her life development as the horoscope so dramatically defines.

Horoscope 4, Theodore Roosevelt

Horoscope 4 belongs to Theodore Roosevelt, the 26th president of the United States (1901–09).[26]

The public image of "Teddy" Roosevelt lives on today as robust and adventurous: Roosevelt was the first-into-battle hero-leader of the "Rough Riders" (a cavalry troop he headed in Puerto Rico and Cuba during the Spanish-American War), but his childhood was decidedly sickly. While we glean from the public record that everything went swimmingly well for this affluent, privileged, drivingly intelligent man, we learn of tremendous debilitation from infantile asthma.

---

25 For full development of the Oriental Planet concept, which is particularly helpful in vocational guidance, please see Tyl, *Synthesis & Counseling*, pages 497–501.

26 Roosevelt was Vice President to William McKinley for his second term. Six months into that term, on September 6, 1901, McKinley was shot by an anarchist named Leon Czolgocz, and died eight days later. Roosevelt took over the presidency on September 14, 1901 (SA Mars conjunct the Midheaven, SA Moon opposed the Midheaven within 8' of arc, SA Ascendant square Mercury, ruler of the Ascendant; tr Saturn opposed Neptune, ruler of the Midheaven; Tertiary Progressed Sun exactly conjunct Uranus, TP Venus exactly conjunct Moon, etc.).

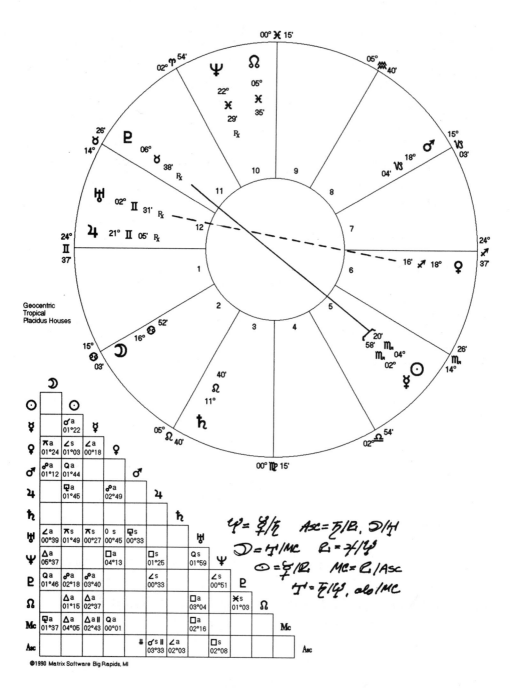

Horoscope 4, Theodore Roosevelt
October 27, 1858, 7:45 P.M. LMT
New York, NY
74W00 — 40N43

Asthma affects approximately ten percent of children and five percent of adults in the United States. Some 3,500 deaths are attributable to asthma each year. About half of all chronic illness in childhood is due to asthma.[27]

Asthma is characterized by a wheezing in the lungs, tightness of the chest, coughing, and difficulty breathing, which can easily bring about panic. It is the leading cause of chronic illness among children and school absenteeism; about half the children who develop asthma do so before the age of ten. No cause for asthma is clinically known.

With all the emphasis on the very young as the birth stage of asthma, prevalent deductions suggest that asthma is linked to psychogenic causes (originating in the mind or in mental or emotional conflict; psychosomatic). Dr. Isadore Rosenfeld in his book *Modern Prevention* adamantly takes a contrary view, and *The Mayo Clinic Health Book* avoids the subject. Yet, doctor after doctor with whom I have discussed this subject see the high probability of a link between early homelife emotional upset and the occurrence of asthma. I think what the doctors are saying is that certain individuals have a *vulnerability* to asthma; that that is the weak spot in their body; and that stress can easily travel there and deposit itself in the lungs and breathing mechanism. Astrology can add that the mind is directing the way, trying to discharge the upset.

Teddy Roosevelt was a privileged young man, born into an affluent family. It *seems* he had very loving parents and everything he wanted. Yet he had this intense asthmatic condition, to such an extent that his father built a small exercise center in their home for Teddy to use to overcome the disease. Biographers all see Teddy's constant physical adventurism—his grand physical attack on the world, even personally leading an expedition into the jungles of South America after his political career, at age fifty-five—as an overcompensatory effort, born in him when very young, to conquer the disease and perpetually to stay ahead of it.[28]

Teddy's Sun-Moon blend promises a magnetism, an emotional expansiveness that attracts others, brings them under his spell (and control); an arena of leadership is strongly established, but not without the sensitivities critical to preserve good relationships. While the Mars-in-Capricorn opposition with the Moon adds a tremendous vitality—and the robustness that was Teddy's trademark—we can also see it *as an agitation of the*

---

27 Mayo, pages 1044–1047; Rosenfeld, page 81–87.

28 Medicine does not understand even the relationship between exercise and asthma. Generally, moderation is the rule; but moderation is something Teddy didn't understand.

emotions, astrologically suggesting anxiety about self-worth (the Moon rules and is in the 2nd). We can see how Teddy projected himself up and out of difficulties, and also we can suggest a threat to the stomach (ulcers, normally; an acid burn, a break or hole in the lining of the esophagus, stomach, or duodenum).

All of this is certainly an echo of the Pluto opposition with Sun-Mercury, Mercury ruling the Ascendant. Whenever we have Pluto in strong developmental tension with the Sun (especially the square), we can expect that there is "a blanket over a grenade," some cover in life development that must be blown off and away from the potentials. In this case, with Pluto ruling the 6th, we would be alerted to some sickness that could have threatened development (and something that parallels the sickness in life development). If the sickness is cured, the potentials will bloom; the Pluto projection then becomes tremendous empowerment.

Indeed, the empowerment can actually be what *cures* the situation: Teddy applied himself heroically physically to beat the asthma ("might makes right"). Mercury becomes the key consideration here: the sickness could be with the lungs, with asthma; the astrologer would have to ask Teddy that question, regardless of the fact that Mercury is in a Fixed Water sign, along with the Sun. Mercury is Mercury, it refers to (rules) the lungs and how they function, and, here, it rules Teddy's Ascendant as well, the core of his well-being.

Our consideration of Mercury's high focus would also reveal that Teddy read voraciously throughout his childhood (he could not risk an asthma attack out at play with other children). Throughout his life, he thought of himself as a *writer;* he published over two thousand works on history, politics, and his travels. He won the Nobel Peace Prize for mediating in the Russo-Japanese War (1906).

These dimensions of his profile bring the 9th House (and 3rd House) to mind, of course, here ruled by Uranus. We can note that Uranus and Venus in Sagittarius are in quindecile (see page 9) aspect (shown in the aspect grid, page 28, with a "0" label). Here is intense absorption, even obsession about international adventure, higher thought, learning, *as well as the confrontation with illness, with Venus ruling the 12th holding Uranus.*

Additionally, we see that Uranus is peregrine, a tremendous corroboration of Teddy's individuality and adventurism. Uranus is also square the midpoint of Node/Midheaven (Uranus=Node/Midheaven): "sudden experiences, rashness, being seen as zany, solving problems innovatively with others."

The Sun is the ruler of the writing 3rd, is conjunct Mercury in the dominating opposition with Pluto, and is trine the Midheaven. Saturn is in Leo (the fulfillment of ambition through dramatic means; e.g., Liberace, Leonard Bernstein) in the 3rd and it too is peregrine!

Teddy's distant cousin, Franklin Delano Roosevelt (see page 205) has a horoscope that is dominated by Mercury: Mercury rules the Virgo Ascendant and the Gemini Midheaven; Mercury is in the 6th House almost precisely squared by Pluto, ruling the 3rd House of movement, locomotion. Franklin's Sun was strongly challenged by squares from a Jupiter-Saturn-Neptune conjunction in his 8th. Mars was square his Ascendant. The registration of physical vulnerability was dramatically profiled.

The astrologer would have had to ask Franklin about Mercury ailments, beginning perhaps with asthma (Mercury was in Aquarius in mutual reception with Uranus in the 12th!). The astrologer could have (would have) also inquired about the potential for a problem with movement/ mobility (infantile paralysis was quite common in that generation). Roosevelt was indeed stricken with poliomyelitis in August 1921. He had just *lost the election of 1920,* running as Vice President with James Cox; Solar Arc Neptune was conjunct his Midheaven and almost precisely square his Ascendant; transiting Saturn was precisely upon his Ascendant.[29] [We will return to Teddy Roosevelt's horoscope in a moment.]

Lower back pain and depression are the two most common weaknesses seen predominantly through Air Sign/Air Planet involvements.

For example, in my horoscope (see page 57), I have *Mars in Libra in the 5th* square a Mercury-Pluto opposition [instantly now, our mind must register the possibility of lower back difficulty; in the T-Square, of course, Pluto, in the opposition axis, is *squaring Mars in Libra*]. After back pains got worse and worse in my early twenties, a spine condition erupted and required drastic surgery in 1969. I saw it coming astrologically, took out special insurance, tried to avoid it, and was in the hospital three days after the pre-existing condition waiting period had expired.[30]

---

29 Cornell, who must have studied many cases of polio (infantile paralysis), specifies Neptune as the "chief afflictor" and, yet, does not mention Mercury involved with the function of movement.

30 This same signature could witness a stressed Mercury, ruler of my 12th, itself in my 8th: a stroke, a cerebral hemorrhage; as well as acute perception and articulation intensity, etc. on another level of analysis.

The focus of the Libran back pain is usually in the area of the belt line, the third to fifth lumbar vertebra, as we have seen. Inquiry and study about a proper exercise regimen for this area can provide the astrologer with very helpful information to pass on to the client with such difficulty, as well as proper medical referral, of course.

Depression is one of the ten leading causes of disability worldwide, as measured in years lived with the disability. In the next twenty years, (unipolar) depression is expected to be second only to heart disease as the world's major cause of disease burden.[31]

Depression can be a *normal* human emotion—a response to loss, disappointment, or failure. Some depressions, however, are *diseases,* and these diseases are destructive to families, to careers, to relationships. Between ten and thirty percent of depressives and manic-depressives kill themselves.[32]

Doctors Klein and Wender, in their superb guide, *Understanding Depression,* tell us that one woman in five and one man in ten can expect to develop a depression or a manic-depression sometime during the course of their lives. The work overview these doctors have presented in their book includes a simple list of diagnostic questions, the answers to which suggest the probability of depression. They caution as well that, while some forms of depression can certainly be treated with knowledgeable self-help, other forms of depression can *not* be treated except by medical evaluation and treatment.

There is little insecurity in astrology that the interrelationship of Mercury and Saturn corresponds most often to depression, natally as predisposition, by transit or Arc in development. Beyond the obvious hard aspects with Mercury, we can be alerted to the potential for depression by Saturn's placement in the Ascendant or squaring or opposing the Ascendant or its ruler; Saturn placed in the 3rd House (the experiential zone for the mind) and/or its aspects to the ruler of the 3rd.

Additionally, we can be alerted by the Midpoint picture: Neptune= Mercury/Saturn.[33] Then, we have pictures that often connote environmental happenings that pull from us deep, possibly depressed reaction: Saturn=Neptune/Pluto which strongly suggests "the presence of grief,

---

31 World Health Organization [WHO] report; *Psychiatric Times,* Volume XIII, November 1996; Michael Jonathan Grinfield.

32 Klein, Wender, page 3.

33 To learn skill with Midpoint delineation, we must appreciate how the components of a picture work together. Here, for example, we have Neptune (confusion) affecting the mind (Mercury) and its relationship with controls (Saturn).

weakness, torment"; Pluto=Saturn/Ascendant, "violent upset, deep anguish, being put down by others"; Ascendant=Saturn/Pluto, "feeling a loss of identity."

Now, refer back, please, to Teddy Roosevelt's horoscope (see page 28): Roosevelt transcended his severe asthma and became the epitome of rough-riding robustness. Yet, in his horoscope there are the Midpoint pictures Neptune=Mercury/Saturn and Ascendant=Saturn/Pluto. Often, when another side of the personality is so overly developed, as robustness and busyness showed with Roosevelt, difficult pictures like these beg to be ignored, the astrologer is intimidated by the positive image. We must know though that in Roosevelt's life development, much anguish was internalized, in his early years and later.

On February 14, 1884, in a brownstone home in Manhattan, while giving birth to a daughter, Roosevelt's wife died, and, *at the same time,* on another floor, Roosevelt's mother, sick in bed with typhoid fever, also died.

This extraordinary day anchored Roosevelt into transformative grief. He changed his life (identity) entirely, leaving New York, going out to the wild West, to the Dakotas, and becoming a cowboy for some two years. Could this have been an adult extension of the upsets he experienced earlier in life?

Note that Roosevelt did not stay in New York to pick up the pieces, even with a newborn daughter. He *abandoned* the scene for two years to put himself together (Uranus peregrine, quindecile Venus ruler of the 5th; Pluto opposed the Sun in the 5th).

And then there are two other measurements that promised he would be back: his Saturn in Leo peregrine, and his Midheaven=Pluto/Ascendant midpoint picture, suggesting eventual power, authority, success, and ego ascendancy.

Horoscope 5, Art Buchwald

Art Buchwald, the highly celebrated internationally syndicated humorist/columnist, is a manic depressive (bipolar depression).[34] His horoscope has Mercury retrograde in Scorpio conjoined with Venus and with the Sun in Libra (Air sign), square the Mars-Neptune conjunction in the 7th. Any contact between Mars and Neptune can establish charisma; here we have the charismatic outflow to the public from the creatively idealized 9th House focus (Buchwald began his writing career in Paris, France). But what might be suggested by the retrogradation of Mercury, ruler of the 6th?

Note that the Moon is in Aries (the reigning need to be "numero uno"). The Moon rules the 7th; the square from Pluto reinforces the public projection mightily; and the Moon's position on the Aries Point guarantees it. This is the registration of extreme (manic) ego expression.

Mars, in the conjunction with Neptune, opposes Uranus, co-ruler of the Ascendant, in its own sign and placed in the Ascendant; Mars is also oriental (intense promotion energy). This is a high-energy, high-nervous orientation (more suggestion of the manic). Note that Uranus is retrograde, though, and that Mars rules the mental/writing 3rd.

All of this seems natural, normal, and routine for a celebrated publicly projected, high-energy humorist writer. All things considered, we sense/see the high-energy, ebullient, self-promotional side of a creative man.

But note the Midpoint pictures: Saturn=Neptune/Pluto; Saturn=Moon/Mercury; Sun=Mars/Saturn (breaking down under stress, the sense of loss); Midheaven=Moon/Pluto (one-sided emotional intensity). Another part of the portrait starts to emerge from the horoscope, the possibility of the depressive pole of his mind-set, perhaps the "other" level suggested by the retrogradation of Mercury and Uranus. Note as well that the Neptune squares refer to the self-worth 2nd where the Moon is squared by Pluto. This is a dramatic focus of self-worth anxiety. Mars echoes this intensely through its quindecile with the Ascendant, the obsession to prove himself.

Buchwald's early life was spent constantly moving, in the company of strangers. Shortly after birth, he was taken from his mother, who was mentally ill with chronic depression, and was placed in a Seventh-Day

---

34 Art Buchwald has presented his case and his effort to promote public awareness of the disease on the "Larry King Live" Television Show, CNN, April 22, 1996.

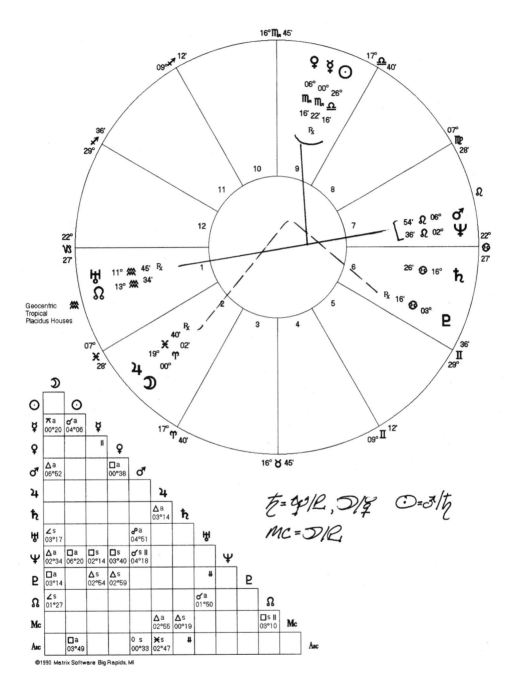

Horoscope 5, Art Buchwald
October 20, 1915, 1:00 P.M. EST
Mount Vernon, NY
73W50 — 40N54

Adventist shelter and then in New York's Hebrew Orphan Asylum, and then to a series of foster homes—all before the age of fifteen. At seventeen, he ran away (transiting Uranus square Ascendant, transiting Pluto opposed Ascendant) and joined the Marines. Buchwald himself now says that what he has really been trying to do with humor is, "I'm getting even. Being funny is the best revenge."

Horoscope 6, Mike Wallace

Horoscope 6 belongs to Mike Wallace, the exceedingly popular, ace news-interviewer on television (*60 Minutes, Twentieth Century*). We can note the suppression below the horizon (unfinished business developmentally), the sensitivity of the Pisces Ascendant, with its ruler Neptune conjoined with Saturn in the 5th, and that conjunction square to Moon-Mercury; the Moon rules the 5th. Again, within this complex, we have Mercury retrograde; what is the other "agenda," the other stream of concerns that work within Wallace's development? The focus on the 5th House suggests concerns with love, the process of giving love, the vulnerability in loving, and/or the relationship of all this with children.[35]

Mars is square Jupiter in Gemini in the 3rd, certainly a corroboration of high-energy communication skill, but Mercury rules the 7th and is retrograde, a withdrawal somehow or a fear of rejection, a second level of consideration; the Moon and Sun are both in Taurus which suggests keeping things as they are to protect against the insecurity of change. There is something "held down on the farm" here, something private.

The Midpoint pictures offer immediate suggestions that Mike Wallace may face depression critically: Saturn=Sun/Moon, Venus/Jupiter, Sun/Mercury; the Midheaven=Sun/Saturn (feeling devalued, the "lone wolf" position); Midheaven=Sun/Neptune (loss of ego strength, possible depression).[36]

The point here in our study is that when we look aggressively into any horoscope, we usually find repetitive measurements; the horoscope wants to "stick together," to homogenize, to say the same thing strongly over and over and over again. When we see disparity or divergence, we must investigate the particularly unusual circumstances.

---

35 Please recall the astro-concomitants of depression in Judy Garland's horoscope (see page 25).

36 Mike Wallace is a diagnosed manic depressive and has presented his case and effort for public awareness of the disease on the "Larry King Live" Television Show, CNN, April 22, 1996.

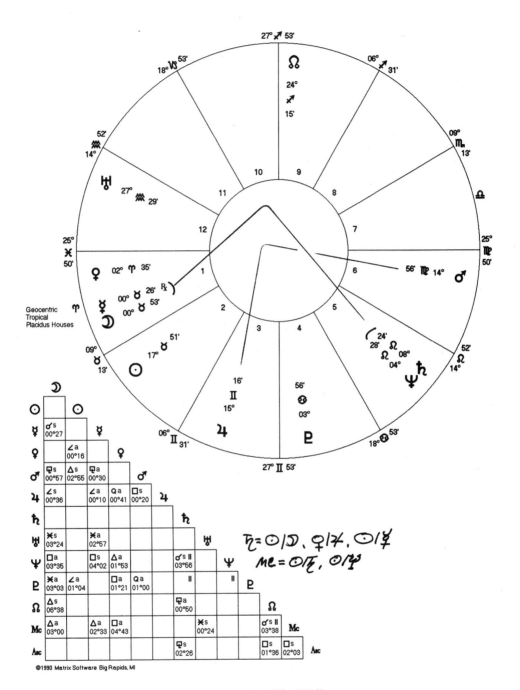

Horoscope 6, Mike Wallace
May 9, 1918, 3:30 P.M. EWT (3–4 P.M.)
Brookline, MA
71W07 — 42N20

Here, we would discuss with Mike Wallace the issues pointing to depression. We would discover together that he fits the general profile of manic depression—beyond just normal mood change.

Mike Wallace was a star in broadcasting from his earliest days in college, especially in commercials and as an announcer for highly popular radio series. In the early 1960s, when he began to report the news, the broadcasting establishment did not take him seriously. Simultaneously, his son Peter, on summer vacation from college, fell to his death in an accident in Greece. Wallace was "forced to rethink his whole life." The first signs of depression appeared.[37]

When Wallace was hired for the new CBS Show, *60 Minutes,* one of his earliest interviews was with General Westmoreland and the concomitant Vietnam-War information disclosure scandal. Wallace and CBS were sued for libel by Westmoreland. This enormous attack on Wallace's work ethic imploded severely, and Wallace was hospitalized for depression.

Wallace won the libel case but kept his depression hidden. He went off his medication, and, in 1983 (with transiting Neptune conjunct his Midheaven and transiting Saturn opposed his Moon), Wallace hit bottom; his depression was severe once again. Medical help and his friends Art Buchwald (see Horoscope 5, page 34) and famed writer William Styron (also a manic-depressive) helped him through to medicated stability.[38]

In Wallace's horoscope, the Neptune-Saturn conjunction in Leo looms large and, in its square with Moon-Mercury, is at the core of the suspicion of depression and the connection with 5th House matters (children, his son). Saturn will dominate in its position square the midpoint of Sun/Moon. The Leo emphasis here brings to mind concern about the heart. But the Sun is comfortably aspected and reinforced by the contact (trine) with Mars, an indication of vitality (see page 34). Wallace's extraordinary vitality and busyness, at age eighty in 1998, beam forth in his television appearances and are the talk of the industry.

---

37 Reported on the television show, "Mike Wallace remembers," CBS, September 11, 1997.

38 William Styron: June 12, 1925 at 10:15 p.m., EST at Newport News, VA. Styron's Moon is in Pisces, Mercury is in Gemini and peregrine. Neptune is square the Midheaven and quindecile the Ascendant.

The Water Family

This element family oversees all the liquids of the body and the process of digestion (including feeding of the foetus and elimination of wastes), the procreative process and the organs involved. With water comprising some sixty-six percent of the body, the reliance on fluids is enormous.

Cancer rulerships include the stomach and the breasts. We can appreciate that an astrological signature of nervousness that is focused in Cancer—Mercury in Cancer squared by Uranus, for example—can implicate a "nervous stomach." By reflex action to Capricorn—the sign opposite Cancer—we can anticipate the sense of being "weak in the knees," possibly even an inflammation of the knee(s), an initial symptom of rheumatoid arthritis.[39]

Echoing the seventeenth-century astrologers, Ingrid Naiman suggests as well that the Moon, the ruler of Cancer, rules the brain. The brain is exceedingly water dependent, sugar dependent; its function is dependent in the main upon storing memory, learning and selecting from memory within the cognitive processing that goes on in our consciousness (Mercury).[40]

I have found that a Moon with fast diurnal motion on the birth date (in excess of 14 degrees) correlates noticeably with mental sharpness, quick response, with what we call "brightness." The Moon *feels* right as significator of the brain and, working with Mercury, probably can signify mental facility.

But let me submit another consideration, that we shall revisit later, in our discussion of suicide (beginning on page 223):

The composer George Gershwin (September 26, 1898 at perhaps 11:09 A.M., EST in New York City) was as bright as one can be; even his music was composed and played with energy and speed hard to match. Even working with an unreliable birth time, we know that the horoscope is dominated by Mercury in Virgo at the Midheaven squared by Pluto, Neptune probably squaring the Midheaven as well, with Saturn close to the Ascendant. The diurnal motion of the Moon was 14.39, and his Moon in Aquarius was comfortably aspected, with no debilitating tension at all. When, Gershwin died (July 11, 1937) of a *brain tumor*, no arc or

---

39 "Rheumatoid" refers to "fluids"; rheumatoid arthritis is a constitutional disease of still unknown cause and follows a progressive course characterized by inflammation and swelling of joint structures. In contrast, *oasteoarthritis* refers to joint debilitation through wear and tear over time.

40 Personal discussion with Naiman.

transit was in touch with his natal Moon. If the Moon rules the brain, why was not the Moon "featured" in the horoscopic scenario leading up and corresponding to with his death? How could we have seen the brain as Gershwin's charm *and* his weakness?

Astrologer Jim Lewis, the creator of Astro*Carto*Graphy (born June 5, 1941 at 9:30 A.M., EDT in New York City), also had a diurnal Moon speed of 14.39; his words were always packed with emotion and pressing power (Mercury=Sun/Pluto), often appearing to border on argumentation (AP=Uranus/Pluto; Pluto rising in Leo). Jim's horoscope was dominated by Mars in Pisces square the Sun in Gemini. His Moon was surprisingly "peaceful" in Libra and comfortably aspected. Jim also died of a brain tumor, on February 21, 1995, without his Moon, ruler of the 12th, being unduly "attacked." Why was the Moon not more prominent?

Civil Rights leader Ralph Abernathy (born March 11, 1926 at 2:15 A.M., CST in Linden, Alabama) shows a health debilitation this way: the Capricorn Ascendant is ruled by Saturn-retrograde in Scorpio, which is in square with *Neptune in Leo*. Pluto opposes the Ascendant and that axis is squared by Mercury in Aries, ruling the 6th. We can surmise a weakness in Scorpio matters (Saturn in Scorpio) and/or in the heart (Neptune in Leo), and/or in the knees or skin (Capricorn Ascendant; see next section).

The Pisces Sun is conjoined with Uranus, an exacerbation of a sensitive constitution and an echo of a potential heart problem, through the Sun (regardless of its position in Pisces).

Abernathy had a stroke—a blockage of blood flow leading to or bleeding in the brain, i.e., a "brain attack" (see "Stroke," page 200). He underwent bypass surgery to relieve a blocked brain artery March 9, 1983. The Moon is well placed in Aquarius conjunct Venus and Jupiter. Why? We can see the overall health vulnerability, connected with the heart, but we can not see that that vulnerability is stroke or brain-specific.

I do not believe we have answers to these questions yet—and there are *many* questions like these. As we define what we do not know at the same time as we define and practice what we *do* know in medical astrology, perhaps more of us will be engaged with these problems and, through careful research, we will come up with further insight.

Here is an important consideration: perhaps there *is no* specific ruler-ship for the brain. Perhaps the horoscope *in its entirety* is the imprint of the brain, with each planet carrying into behavior a portion of that consciousness. In that entirety, the brain becomes the *mind*, the concept of being that is more than the functional parts of the organ.[41]

For example, there are astrological measurements that correspond to purposeful or inexplicable alteration of consciousness. These measurements usually involve the Arc or Transit of Neptune in touch *with an angle of the horoscope*—our orientation in space and time—by conjunction or square, even more predictably than when the Arc or Transit of Neptune is in high tension contact with the Sun or the Moon (or Mercury; further discussion later). The liver is the liver, the heart is the heart, the lungs are the lungs, but the brain becomes the mind, the seat of consciousness, the ALL of us.[42]

We hear about the mind working against disease: the benefits of visualization and prayer that have indeed been clinically tested affirmatively. Does the transit of Neptune contacting Moon-Mercury, for example, suggest the inspiration that can be originated to mobilize mental resources to fight disease? Does the same transit have the potential to distort the consciousness factor to open the body to the intrusion of disease, e.g., psychosomatic illness? Medical science knows that the mind can shut down the immune system! The fact that we answer affirmatively to both questions shows you how demanding astrology is, how the art of interpretation transcends stark measurements.

In our studies of the disease cancer later in this book, we will see cancer not as an accident, a viral contagion, or a localized cellular scourge. Cancer will be seen as a programmed, incipient *alteration of who we are*, focused at a weak point within us as a beginning of total system take-over.

Scorpio rulerships include the reproductive organs of both men and women (including most importantly the prostate gland (see page 81) and testicles (see page 100) in the male; the ovaries, cervix, uterus, and the

---

41 Indeed, the study world of Jyotish (Vedic Astrology), so well developed in conceptualization of the Moon (Chandra or Soma), beautifully and firmly relates the Moon to consciousness. The Moon is the single most important influence in Hindu astrology. [See *Ancient Hindu Astrology for the Modern Western Astrologer* by James T. Braha.]

42 An analogy: we know that Washington D.C. is the capital of the United States. The Treasury Department part of the government there "rules" the money situation for the entire country; the Supreme court part legislates the law of the land; the Department of Commerce part runs business, etc. But Washington is the ALL, the capital of the whole, the head, the brain. We can say that without Washington—without the capital—there is no United States; it is our national, conscious location within time and space. Study of Washington is the study of ALL of who we are as a nation.

clitoris in the female; the anus, colon, alimentary canal (leading to the anus); venereal disease (including Herpes and AIDS); the considerations and enactment of abortion; and psychoanalysis/psychotherapy.

As ruler of Scorpio, Pluto takes on rulership of many functions of the body that become urgent in the begetting and losing of life. Later in this work, we will see this dramatically, but at this stage we must recognize Pluto's rulership of Scorpio as an "everpresence" in the horoscope, a beacon illuminating the concerns listed above. Pluto is an overwhelmingly important part of signatures announcing the onset of critical illness.

Mars, as co-ruler of Scorpio, brings the concept of inflammation, the function of surgical intrusion, and the sense of attack into the Scorpio realm; the sex act, inflammation of the bowel. Mars carries the sense of stress (inflammation etc.) into whatever sign it occupies: stressed in Libra, for example, Mars can suggest hemorrhoids, the inflammation and swelling of vein clusters in the anus (the veins being ruled by Venus, ruler of Libra), and/or kidney or bladder difficulties. Mars in Taurus: a throat open to frequent infection (or the thyroid, according to some references), even an increased vulnerability to venereal disease through Venus-relationship to Taurus and Mars reflex reference to Scorpio, the sign opposite Taurus.

Pisces rulerships include most importantly the blood, the lymphatic system, and—curiously, but reliably—the feet; the concerns of alcoholism and hallucination; the circumstances of evasive diagnosis, dream trauma, anaesthesia.

Neptune, as ruler of Pisces, specifically symbolizes the function of the blood (the rulership originally given to Jupiter, co-ruler of Pisces, before the discovery of Neptune). So many, many times over the years, when identifying a difficult Neptune placement (curiously in or relating to the 6th House) I have enquired about a possible inherited blood condition and received corroboration.

In a client consultation recently, with a woman who has had many years of medical experience and is just completing her studies to be a Naturopath, I noted her Neptune in the 6th *exactly quindecile her Ascendant*. This Neptune was also square her Capricorn Moon which was conjunct her *Midheaven*. In the consultation proper, this Neptune significator and its condition suggested the long-time high-focus and upheaval this woman has encountered in trying to work through early development problems (keyed by Saturn retrograde conjunct Pluto in the 4th, ruling the 10th), trying to find her administrative power, her Self outlet (Aries Ascendant; Moon in Capricorn at the Midheaven, Mars conjunct the Capricorn Sun). Her constant changes of jobs are finally falling away as she sets out to be her own person as a Naturopath.

I enquired, "Let me ask you a question that may suggest a specialization in your field that could set you apart more from other Naturopaths: might you specialize in the study of the blood, working with blood...?" She responded with great excitement: I had touched on a subject that *had* developed as a specialty throughout all her earlier employment; she was indeed following this path strongly in her new work!"[43]

Horoscope 7, Female

Horoscope 7 (page 44) is a female who shows very clear weakness in the symbolic terms of Scorpio: Mercury, ruling the Ascendant (a center of health awareness, naturally; the beginning of life), is in Scorpio, is retrograde and conjoined with Mars. Mars in Scorpio is symbolically very powerful and alerts us immediately to inflammation, surgery, danger to the ovaries. This picture is enormous emphasized by Uranus in the 12th square to Mars-Mercury and by Pluto in the 12th square to the Sun, *ruler of the 12th*.

These measurements insist that the health profile be checked: "I am not a medical doctor, but sometimes the horoscope speaks helpfully about the weak parts of the body, especially when it is under stress, emotional, vocational, etc. Do you have a medical history about gynecological concerns? Your ovaries?

The problem this woman had endured was keyed by "life-threatening internal bleeding." She had been operated on for endometriosis (bits of tissue from the uterus becoming implanted in other pelvic organs; perhaps caused by menstrual flow backed up to the fallopian tubes. The implantations develop on the outside of the ovaries, the fallopian tubes, or the uterus, and are a serious health threat and work against pregnancy). During the operation, the surgeons discovered that both her ovaries had ruptured.[44]

---

43 Additionally with this client: I noticed that the Mars-Sun conjunction in Capricorn was tightly semisquare with the conjunction of Venus and Jupiter. I asked if there were any history of diabetes for her or her immediate family (see page 19): she said that, yes, her father had adult onset diabetes. A warning?

44 At the time of hospitalization, SA Mars was square to the Ascendant; SA Uranus was applying to conjunction with the Ascendant. These arcs and transits will be the specific focus of our work in the second part of this book.

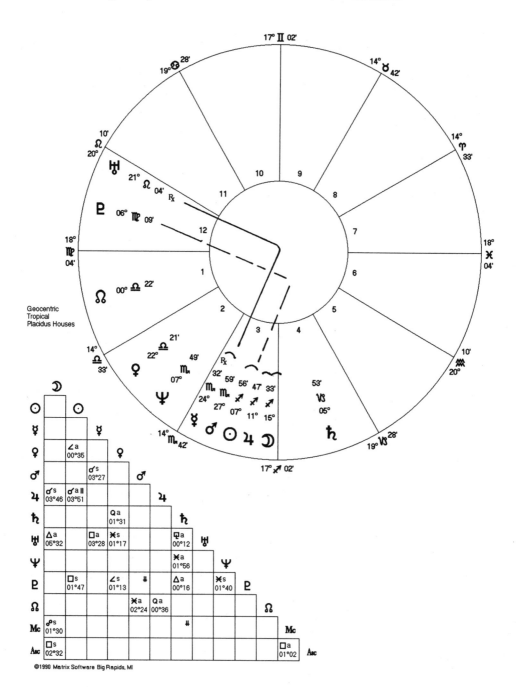

Horoscope 7, Female

Horoscope 8, Female

Horoscope 8 (page 46) guides our learning through a more subtle configuration. The points of developmental tension that can manifest as physical weakness are suggested by Mercury tightly in opposition with Jupiter, ruling the 12th and 6th Houses, respectively; Pluto square the Moon, ruler of the Ascendant (allergies, stomach); Mars is exactly opposed Uranus, and this Uranus is conjoined with Jupiter. Astrologically, in synthesis, we can see the Mars-Uranus aggravation ushered into Jupiter(-Mercury) concerns through the Uranus-Jupiter conjunction. This introduces possible concerns about the liver.

Neptune makes a quincunx (150 degrees, the sense of "necessary adjustment") with Jupiter; Neptune is square with Saturn (over the sign-line) in the 6th House. We can see Neptune feeding the sense of Saturn into Jupiter in Pisces through its quincunx. This is how aspect channels transmit significances for synthesis; the astrologer "pools" the significances of the flow-chart.

When transiting Pluto conjoined natal Saturn as transiting Saturn opposed natal Sun—both very closely—this woman was operated on for a benign tumor pressing on her spine (Saturn); the surgeons also discovered *inoperable liver cancer.*

With a challenged Jupiter or a strong focus of developmental tension in the sign of Sagittarius, we can feel sure that liver performance will show abnormality at one time or another in the life. [We can always inquire helpfully about cholesterol levels.]

Most people do not know that the liver produces its own cholesterol. In response to the diet, the liver can diminish the amount of cholesterol it creates, thus compensating for cholesterol consumed in the diet; it can excrete cholesterol directly into the bile, into the intestines, and out of the body; or the liver can deliver the ingested cholesterol directly into the bloodstream where it can begin to accumulate in the walls of the arteries to form the plaque that ultimately leads to heart attack.

The way the liver chooses to manage cholesterol is as yet unpredictable. To stabilize the cholesterol count, in addition to a stringent diet as free as possible of animal fats, medication is often needed. Full information about cholesterol, High and Low Density Lipoproteins—and, as well, infectious Hepatitis—is essential for everyone to have and can be picked up in your pharmacy, doctor's office, bookstore, public health facility.

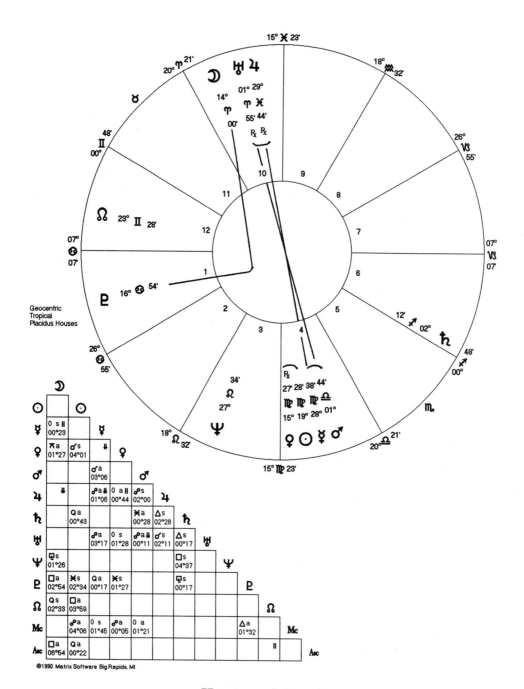

Horoscope 8, Female

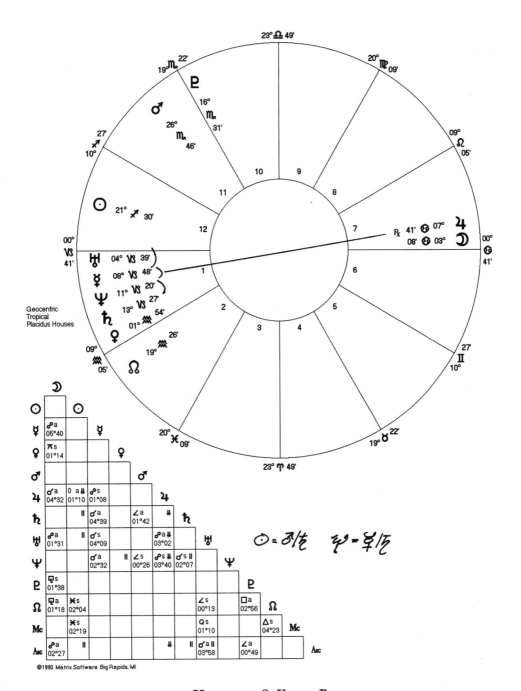

Horoscope 9, Young Boy

©1990 Matrix Software Big Rapids, MI

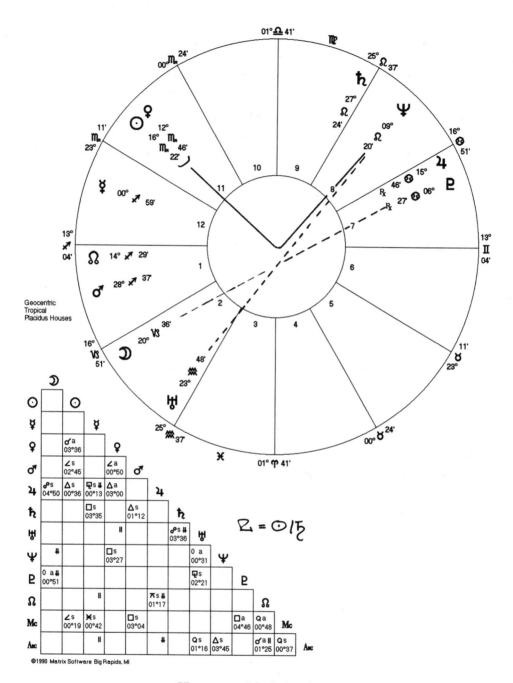

Horoscope 10, Spiro Agnew
November 9, 1918, 9:00 A.M. EST
Forest Hill, MD
76W23 — 39N35

Horoscope 9, Young Boy

Horoscope 9 (see page 47) shows a seven-year old boy who was born HIV-positive and has developed leukemia (cancer of the blood cells) and squamous cell carcinoma on his right lung. This diagnosis suggests Pluto, Neptune, and Mercury, respectively. The horoscope presents Pluto in Scorpio, *semisquare the Ascendant*; the Ascendant ruler Saturn is conjoined with Neptune, and the two of them oppose Jupiter, ruler of the 12th. Note that the Sun in the 12th is in tight quindecile with Jupiter. Finally, Mercury is conjoined with Uranus, which also "aggravates" the Ascendant.

This young horoscope also supports the midpoint picture Sun=Mars/Saturn, a distinct promisor of body health breakdown, especially within measurements that suggest threatening debilitation; and Neptune=Mercury/Saturn, "depression, a sad spirit looking for a ray of hope."[45]

Horoscope 10, Spiro Agnew

Horoscope 10 is the horoscope of Spiro Agnew, Vice-President to Richard Nixon. Agnew died of leukemia. The blood vulnerability is clearly defined by the square between the Sun-Venus conjunction and *Neptune* (note that Venus rules the 6th) along with Neptune's quindecile contact with Uranus (with Uranus opposed by Saturn). The system is weakened generally as well by the quindecile between Pluto and the Moon, and we can note that Pluto=Sun/Saturn, "a threat to health, and a pressure to change one's value system."

---

45 With the inherited AIDS condition, there is much to say for seeing the 12th House Sun, ruler of the 8th, quindecile the difficult Jupiter, ruler of the 12th. This Jupiter is conjoined with the Moon (the Mother), the final dispositor of the horoscope. Note that the parental rulers, Mars and Venus are peregrine.

The Earth Family

The general Earth-family overview of references includes the bones, the muscles (with Mars considered strongly with *the function* of the muscles), and nutrition—everything that builds our body's structure and gives us power. The medical word for this purview is "anabolic," coming from two Greek words meaning *male-producing build-up,* i.e., "constructive metabolism."[46]

Symbolic king in the Earth Family certainly is the planet Saturn, conclusively given rulership over the bones, our skeletal structure (and thus referential to the spine, the back in general), the gall bladder (storage place for the bile used by the liver), the teeth, the knees that help coordinate the body's movement, the skin that defines the body, and the minerals calcium and sulfur (among others).[47]

Horoscope 11, Arnold Schwarzenegger

Horoscope 11 is the horoscope of Arnold Schwarzenegger, the winner of myriad world wide body-building titles and, as well, for many years now, the world's most popular movie star. The achievement of this man—the sheer power of his body and his career—have been astounding: the son of a policeman in Graz, Austria is now known throughout the world, is married to a Kennedy, and is in every sense of the word a Hollywood and business-world tycoon. His horoscope is a portrait of enormous strength *and critical weakness.*

Arnold's rise to epic prominence has been described as awesome reward for obsessive drive, compulsion, extraordinary self-application and business genius. It is not surprising that Schwarzenegger's horoscope has *four quindecile aspects:* Moon with Mercury, Mars, and Ascendant; Neptune with the Midheaven. These quindecile accents alert us to the Moon in Capricorn (the reigning need to make things happen) in the 6th (workaholic position) that is consumed with learning (Mercury rising trined Jupiter) and empowered mightily by Mars (muscle power, intensified by Uranus), in an effort to put the self forward dominantly

---

46 Sports news often reports the issues of athletes using "anabolic steroids," the illegal drugs related chemically to the male sex hormone testosterone, which promotes the buildup of muscle tissue. Legitimate medical uses of anabolic steroids include treatment of skeletal and growth disorders and certain types of anemia (and efforts to offset certain types of irradiation and chemotherapy).

47 See Nauman, pages 195–228.

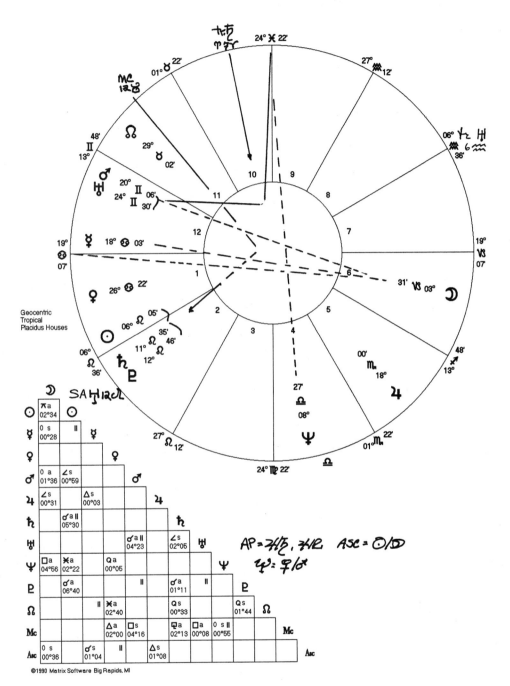

Horoscope 11, Arnold Schwarzenegger
July 30, 1947, 4:10 A.M. CED
Graz, Austria
15E27 — 47N05

©1990 Matrix Software Big Rapids, MI

(reinforced by Ascendant=Sun/Moon; i.e., the Ascendant square the midpoint of Sun-Moon).

Neptune rules the Midheaven (profession) and is quindecile to the Midheaven and square the Moon: here is enormous vision in terms of ego dominance through the profession; here is the introduction of the motion picture industry (Neptune), the earlier years of show business body-building performance.[48]

Fulfilling the expectations we have from the network of aspects described above, we can note the power core of this entire horoscope: the Leo Sun pulled into the Saturn-Pluto conjunction, sextile Neptune (supporting the vision). This is power; this is termination of the status quo in order to advance as far as possible.

Uranus-Mars and Saturn-Pluto work together here: note that Saturn makes contact with Uranus through a semisquare (Mars-Uranus parallel Pluto). This is "pumping iron" (the mineral ruled by Mars), and the pump is directed powerfully into the profession: Mars-Uranus are tightly square the Midheaven.[49]

With the Moon in Earth-sign Capricorn, central to the horoscope aspect patterns and ruling the Ascendant, we feel the pervasive focus of structure, of body power. It is all there.

And something else is there too, something alarmingly contradictory: with such focus on the triple conjunction in Leo, we must be alerted *to potential difficulty with Schwarzenegger's heart!*

Schwarzenegger had open heart surgery on April 16, 1997: transiting Uranus was at 6 Aquarius exactly opposed his Sun in Leo; SA Uranus was at 12 Leo exactly conjunct his Pluto in Leo; SA Midheaven was at 12 Taurus exactly square his Pluto; transiting Saturn was at 7 Aries opposing Neptune, and more.

[A review of Solar Arcs, used more and more intensely throughout the rest of this study, is presented on page 79.]

---

48 Please recall Judy Garland's peregrine Neptune, ruler of her Midheaven (see page 25).

49 Mars is applied power, the work accomplished by the muscles.—There is confusion about ruler-ship of "muscle." Earth Family yes, keyed to Saturn by some theorists, keyed to Mars by others. While we must be aware that these points of confusion exist and are gradually being worked out, we must not let them get in the way of our work: we must negotiate analysis carefully, knowing what we don't know as well as what we do know. This point about muscles can probably come down to "Saturnine" in terms of strategic strategy or weakness from malnutrition or cramping; "Martian" in terms of achievement or a debilitating tear.

Skin Cancer—Melanoma
Horoscope 12, Male

Saturn's rulership of the skin is undisputed. Horoscope 12 is the horoscope of a patient with melanoma, the most deadly but least common cancer of the skin. Usually, melanoma arises painlessly from cells that produce the skin's pigment (melanin). Approximately seventy percent of these dark, splotchy cancers appear on normal skin and about thirty percent arise from an existing mole that has underdone sudden changes somehow.

When observed and treated early, the recovery rate is very high. If not, melanoma is quickly lethal: the cells eat down through the skin, enter the blood stream, and flow quickly to vital organs, including the brain. But epidermal melanoma cancer is growing in occurrence; in certain regions of the country with a great deal of sunlight, it is reaching epidemic proportions. More and more people are observing changed moles on their body, recreational sun-exposure times are catching up with the aging post-World War II generation, and modern-day tanning beds are taking their toll.[50]

Stressed Saturn positions or positions within Capricorn and/or relating to the 12th House or 6th should urge us to inquire about the past history of skin cancer (the disposition to skin cancer is inherited) and to advise about the high potential of its occurrence.

This horoscope shows Saturn opposed by Neptune, ruler of the 12th. Pluto is square to the Sun.

Please note the "solarized" notation (⊙) on the chart: it indicates an *untimed* horoscope. I am introducing untimed horoscopes gradually in this study as well, in preparation for the timing section that is the major focus of this book, and to show that we can indeed learn much and do much good from untimed horoscope. When we arbitrarily use sunrise for the chart time, we are accentuating the Sun, the giver of life, and *we are introducing an Ascendant and 12th House bias to the chart.* This bias becomes a strong focus on the health core of the chart. The "Solarscope" is extremely effective in helping with anticipation of critical illness, as we shall see.

Note that these aspects we have observed will occur regardless of the time of the client's birth that day; Saturn opposed by Neptune and Pluto square Sun do not go away. Note also that the Aries Point=Sun/Saturn, potential ill health is pushed forward strongly into prominence. The

---

50 *Phoenix Magazine*, August 1955, "Beyond Skin Deep" by Peter Aleshire.

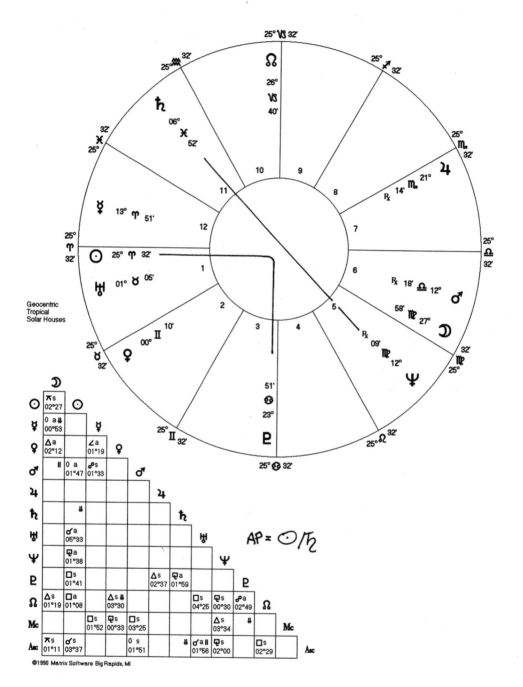

Geocentric
Tropical
Solar Houses

AP = ☉/♄

©1990 Matrix Software Big Rapids, MI

Solarscope 12, Male ☉

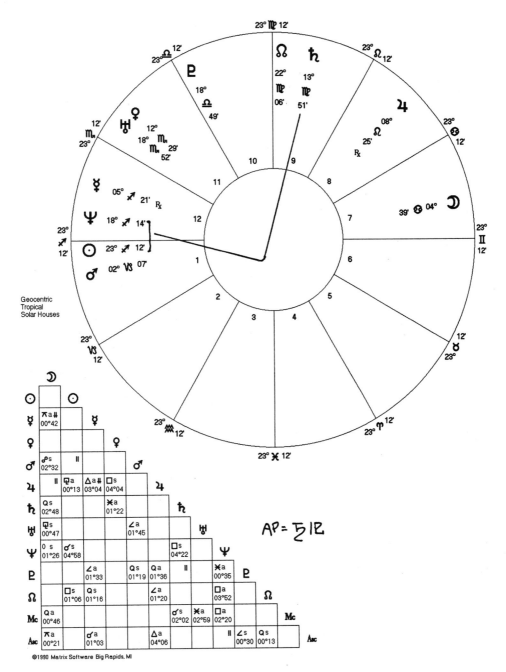

Geocentric
Tropical
Solar Houses

AP = ♄ 12

©1990 Matrix Software Big Rapids, MI

Solarscope 13, Male ☉

melanoma was diagnosed with transiting Saturn at 22 Pisces, which, with high probability, opposed this Virgo Moon position in the Solar 6th.[51]

Solarscope 13, Male

Solarscope (untimed) 13 is another patient with skin melanoma: Saturn in Virgo squared by Neptune in the Solar 12th, conjoined the Sun. The Aries Point=Saturn/Pluto, Pluto ruling the Solar 12th. Diagnosis occurred with transiting Saturn at 18 Pisces, exactly square Neptune.

In both these cases, Saturn is dominatingly aspected. In my horoscope shown here (number 14, on page 57), I have natal Saturn at the Midheaven opposed Neptune. When Saturn transited its natal position for the second time and then went on to square my Sun one and one-half years later, I developed two separate skin cancers, neither a melanoma, but each requiring surgical removal. From the Moon in Leo position, reinforced by the opposition with Venus, the Moon ruling my Ascendant, one could infer my love of the sun, and, as well, every doctor admonishing me to be careful of the sun, telling me that injuries of the skin from the sun are absorbed *cumulatively over a lifetime.*

Is this Saturn-Neptune opposition contact a sub-generational disposition to vulnerability, since all people born April-August 1935, February–May 1936, or August 1936–March 1937 have Saturn in opposition with Neptune, to one degree or another? The answer is probably affirmative, especially when the Ascendant, the 12th House, and the Sun are under high developmental tension by ruler aspect or placement. As we shall see, the catalyst to bring vulnerability out into the open can be provided ostensibly "out of the blue" *by Arcs and Transits into the vital areas of health concerns that we are studying.*

Continuing with my horoscope, we have seen the manifestation of my spine problem (see page 31) and now the skin cancers. Here is a Capricorn Sun with a stressed Saturn: the suggestion of problems with the bones, with the knees in particular (severe osteoarthritis), is emphatically indicated. Here is a Saturn stressed with Neptune involvement (blood): the suggestion of problems with blood pressure is certainly tenable...and also correct.[52]

---

51 The Moon would receive this opposition from transiting Saturn within orb at any birth time from midnight forward to 6 A.M.

52 Erratic high blood pressure; not low, as one would think from Saturn's involvement. We can not yet explain these nuances astrologically.

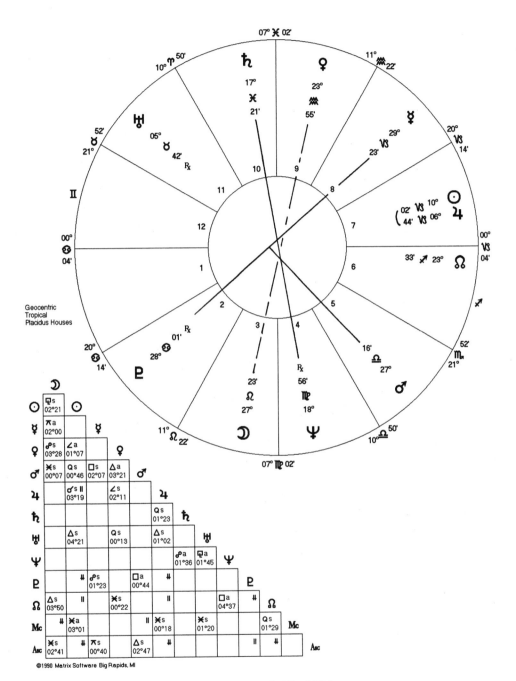

Geocentric
Tropical
Placidus Houses

©1990 Matrix Software Big Rapids, MI

Horoscope 14, Noel Tyl
December 31, 1936, 3:57 P.M. EST
West Chester, PA
75W36 — 39N58

Aspect Routings

Another point of confusion easily arises when we discuss the outer planets. When we are dealing with Saturn, Uranus, Neptune, and Pluto in aspect with one another (or the other planets), which planet is "doing the damage in our drama," if I may abbreviate the thought? Which planet is *doing the aspecting?*

This question is important because the aspecting planet—whichever it is—*leads our analytical thinking.* For example, "Mercury opposed by Saturn" or "Saturn opposing Mercury" portrays Saturn homing in on Mercury. The "heaviness" of Saturn somehow overpowers Mercury in our way of appreciating these symbols in the drama of synthesis.

Uranus "does something to Venus" when it aspects the inner planet, *not the other way around.* Pluto does something to Venus when it aspects the inner planet, not the other way around.

This is also a clear problem in Solar Arcs (and transits). For example, when Saturn arcs (or transits) to contact with the natal Mercury, we can expect that, through some kind of trial or duress, some maturation through depression, some sense of heavy responsibility over time, wisdom is ideally brought into the picture. On the other hand, when Mercury arcs (or transits) to contact with natal Saturn, we can expect that the thinking process gets involved with discipline, hard work, deep analysis.

When Venus arcs (or transits) to natal Uranus, we can expect that grace is added to individuality of expression, that one will gain appreciation by others and be desired. When Uranus arcs (or transits) to natal Venus we can expect intensification of love desires and emotional, adventurous excitement.

So, returning to Arnold Schwarzenegger's horoscope (see page 51), what are we distilling out of the major aspects? Saturn is conjoined with Pluto; I feel that this power aspect is the same as Pluto conjunct Saturn: hard, hard work, potential loss for gain in grand proportions (here the break-down of muscle tissue to rebuild the muscle bigger and better; the importance of minerals in the process).

Jupiter is square Saturn-Pluto—or is *Jupiter* squared by Saturn-Pluto? I have found repeatedly over many years that any time Jupiter and Saturn are in strong aspect to one another, the concept of *proving a point* is introduced into the life; any time Jupiter and Pluto are in strong aspect to one another, the concept of robustness, busyness, or, most commonly, *resourcefulness* is introduced into life activity.

With Mars and Uranus here we see the enormous intensification (Uranus) of Mars activities and applied energy (and medically, the intensification of muscular build-up) channelled into divers directions (Gemini) professionally (Aries in the 10th). We can see the energizing (Mars) of all things adventurous (Uranus), especially in a foreign country (Uranus rules the 9th). The quindecile between Mars and the Moon suggest that his overwork of muscle and his overwork in diversified interests professionally (Mars-Uranus square the Midheaven) are passionately obsessive.

All of this is for identity development to the utmost: the Moon is quindecile to the Ascendant, which means then that Moon=Mars/Ascendant, "emotional temperament, ego drive to make things happen." We also see Ascendant=Sun/Moon; *any planet or point configurated by conjunction, square, or opposition with the Sun-Moon midpoint is going to incline to horoscope dominance;* here the Ascendant, the ego projection, dominates.

We can note as well that AP=Jupiter/Saturn. "Mr. Schwarzenegger, this colossal development of yours on so many fronts, what point has it all been making in your life, through your life?" Schwarzenegger will be all too happy to explain most revealingly.

We have an instinctive and well-schooled tendency to relate natal aspects of Jupiter to "augmenting or assimilating something," more than to "receiving something"—or we would say that Schwarzenegger's Saturn-Pluto conjunction in Leo is "pounding away" at his Jupiter in Scorpio: his religious belief system, perhaps; his liver; a concern with his reproductive system(?).

We have the instinct to see Saturn as controlling, Uranus as intensifying, Neptune as obfuscating (camouflaging, bewildering), and Pluto as empowering. Relationships between these outer planets are generational image-keys for sure.[53] However, our concern here is with cursory medical diagnosis: do our eyes go to my Saturn because of Neptune in opposition to it, or do our eyes go to Neptune because of Saturn's opposition to *it*? I have had terribly bad knees since age fifty-five to fifty-seven (but initially

---

53 See Erin Sullivan's *Dynasty* (Arcana, 1997) for a full exploration of family and generational astrology.

aggravated early on in my teens and early twenties in athletics) and I have had to control elevated blood pressure with medicine for the past thirty years. *Both arms* of the Saturn-Neptune opposition have manifested the tension of the aspect.

In my horoscope, we instinctively see Mars in Libra squaring the opposition between Mercury and Pluto; Mars energizes the potentially powerful perception symbolized there. We do not see as easily Pluto squaring Mars in Libra; since we always try for organization, for seamless synthesis, we do not instinctively break apart the T-Square. But we have already discussed that I had critically severe lower back problems that required surgery, and that I protect the lower back even today many years later. Mars in Libra *does* receive the tension from Pluto in Cancer. But there is no stomach concern whatsoever throughout my entire life; i.e., it does not seem that Mars aggravates the Pluto reference to the sign Cancer, and the Moon is not challenged.

Dual Rulerships

As we have seen so far in our discussion of cursory diagnostics, we have the confusions of labels and the different reference "feel" between sign and planet. Perhaps sign *is* organ and planet *is* function, but as yet it does not hold up. And then we have the problem of dual rulerships, key planets ruling more than one sign.

Mercury rules Gemini and Virgo, an Air sign and an Earth sign. Traditionally, we look to Gemini, to Mercury in Gemini or referring to Gemini from another sign as a symbolism for the lungs, breathing, communicating; the shoulders, arms, and hands and their activity; moving about; nerve function. Traditionally, we look to Virgo, to Mercury in Virgo or referring to Virgo from another sign as a symbolism for diet, eating disorders (anorexia, bulimia); blood circulation (with the Sun), hygiene; mental orientation, including intelligence, discernment, dyslexia, dementia, and delirium (with other planets keying the focus, of course).

Venus rules Libra and Taurus, an Air sign and an Earth sign. Traditionally, we look to Libra, to Venus in Libra or referring to Libra from another sign as a symbolism for the lower back, the kidneys, the bladder, hemorrhoids; the hair, and, with Mars, surely plastic surgery.[54]

---

54 Cornell adds the sign Capricorn for "hair," i.e., Venus in Capricorn, since the hair is an appendage of the skin (a Capricorn concern, specifically manifested through Saturn).

Taurus, Venus in Taurus or referring to Taurus from another sign traditionally symbolizes the throat, the thyroid gland; sugar metabolism.

There are many more symbolisms issuing from the planets than we are dealing with here, of course. We are concentrating on an orientation to cursory medical diagnosis of most common concerns, i.e., delineation of the major weak places in a person's body through study of the horoscope.

Synthesis Guidelines

Within all of these overlapping concerns about aspect routings, rulership networks, symbolisms of organs and functions, *three practical guidelines do emerge*—not just for medical astrology, but for life analysis as well:

- Planets interact most meaningfully in terms of developmental tension between two planetary groups: the planetary group of *the Sun, Moon, (Ascendant), Mercury, Venus, and Jupiter* in touch with the planetary group *Mars, Saturn, Uranus, Neptune, and Pluto.*

- The specific quality of "hard" aspect between two (or more) planets does not play as important a role in judgment as does *the FACT OF CONTACT between the two planets.*

- The suggestions of potential organic or functional weakness exist significantly *within the planetary symbolisms themselves, regardless of the sign that each planet is in.*

Just consider in astrology how much symbolic content has been given to each planet! We see Saturn, for example, and our mind is flooded with understandings of the Earth Family, the Sign Capricorn, the empirical evidence of Saturn itself and its aspects with all the other planets. Then, we see Saturn in contact with another planet and we are flooded with all we know about *that* symbol. The two come together in contact of some kind and the mix is made. When we add *time* to this mix, (i.e., the aging process), synthesis of the analysis of potential illness becomes even more powerful.

In studying the contact between planets, we are pursuing the chief channels of developmental tension: the square, opposition, quindecile, conjunction, sesquiquadrate, and semisquare. *We create enough synthesis of developmental tensions to support an educated question to the client,* a question that may unlock a world of warning keyed to time measurements in the near future.

Simplifying Structures

An easy example: probably because the Sun and Moon were called the "Lights" in traditional astrology, the Sun was given rulership of one eye and the Moon was given rulership of the other. We have consulted with clients who have the Sun in touch with Saturn or the Moon in touch with Saturn, and there has certainly been the presence of weakness/disease in the eyes. I have two such horoscopes at hand right now: a woman with Saturn in between Sun and Moon in conjunction (her twin brother has the same configuration, of course) and another woman with Saturn conjunct the Sun, and all of them have conspicuous difficulty with their eyes.[55]

Look again at Horoscope 1 (see page 12): this woman was born with Saturn opposed her Sun. She told me that her extremely bad eyesight had been discovered in the first grade when she simply could not see her teacher unless she was in the first row of the classroom. Teddy Roosevelt (see page 28) wore glasses (sometimes a monocle), note Pluto opposed Sun; Art Buchwald has eye problems (see page 35) with Pluto square his Moon and Neptune square his Sun; the same thing with Mike Wallace (see page 37) with Neptune and Saturn square his Moon [and traditional astrology places the eyes—vision—symbolically in the 1st House]; Arnold Schwarzenegger undoubtedly wears contacts (see page 51) with Neptune square Moon and Saturn conjunct the Sun.

Horoscope 15, Female

Look at Horoscope 15: this woman is eighty-five years old in 1997, hale and hearty, bright and feisty. She has severe glaucoma.

Glaucoma is a group of diseases of the eye which cause progressive damage to the optic nerve through increased pressure (Neptune) within the eyeball. As the optic nerve deteriorates, blind spots develop. In the United States, glaucoma is a leading cause of blindness; about three percent of Americans older than sixty-five—about two million people—are affected.[56]

While most adults after the age of about forty-two seem to need help with their eyesight (including me, without a hard aspect with my Sun or Moon), the cases presented here so far are cases of eye problems and/or lifelong vision difficulties *beyond the norm*. Since we take for granted in

---

55 Traditional references labeled the Sun as ruler of the right eye in the male and the Moon as ruler of the right eye in the female, but I believe this was more for symmetry and Hermetic neatness, than it was corroboration of empirical evidence.

56 Mayo, page 550.

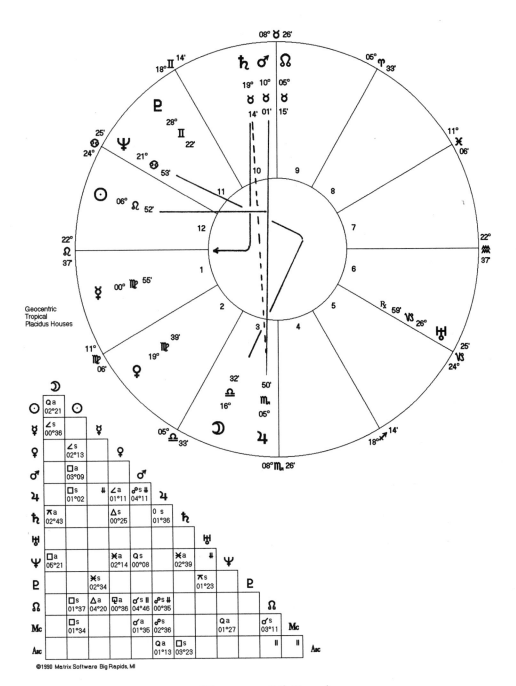

Horoscope 15, Female

modern times that older people need glasses to help keep vision keen, we tend to overlook the potential and presence of eye disease.[57]

Note that this lady has Neptune square to her Moon, ruler of the 12th, and the Sun squared by Mars. She has heart problems (Mars square the Sun in Leo; Saturn square the Leo Ascendant), and, following up on the Saturn in an Earth sign square the Ascendant, she has just developed skin cancer in five different spots on her body (during the period when transiting Uranus opposed her Sun).

Note that this lady has Sun in contact with *Jupiter*, Mars in contact with *Jupiter*, and *Jupiter* in quindecile with Saturn, ruler of the 6th. This is a strong focus on Jupiter, on the liver. My client has adult onset diabetes (see page 19). Note please: *Venus is semisquare Jupiter.*

Notice how little mention, for the last two pages, is now being made of the *signs* holding the key planets! Notice how much understanding is flowing *into the symbols alone* through their contact with each other!

Finally, the lady claims to have had colon cancer when transiting Saturn opposed her Ascendant, but there is no Pluto indication of note. We get to Scorpio through reflex action from Saturn in Taurus, i.e., to the opposite sign, Scorpio, and we note again the stressed Jupiter in Scorpio making a quindecile with Saturn.

From my experience, this is too circuitous networking for colon problems. Interestingly, the woman's lifelong friend whispers that my client never had cancer; she just made a self-aggrandizing situation out of her colon problems (the Leo Ascendant). But, as we shall see, the activation of an angle by transiting Saturn at the time claimed for her colon cancer does defend her credibility.

Horoscope 16, Female

Horoscope 16 is the daughter of the lady discussed just above (Horoscope 15). With Saturn opposed the Sun, we can expect eye problems, eye disease. Glaucoma is *inherited,* it runs in families, and this lady at age sixty-three has indeed developed glaucoma and has had eye surgery.

Additionally, this daughter has had a polyp removed from her colon (see Mars conjunct Pluto, especially sensitized as ruler of the Ascendant

---

57 In my latest physical checkup, the internist searched into my eyes. He said, "You have the beginnings of cataracts there." I knew that he was wrong, astrologically: my horoscope does not support that potential although my age may invite it. I made an appointment with an eye surgeon and went through every test in the books: there is no cataract; there was nothing of any concern. We will be talking about mis-diagnosis by doctors later in this study.

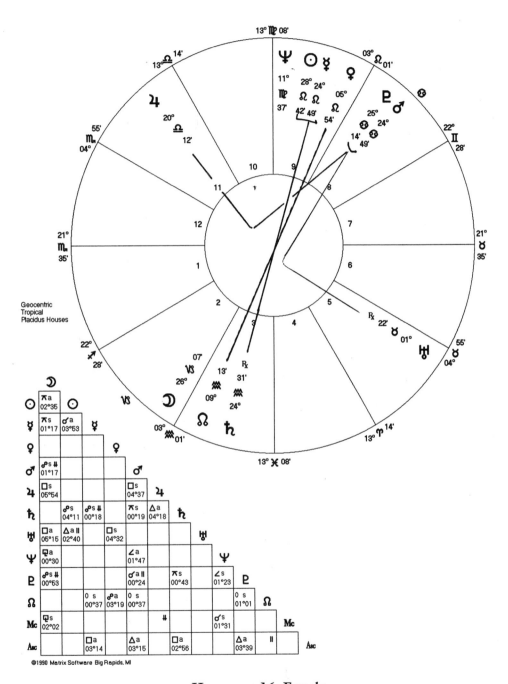

Horoscope 16, Female

and 12th and receiving the square from Uranus); she has had kidney problems (Mars-Pluto square to Jupiter in Libra, with Venus receiving the square from Uranus and ruling the 6th) to the point that an organ donor was standing by; and she has had severe gynecological crisis with an ectopic pregnancy (when the fertilized egg implants itself anywhere other than the lining of the uterus, usually in the fallopian tube (Libra); occurring in 1 out of 100 pregnancies[58]) corresponding to the already observed Pluto tensions, especially the relation with Jupiter in Libra and the Venus disposition. This latter crisis occurred when transiting Neptune was tightly square Pluto from Libra, when transiting Uranus was conjunct Pluto, and transiting Saturn was square Venus!

Horoscope 17, Hazel

This is the horoscope of an indomitable, alert, productive, indeed feisty lady ninety years old in 1997. She has a fascinating profession: she is a lifelong researcher, writer, and lecturer about haunting spirits—personal possession and haunted houses. Hazel is a ghost-buster! Not only has she stood up to thousands of spirits, but she has stood up to Nature, to the aging process, which naturally has tried to invade her health through the weakest places in her body many times over during her long lifetime.[59]

We can enumerate these weak places easily, i.e., the bodily organs and functions which we would cite as part of an astrological overview of her health profile:

1. *The blood pressure* (Neptune, ruling the 6th, opposed by Uranus, quindecile with Venus, ruler of the Ascendant): Hazel has very low blood pressure, but it has not been problematic.

2. *The lower back* (Moon in *Libra* quindecile Saturn, *Venus* quindecile Neptune; Moon square Neptune; Uranus and Neptune square the *Libra* Ascendant; Saturn-Sun conjunction in the 5th): Hazel has back problems, "The doctors told me long ago when I was in my forties (a half-century ago; when Neptune was transiting Libra), that I would need a complete spine fusion!" Hazel beat the prognosis with a strict and continuous regimen of back exercise.

---

58 Mayo, page 199.

59 Hazel Denning, author of *True Hauntings: Spirits with a Purpose*, Llewellyn 1996, has the following "hidden" measurement signatures which certainly correspond to her writing and unusual profession: AP=Moon/Mercury, Neptune/Pluto, Saturn/Ascendant; Ascendant= Neptune/Midheaven.

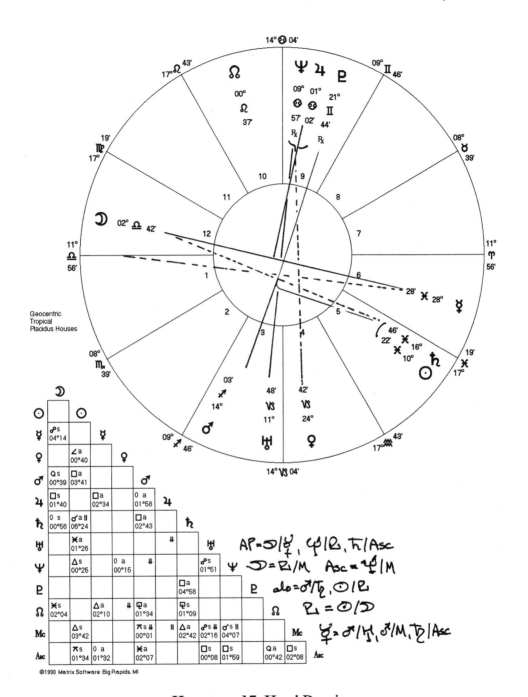

Horoscope 17, Hazel Denning
March 1, 1907, 8:20 P.M. CST
Woodstock, IL
88W27 — 42N19

3. *The stomach* (*Moon* ruling Cancer, its tension structure; Neptune in Cancer, opposed by Uranus): Hazel has severe digestion problems ; "it's the weakest point in my body, and I am very careful about it."

4. *The knees* (reflex sign response opposite the Cancer focus, Uranus in *Capricorn* opposed by Neptune, *Saturn* conjunct the Sun, squared by Mars, the Sun and Saturn in the 5th): Hazel has no knee problems(!).

5. *The eyes* (Saturn conjunct the Sun, Moon squared by Neptune; Ascendant squared by Uranus and Neptune; *Pluto=Sun/Moon*): five years ago in 1991–92 (with transiting Uranus and Neptune squaring her Ascendant and Midheaven), Hazel experienced macular degeneration (the most frequent cause of legal blindness, an increasing blurring of central vision). She says, "I will NOT lose my sight; I took up an intense vitamin therapy, meditation... and it has worked."

6. *The lungs* (Saturn square Pluto in Gemini, Mercury quindecile the Ascendant, from the 6th, ruling the 12th): no problems with the lungs(!).

7. *The liver* (Neptune conjunct Jupiter, which is receiving a quindecile from Mars in Sagittarius; see page 17): Hazel says, "Yes, I've always had a dangerous condition there, since I was fourteen [with transiting Saturn conjunct the Moon and exactly square Jupiter]; I have always been told that my liver is 'underfunctioning'."

We can not explain why Hazel has not experienced serious problems with her knees or lungs. Perhaps her resistance to these particular problems is an inherited genetic strength and that is indicated in the aspect routing that is not pronounced enough for us to see.

Our study is bent on identifying the *potentials,* and for Hazel, the problems with her back, stomach, eyes, and liver were very clearly indicated indeed. I was able to enumerate them all without ever having met Hazel, corroborating the findings by telephone.

It is natural that, as we learn and practice cursory diagnosis techniques in astrology, these after-the-fact torrents of synthesis can be intimidating. How can we possibly look into these things—these multiple disease/weakness potentials—*ahead of time,* especially with a young client with so much life time ahead and a relatively fine health record? How can we do that with the proper rationale; how can we present the possibilities with grace and responsibility without alarming our clients unduly; how do we create a referral atmosphere instead of a panic situation? These issues are covered in the last section of this book. It is not as difficult as it may seem now.

Aging

Naturally, the longer we live, the more such patterns of illness will develop in us all; the horoscope will parallel the breakdown of our physiological (and mental) makeup. Over time, more and more of the tension structures in the horoscope will mirror complications in the body's systemic integrity. This is the progress of aging (senescence).

People in the United States and Great Britain are living *twice* as long now as they did in Victorian times. Aging has become a crucial study area for science and bureaucracy, trying to prolong life and working to accommodate the growing numbers of people living into older age.

The reason that we are living longer is not so much that we are improving structurally in mind and body over ancient times as it is that life around us has improved dramatically: food harvests, medical discoveries, our combat against diseases bacteriological, social, and political. We come closer and closer to fulfilling the maximum life span that has probably not changed from time immemorial.[60]

Insurance actuarial tables dramatically reflect the reality of aging: for 100,000 males and 100,000 females born in the West, there is a life expectancy today of 70.5 years for males and 76.7 years for females (1988 statistics). One hundred years *earlier,* life expectancy was 43.9 for males and 46.3 for females.[61]

At age twenty in today's world, we can expect to live some fifty-one years more; at age forty, some thirty-two years more; at age sixty, some sixteen years; at eighty, some six years. There is a shift in the numbers as we age. I see this as our *gaining* life time—and perhaps skill and efficiency in living—by *surviving* life time.

---

60 Gosden, page 5. There has been a sixfold increase in centenarians over the past thirty years; page 75. The twentieth century is probably the first century in which people in the West could count on living to see their grandchildren grow up. For every 100 boys born a century ago, only fifty would live to forty-four or more years; page 81.

61 Gosden, page 76.

Where we live has much to do with how long we live. Japan's economic success over the past forty years has something to do with its place at the top of the life expectancy list; whereas, in contrast, life expectancy in a Nigerian village is just forty-three years, with nearly one-fourth of all children dying before their fifth birthday. Roger Gosden, prestigious professor and researcher from Cambridge, Edinburgh, and Duke Universities, says, "Life expectance overall is affected as much by social differences in wealth as by gross national product or other macroeconomic indicators. That is why the United States, with its enormous economic gulf between rich and poor, comes way down the list at number fifteen. Countries with the most equitable distributions of wealth, such as Iceland, Switzerland and Sweden, appear near the top of the list.

"Ever rising standards of living, however, will give diminishing returns as we get closer to our biological limits for survival. Over the twentieth century, infants gained about twenty-five years in life expectance, adolescents fifteen years, forty-five-year-olds six years and sixty-five-year-olds only two. The social and medical battles against infectious diseases have been relatively easy compared with the intractable problem of the aging process itself. We shall have to wait for a radical biological intervention before the life statistics of elderly people can be substantially improved, because if one disease, such as heart disease, does not trip us up, something else, like cancer or stroke, will."[62]

When we study the mathematical ratios that capture the aging process, we see that it gets progressively more difficult for us to reach the next age group. *The probability of dying from natural causes doubles every eight years during adult life.*

These kinds of equations were developed early in the nineteenth century by an Edinburgh actuary, Benjamin Gompertz, and are respected and applicable yet today. The numerical picture is constant for all the different racial groups and populations around the globe and has not changed, at least since Victorian times. The numerical picture does not define age per se, but *the accumulation of all terminal diseases;* over time, the velocity of nerve impulses, the maximum heart rate, the kidney blood flow, the maximum breathing capacity, and the maximum work rate, the ability to hear, to see, to smell, shrinkage and dehydration of the brain, as well as female fertility all drop off at different rates.

---

62 Gosden, page 78.

There have been fascinating theories and engaging research into the possible concomitants of aging to be found in early life experience. In the 1950s California medical physicist Hardin Jones suggested that *a person's biological age is programmed by disease experience early in life;* that improvements in life expectancy were mirroring the steady decline in infant mortality that had occurred over the past century. *He also found that favorable experiences early in life have a greater impact than being a rugged survivor of a hostile environment.* Gosden then suggests that "while a healthy infancy does not slow the aging clock, it may reset the time at which the life span begins to tick away."[63]

These findings by Jones become very important in this study as I postulate and track the concept of "accumulated developmental deficit" in relation to critical illness.

The research into senescence has been propelled by the discovery of hormones (from the Greek *to stir up, to excite*). Hormones are products of living cells that circulate in body fluids and produce special effects. Discovery and work with hormones began in the last decade of the nineteenth century and continue still.

The initial fad of hormones was for rejuvenation of the male energy profile, male sexual vigor. Sex gland grafting with tissues from animal testes was the rage early in the twentieth century, sparking modern laboratory expeditions for the Fountain of Youth, the Elixir of Life. Present-day hormone therapies powerfully and sensitively work with female ovulation and menopause, birth control, libido for both genders, muscular growth, and more. Side effects abound in hormone therapies, and these side effects have often been harnessed to good work; the birth control pill in women, for example, reduces the risks of getting cancer of the ovaries and uterus, reduces thyroid problems, rheumatoid arthritis, peptic ulcers and fibroids.

We can appreciate the progress of aging dramatically when we consider that a modern woman will typically experience 400 or more menstrual cycles and ovulations in her lifetime—*three times as many* as her ancient forebears and the remaining bands of hunter-gatherers in Africa today (where pregnancies are spaced by extending post-partem suckling

---

63 Gosden, page 97. Researchers also have found that babies weighing less than 6.6 pounds at birth suffered from ten times as much heart disease, high blood pressure and diabetes as those who weighed more than ten pounds at birth. This difference persisted even after taking smoking, alcohol, and social conditions into account.

periods). Prosperous lifestyles in the West encourage earlier puberty and possibly a later menopause, which add up to another fifty or so menstrual cycles and more estrogen exposure (the female sex hormone produced by the ovaries). Are the ovaries working far, far more than their originally designed "job description" specified?

And then there is the world of cells that live and die within us just as we do ourselves. We need to recall Astrology's Hermetic basis of the microcosm reflecting the macrocosm; it holds an important position in our considerations of aging and dying, i.e., the life and death of the cells—the hundred trillion or more cells—that make up our body. The cells are the smallest living units in our make up, incredibly tiny (ten thousand of them clustered together are just visible to the unaided eye), yet every one of these cells, all-pervasive in our body, contains within it, in the form of the molecule called DNA, a kind of chemical hologram of *an entire individual human being.* Theoretically, each cell has the information necessary to reproduce the entire being, of which it is but the hundred-trillionth part![64]

These cells live and die and are recycled within our body, just as the body itself will be recycled in its entirety through the soil and through plants to provide nutrients and oxygen to nourish human cells yet unborn.

This book is not the forum—nor is my expertise specialized enough—for rich study of hormones and their use in medical healing, of cells and their reproduction. The essence of the hormone issue in particular with regard to our study of critical illness throughout the aging process is that *sex organs are the powerhouse of the body, and hormone deficiency is the root of aging.*[65]

Does this medical fact suggest to astrology that aging has some *specific* reference to the 5th and 8th Houses, the Houses through which we read the sexual profile? Through the natural distribution of signs, those Houses are ruled by the Sun (Leo, 5th), the "Life Giver," and Mars-Pluto (Scorpio, 8th), the "Energizer."[66]

After studying many, many horoscopes for only the concept of aging, I feel I can not find any specific astrological correlation with the Houses. *But there is no doubt whatsoever,* as you will soon see, that

---

64 Clark, page 7.

65 Gosden, page 198.

66 Alan Leo gave these epithets to the planets in 1918, The Art of Synthesis. Additionally: the Moon: Mother; Mercury: the Thinker; Venus: the Unifier; Jupiter: the Uplifter; Saturn: the Subduer; Uranus: the Awakener; Neptune: The Mystic.

the Sun shines as the giver of life and Pluto shades with the power to take it away.

Surely, we are again stalking something as evasive as the separation of brain and mind—the organ and the pervasive presence of consciousness, and the layering of the unconscious (id, super ego, ego) that *permeate* our being, our horoscope, every symbol in it. Again, perhaps that gestalt (*whole form*) is bound to *the angles of the horoscope,* the definition of our portion of time and space in this incarnation.

Perhaps astrology does not know enough about the aging process because the bulk of the clients we see in our practice is inordinately highly focused on people *under* fifty years of age? Additionally, the astrology we have so strongly inherited from turn-of-the-last century England was fashioned at a time when life spans indeed averaged *below* fifty!

As our faculties fail in senescence, one organ or process that fails relates to another organ or process that is failing, sometimes causally. The overall process of debilitation speeds up; the inexorable force of Nature—planting our seed, giving birth to our own kind, and then leaving the land to free up resource-supply for those growing behind us—*this force* overtakes us.

The tensions in the developmental process, so clearly indicated in the horoscope, stimulate growth, *but they also invite stress and breakdown.* It becomes a matter of degree: *how much* developmental tension is there in relation to how much we need and can use advantageously, to how much we internalize and suffer in terms of frustration and breakdown. Inexorably, even "good" things in life get "old."

We know that strong aspects to the Sun (natally or in time development systems) will manifest exceedingly often as eye disease and difficulties with vision. We know that strong aspects to the Sun will manifest exceedingly often as heart concerns. Does this suggest that eye disease and heart problems relate to one another?

How do we know which to inquire about? Do we inquire about both?

We do know that strong aspects to the Moon will also manifest exceedingly often as eye failures...but also as stomach problems. Again, do they go together even though they may be separated in development by time, i.e., in the process of aging? Or is there some kind of genetically predisposed preselection that governs the body's choice in its breakdown?

Why is it that diabetes is presaged so very often through the interrelationship between Venus and Jupiter, but so many people have diabetes *without* that signature? With a stressed Venus, Mars or Saturn in Libra, we are seeing that it is reasonable that, over time, bladder, kidney, and lower back problems will all manifest more often than not, *especially with the predisposition accentuated by non-medical tensions in early life development.*

The non-answer replies to these questions are bound up with clarification of the purpose served by astrology in the context of illness, aging, and death. While there are inspired individuals among us who can heal others, guided by astrology, I believe that we are not yet, all of us, by definition or by expectation, healers; our astrology is reflectively informative and spiritually confirming more than it is specifically remedial. Yet, our astrology *can* relate dynamically and helpfully to other disciplines in the study of and service to humankind: to individual psychology, especially; to relationship counseling; to vocational guidance; perhaps to nutrition (diet). With our astrology, we are able to be a major part of the effort to celebrate life.

Above all, it is in the dimension of *timing* that astrology can excel, bringing to other disciplines, including medicine, the dimension of early warning of systemic breakdown. This is the thrust of this book, and we are developing our understanding carefully.

Astrology can say with Dr. Charles H. Mayo, "That which can be foreseen can be prevented."

2.

EARLY-WARNING PATTERNS
IN THE HOROSCOPE

T here is almost always confusion within symbolism, whether or not it is astrological. To discern the core significance of symbolism is the challenge and the exercise—the art—of applying that symbolism. But there is little confusion about time, and it is through astrological timing that we can discover highly reliable symbolic patterns of systemic breakdown. By detecting these patterns, astrology is able to give early warning of critical illness; astrology is able to help save lives.

The Dark World of Cancer

Horoscope 18, Norman Schwarzkopf

Chart 18 belongs to retired General Norman Schwarzkopf: the Sun-Moon blend promises a tremendous amount of energy to make things happen, to administrate progress, to command ego recognition in the most practical way possible; there is no "fooling around" here; what you want is what you get. This image is reinforced by the Leo Ascendant and the Moon's "workaholic" position in the 6th House; by the Mars conjunction with Pluto and the Mars-Pluto opposition to the Moon, with Mars ruling the Midheaven. All this is taken to extreme ego-focus by the quindecile of the Moon with the Ascendant; and to paradoxical

---

67 Additionally, this should register immediately as the Ascendant=Moon/Saturn, a paradoxically

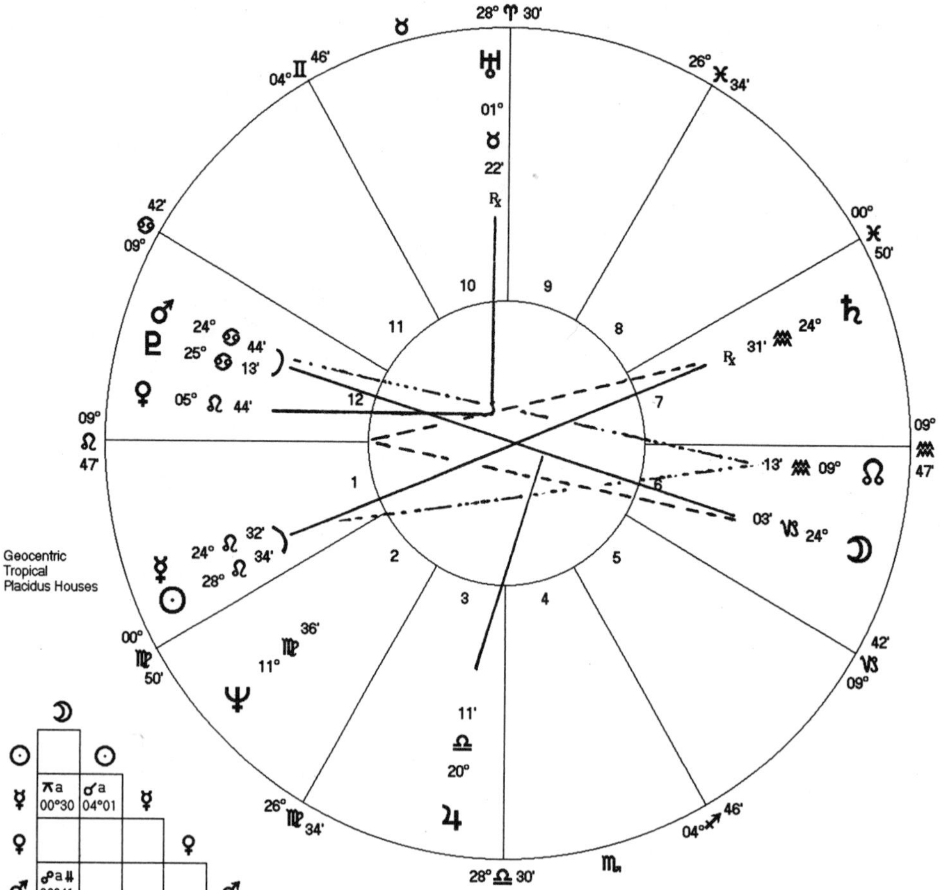

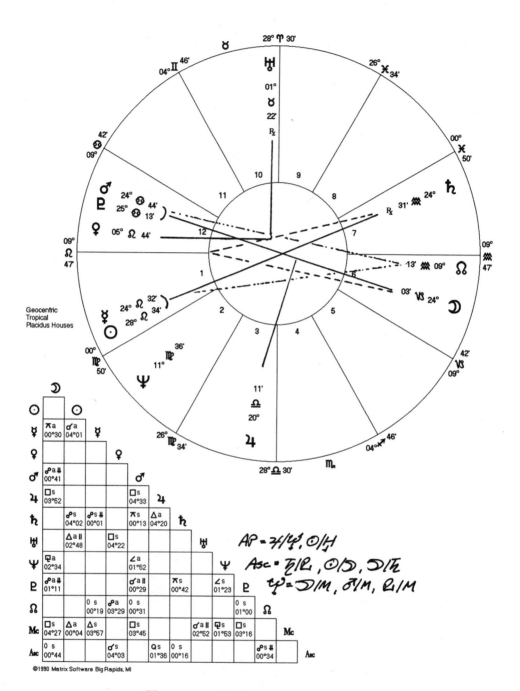

	☽	☉	☿	♀	♂	♃	♄	♅	♆	♇	☊	Mc
☉												
☿	⊼a 00°30	☌a 04°01										
♀												
♂	☍a # 00°41											
♃	□s 03°52				□s 04°33							
♄		☍s 04°02	☍s # 00°01		⊼s 00°13	△a 04°20						
♅		△a ‖ 02°48		□s 04°22								
♆	⚼a 02°34				∠a 01°52							
♇	☍a # 01°11				☌a ‖ 00°29		⊼s 00°42		∠s 01°23			
☊			0 s 00°19	☍a 03°29	0 s 00°31					0 s 01°00		
Mc	□s 04°27	△a 00°04	△s 03°57		□s 03°45			☌a ‖ 02°52	⚼s 01°53	□s 03°16		
Asc	0 s 00°44			☌s 04°03		Qs 01°36	0 s 00°16				☍s # 00°34	

AP = ♃/♆, ☉/♅
Asc = ♄/♇, ☉/☽, ☽/♄
♆ = ☽/M, ♂/M, ♇/M

©1990 Matrix Software Big Rapids, MI

Horoscope 18, Norman Schwarzkopf
August 22, 1934, 4:45 A.M. EDT
Trenton, NJ
74W45 — 40N13

reserved (hurt) or vengeful self-presentation through Saturn's quindecile with the Ascendant as well.[67]

This image is challenged, frustrated, threatened by the Saturn retrograde opposition with the Sun-Mercury: the king complex is jeopardized by the difficult father relationship Schwarzkopf had in the early home; the self-worth profile is challenged (Mercury, opposed by Saturn, rules the self-worth 2nd House holding Neptune, which in turn is sesquiquadrate to the Moon). Schwarzkopf *must* prove himself to his father, and to the world.

Another jarring image is symbolically suggested by Ascendant= Saturn/Pluto, Sun/Moon, Moon/Saturn: this is hard, hard work, every challenge taken personally, tremendous conflict with the father figure, all eventually to work out in some way through the matured personality, but not without deep grief and sadness.

The Aries Point involves Jupiter/Neptune and Sun/Uranus suggesting a publicly known self-indulgent and revolutionary spirit.

The Neptune ties with Moon/Midheaven, Mars/Midheaven, and Pluto/Midheaven all threaten for something "to go wrong," something that might undercut his heroics, his personal power. This intrusion in the scheme of things could well have to do with *critical illness:* the Moon rules the 12th, Saturn rules the 6th and both are involved with major tension aspects involving Mars, Pluto, and Saturn.

Cursory diagnosis orientation shows tension (potential weakness) with the Sun and the Moon, the eyes; the heart (reinforced by the Sun and Leo prominence); the stomach (reinforced by the Moon and Cancer prominence); and specifically the sex organs (the prostate gland, the testicles) and the colon (Mars conjunct Pluto in the 12th). The Uranus square with Venus suggests lower back, bladder, kidneys; possibly the throat region, the esophagus. References from Saturn and the Moon combine strongly to suggest knee problems.

Let us assume that General Schwarzkopf has come to see you for a horoscope consultation on his birthday, August 22, 1993. He is filled with energy, commanding the room, dominating the conversation as you go through the analysis. The *additional* chart you have drawn is shown as Chart 18a, the Solar Arcs for his birthdate August 22 in 1993.

---

67 Additionally, this should register immediately as the Ascendant=Moon/Saturn, a paradoxically reserved (or hurt) self-presentation.

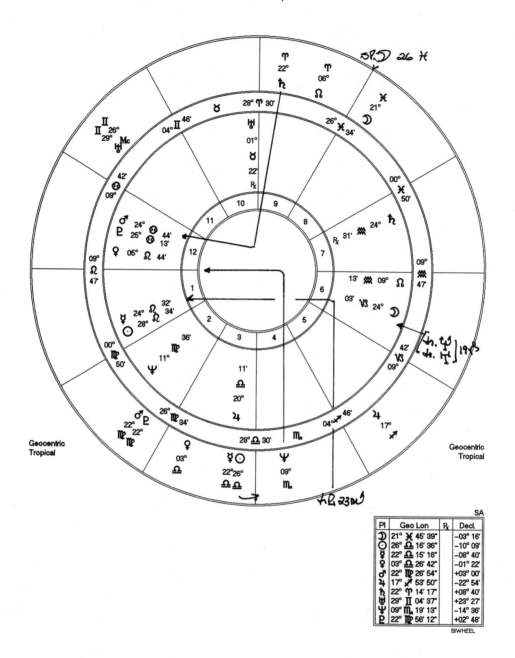

Pl	Geo Lon	Rx	Decl.
☽	21° ♓ 45' 39"		–03° 16'
☉	26° ♎ 16' 36"		–10° 09'
☿	22° ♎ 15' 16"		–08° 40'
♀	03° ♎ 26' 42"		–01° 22'
♂	22° ♍ 26' 54"		+03° 00'
♃	17° ♐ 53' 50"		–22° 54'
♄	22° ♈ 14' 17"		+08° 40'
♅	29° ♊ 04' 37"		+23° 27'
♆	09° ♏ 19' 13"		–14° 36'
♇	22° ♍ 56' 12"		+02° 48'

SA

BIWHEEL

Solar Arc Chart 18a, Norman Schwarzkopf

Inner Chart
August 22, 1934, 4:45 A.M. EDT
Trenton, NJ
74W45 — 40N13

Outer Ring
SA: August 22, 1993

Solar Arc Review

- Solar Arcs comprise a masterful prediction system in astrology, forgotten for the most part in American teaching during the first half of this century. The development of Solar Arcs is thoroughly covered in Tyl, *Prediction in Astrology* and is presented as well in Tyl, *Synthesis & Counseling in Astrology*.

- The natal position of the client's Sun is subtracted from the Secondary Progressed position of that Sun for a specific date in life development. The arc so defined is then added to the natal position *of each planet, the Ascendant, the Midheaven, and the Nodal Axis (counterclockwise motion)*. These new Solar Arc positions preserve the natal relativity each to each other, and all share the symbolic progression increment of the SP SA Sun. These SA positions are placed in the outer ring of the horoscope; they form innumerable new aspects with the natal positions, outperforming to a high degree the relatively immobile positionings of Secondary Progressions.

- The SA development can be abbreviated by eye as one degree movement forward or backward in the horoscope equalling one year of time. For births in the Northern or Southern hemisphere between May and September, the Arc is slightly slower than one degree per day/year and accumulates one whole degree/year of "error" in some thirty years of lifetime. Therefore, thirty-two years of life would correspond to the 31-degree accumulation of the slow "Summer" arc ("Winter" in the Southern hemisphere). Of course the computer does the computation automatically, precisely; but this rule of thumb is important for abbreviated estimation of Solar Arcs.

- The SA development for births between October and April are quite reliable at one degree equalling one year. therefore, fifty-two years of life would correspond to the 52-degree accumulation of the even "Winter" arc (of the "Summer" arc, SH).

- Solar Arcs are almost always limited to conjunction, square, opposition, semisquare, and sesquiquadrate aspects, i.e., the aspects of highest tension, with the natal planetary and angular positions. Solar Arcs are also directed to hard aspect relationships with natal *midpoints*. In all, some 1,014 new aspects are possible as life develops through Solar Arc symbolism, and interpretive images for all these Arcs are presented in the Tyl books mentioned above.

In horoscope 18a, you see dramatically clearly SA Neptune in the outer ring in the 4th House square the Ascendant. This is serious: with only the rarest exceptions, anytime arcing (or transiting) Neptune conjoins or squares an angle of the horoscope, a period of high sensitivity occurs; there is the sense of ego disappearance, the identity gets lost somehow; one feels victimized.[68]

SA Neptune is "attacking" the Ascendant here, the core of health concerns and identity (you would have already checked major "hits" to the Ascendant throughout your analysis; for example SA Pluto= Ascendant at 14½ (25 Cancer 13 to 9 Leo 47 is 14 degrees and 34 minutes, roughly 14½ years of age).

You time the SA Neptune=Ascendant more carefully: Neptune at 09 Scorpio 19 to the Ascendant at 09 Leo 47 is 28' of arc, i.e., just six months *after* the August 22, 1993 date of the Solar Arc chart, which is *February 1994.* [Abbreviating 1 degree=1 year, i.e., 60'=12 months; 5' of arc=1 month forward or back from the Chart mark.]

In your preparation, you looked ahead in the Ephemeris to *February– March 1994,* six months into the future. You saw the following[69]:

1994					
	MARS	JUPITER	SATURN	URANUS	NEPTUNE	PLUTO
MONTH	LONG	LONG	LONG	LONG	LONG	LONG
JAN	09 ♑	10 ♏	27 ♒	20 ♑	26 ♑	27 ♏
FEB	03 ♒	13	00	23	22	28
MAR	25	15	04	25	23	28
APR	19 ♓	13	07	26	23	28
MAY	13 ♈	10	10	26	23	27
JUN	06 ♉	06	13	26	23	26
JUL	28	05	12	26	22	26
AUG	19 ♊	06	11	24	22	25
SEP	10 ♋	10	09	23	21	25
OCT	28	15	07	22	21	26
NOV	14 ♌	22	06	23	21	27
DEC	27	28	06	24	22	28

---

68 Also, please note that SA Saturn at 22 Aries 14 is beginning to apply to a square with natal Mars-Pluto in the 12th; SA Sun is just past square with Pluto. The "equals sign" (=) in Solar Arc equations and Midpoint pictures connotes the relationship of the left side of the equation to the right side of the equation by conjunction, semisquare, square, sesquiquadrate, or opposition.

69 The 100-year Transit Tables in *Synthesis & Counseling in Astrology,* with the first-of-the-month positions for all the planets Mars through Pluto is extremely helpful in speed-measuring transits to come or transits past.

- Tr. Pluto square n. Sun, 2–4/94
- Tr. Neptune opposed Mars-Pluto, 2–6/94
- Tr. Uranus opposed Mars-Pluto, 2–6/94
- Tr. Saturn opposed Ascendant, 5/94

This is extremely strong transit activity, fulfilling the astrological maxim that for critical occurrences in life, more than one major aspect apply.

You checked the SP Moon position as well (26 Pisces on August 22, 1993) and noted that it was uninvolved with the projections coming up in the Spring of 1994 [you can progress the SP Moon position forward or back by eye at the rate of 1 degree per month of real time; i.e., here 26 Pisces + 6 degrees for six months to 2 Aries.]

It is extremely clear that General Schwarzkopf is under extreme pressure, possible danger with regard to his health at the time of consultation, perhaps brought to its "astro-mathematical peak" in April 1994: the Ascendant is deeply challenged by SA Neptune; the Moon's opposition axis with Mars-Pluto in the 6th–12th axis is pointedly excited by transiting Neptune and Uranus. The target seems to be natal Pluto, *with transiting Pluto exactly square the Sun as corroboration.*[70]

General Schwarzkopf delayed acting on your recommendation of a thorough physical examination, which he had surely been putting off for too long; he waited until March 1994, when he did visit the MacDill Air Force Base Hospital in Tampa, Florida. Schwarzkopf was concerned and uncomfortable with nagging tendonitis in one *knee*.

Prostate Cancer

While he was at the hospital, he decided to visit the base urologist for an exam. "I feel something not quite right," the doctor said, after making a routine rectal exam (access to the prostate gland through digital pressure and feel is accomplished through the rectum). "But if it's cancer, I can tell ninety percent of the time, and I don't think so."[71]

---

70 Additionally in March 1994, Schwarzkopf had SA Neptune=Saturn/Pluto, "a very difficult measurement picture, suggesting an unstable life situation because of the inexplicable, because of fear."

71 *TIME* magazine account; April 1, 1996.

Shwarzkopf had recently undergone a PSA (prostate-specific antigen) test and registered a count of only 1.8, well below the level considered suspicious for cancer (see page 93). To play it safe, the urologist performed an ultrasound exam, took a biopsy of the prostate gland, and sent it off to a pathologist.

Schwarzkopf left the hospital relaxed and optimistic, but a week later, the doctor called and said, "I don't know how to tell you this, but you have prostate cancer."

Schwarzkopf is quoted with this reaction: "For me, it was like war. The first thing you do is learn about the enemy." He was operated on immediately. His life changed: after some six months of convalescence, Shwarzkopf rechanneled his professional strengths and charisma to help the fight against Prostate Cancer and to inspire young leukemia patients everywhere fight their disease. He achieved much publicity for himself and his program; Schwarzkopf was on the cover of *TIME* magazine, the April 1, 1996 issue, "The Battle Against Prostate Cancer"; his SA Sun had advanced to 28 Libra 52 *opposed his Midheaven* ("ego recognition, potential glory, success, fulfillment").

Now, if we had this birth data *without* the birth time, how reliable would our analysis be? Would we be able to see the problem coming? The Ascendant and Midheaven would be different of course; we would lose the powerful SA Neptune square to the Ascendant, the major alert to a challenged system.

Chart 18b is the Solarscope for the "consultation" with General Schwarzkopf six-seven months before his crisis. The chart shows the application of SA Saturn to square with the Mars-Pluto and Moon opposition, with the Moon ruling the 12th and Saturn ruling the 6th; the separating SA square of the Sun with the same axis, suggesting the *earlier illumination of difficulty*. We can feel that these two arcs mark the larger time period of difficulty, i.e., from two years back (SA Sun=Mars; difficulty illuminated) to two and one-half years into the future, a crisis of change. *Something is happening.*

The build-up of transit activity to the Sun and into the Moon opposition axis with Mars-Pluto is clear, exactly the same as for the timed horoscope. We would be alerted similarly to the Spring period of 1994.

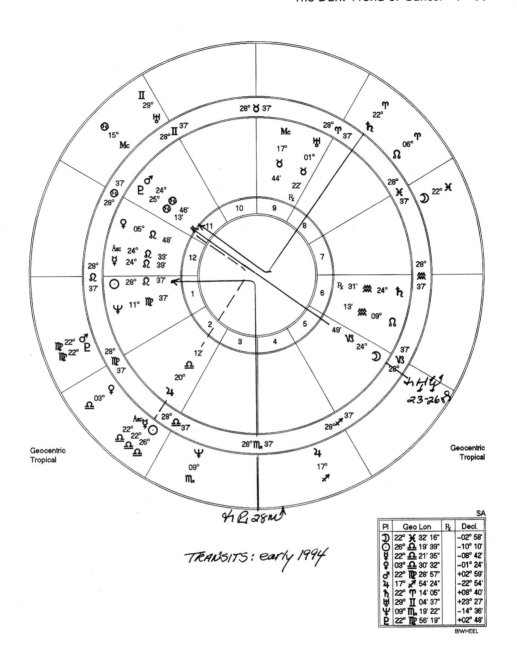

TRANSITS: early 1994

PI	Geo Lon	Rx	Decl.
☽	22° ♓ 32' 16"		−02° 58'
☉	26° ♎ 19' 39"		−10° 10'
☿	22° ♎ 21' 35"		−08° 42'
♀	03° ♎ 30' 32"		−01° 24'
♂	22° ♍ 28' 57"		+02° 59'
♃	17° ♐ 54' 24"		−22° 54'
♄	22° ♈ 14' 05"		+08° 40'
♅	29° ♊ 04' 37"		+23° 27'
♆	09° ♏ 19' 22"		−14° 36'
♇	22° ♍ 56' 19"		+02° 48'

SA

BIWHEEL

Solarscope Chart 18b, Norman Schwarzkopf ☉

Inner Chart
August 22, 1934, 4:45 A.M. EDT
Trenton, NJ
74W45 — 40N13

Outer Ring — Consultation
SA: August 22, 1993
Transits: Early 1994

As we shall see continuously, with the built-in bias of untimed horoscopes set for the Sun on the Ascendant, using Solar Houses (Equal Houses), aspects and arcs to the solar center of the horoscope and the 12th House zone are extraordinarily telling and reliable in pursuit of the patterns of critical illness.

Horoscope 19, Male

For example, Horoscope 19 is untimed but very revealing. The outer ring of Solar Arcs is cast for the man's birthday in 1994.

Natally, we see Sun squared by Pluto (the image of a "blanket over a grenade"). In the Solarscope, this will hit at the heart of the health profile at the Ascendant, and, indeed, in any horoscope, through contact with the Sun, suggest an attack on the life-giver, somehow, somewhere, sometime.

This Sun-Pluto contact here alerts us to Pluto concerns in the male: to the reproductive organs, the prostate gland and the testicles, and the colon.

The quindecile between Pluto and the Moon (simply check what looks like a "very wide opposition" by adding 15 degrees to Pluto (see page 9) to come to 20 Leo opposite the Moon) is invalid here since the Moon's position is unsure due to the lack of birth time. If this were a timed horoscope, *this quindecile would be a critical companion significator of the attack on this man's health.*

The quindecile between Mars and Neptune (add 15 degrees to Neptune or subtract 15 degrees from the Mars position) is very important here since Mars is in its own sign, rules the 6th, and is in the 6th. Its retrogradation introduces into the analysis yet another level of consideration.

Did your eyes pick up the Venus-Jupiter opposition? This suggests strongly the high potential of diabetes occurring in the man's family history and/or in himself (see page 19).

As the cursory analysis develops we sense the vulnerability to several critical illnesses.

The arcs "for the consultation" show SA Pluto just separating from natal Neptune; we will see develop in our study that this is a critical contact for matters of illness. This arc suggests strongly that *something has been developing* that is Plutonic and yet unseen, undiagnosed.

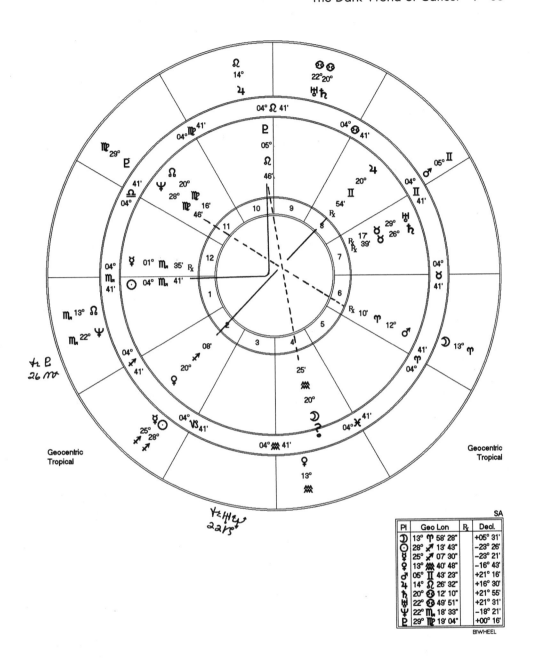

Solarscope 19, Male ☉
Outer Ring
SA: October 28, 1994

Always in prediction, we look for angular contact *first,* through arcs or transits, through conjunctions or squares. These are the most telling time measurements. Here, we have minimal arc activity beyond Pluto=Neptune.

But look carefully at the transits noted here: transiting Pluto (again, Pluto) is exactly opposed Saturn, and transiting Neptune and Uranus are on their way to the fourth cusp, an angle of the Solarscope, i.e., *square to the natal Sun.*

We check the ephemeris and see that transiting Uranus comes to the fourth cusp and square with the Sun in March 1996; and, at the same time, transiting Saturn will have moved to 25–29 Pisces, *opposing natal Neptune.*

There is simply no doubt about this confluence of serious measurements. The man must be referred for medical checkup, specifically for Plutonic concerns, immediately. The Pluto arc over Neptune was undoubtedly the beginning period of a crisis that would peak in March 1996.

This man was diagnosed for prostate cancer in March 1996 and was operated on May 1, 1996, with transiting Uranus at 4 Aquarius 33, *8 minutes of arc from precise square with the natal Sun.*

To follow up on the diabetes concern (Venus-Jupiter opposition): this man's mother had been diagnosed to be "borderline diabetic." He himself experienced intense reactive hypoglycemic symptoms: weakness, fidgeting, irritability between meals; even in his doctor's office when being tested for diabetes, he required medication on the spot! He is diagnosed not as diabetic but borderline, as his mother was.

Horoscope 20, Ed Kaps

Horoscope 20 is the horoscope of Ed Kaps, founder of the nationwide Prostate survivors "Us Too!" support groups and a member of the Board of Directors of the American Foundation for Urologic Disease. Ed started the support group with Senator Bob Dole at the Capitol building in Washington, D.C.

Kaps happens to live nearby. I learned of him through the local newspaper, made contact, and told him about my work. I invited him to my office to see my presentation about astrology and early warning about critical disease, specifically prostate cancer. I explained my findings in layman's terms—using a "good guys-bad guys" scenario with the planets—and he was impressed with how the patterns unfolded. But then came the proof of the pudding: "Ed, do you know what time *you* were born?"

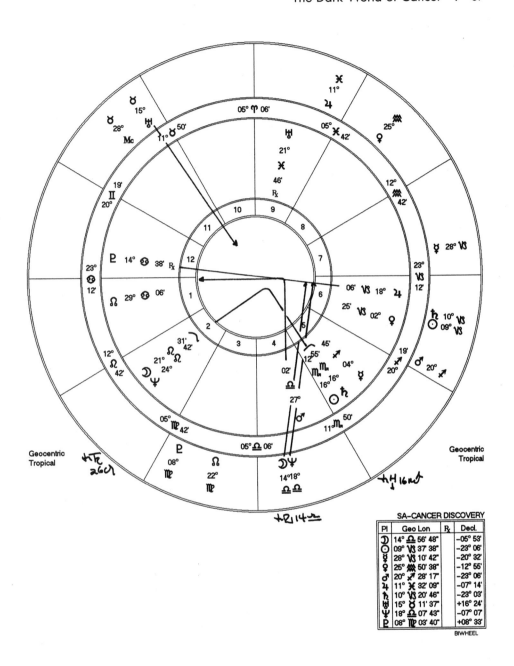

SA-CANCER DISCOVERY			
Pl	Geo Lon	℞	Decl.
☽	14° ♎ 56' 48"		–05° 53'
☉	09° ♑ 37' 38"		–23° 06'
☿	28° ♑ 10' 42"		–20° 32'
♀	25° ♒ 50' 38"		–12° 55'
♂	20° ♐ 28' 17"		–23° 06'
♃	11° ♓ 32' 09"		–07° 14'
♄	10° ♑ 20' 46"		–23° 03'
♅	15° ♉ 11' 37"		+16° 24'
♆	18° ♎ 07' 43"		–07° 07'
♇	08° ♍ 03' 40"		+08° 33'

BIWHEEL

Horoscope 20, Ed Kaps

Inner Chart
November 8, 1925, 9:00 P.M. CST
Joliet, IL
88W05 — 41N31

Outer Ring — Cancer Discovery
SA: July 15, 1978

Ed had come prepared. He knew his birth time and the month when his cancer had been diagnosed.[72] I immediately put his data into the computer and sat through about twenty seconds of extraordinary tension! Would his horoscope show the pattern that I had seen emerging through scores of research tests? As the double-ringed chart came out of the printer, I saw immediately what you see here in Horoscope 20; *there it was!*

Natally, note the opposition between Jupiter and Pluto at the horizon. This is the suppressing "lid" on the northern hemisphere below the horizon, the unfinished business in the early home, the tensions in development that undoubtedly exacerbated vulnerability to critical illness. This is echoed powerfully by the conjunction between Saturn and the Sun, in Scorpio, disposed by Pluto. (And as well by Venus in Capricorn peregrine, ruling the parental 4th House and Mars in the 4th squaring the Ascendant, ruling the parental 10th.)

In turn, the Moon-Neptune conjunction squares the Sun-Saturn conjunction, a bit widely but significantly within the growing analysis. It is key here to note that the Moon, ruler of the Ascendant, is strongly challenged by this four-planet aspect configuration. The Mars square to the Ascendant challenges the health center further.

As our work develops, we will see the subtle *negative* involvement of Jupiter very often within the patterning. It is as if Jupiter symbolically builds up the concept of excessive cell division. Here the reference could be specifically to the reproductive organs, the prostate gland and testicles, and the colon, or to the liver (Jupiter and its functions). Jupiter rules the 6th and is in the 6th. The Plutonic target is reinforced by the Sun-Saturn conjunction in Scorpio.

Cell division is triggered by proteins that are called growth factors. These proteins fit into receptor proteins embedded in the cell wall and all sorts of triggered reactions take place causing the DNA to produce proteins that participate in cell division. Additionally, there are growth-inhibiting factors as well (sometimes called tumor suppressors). Things can get out of control if there is a defective gene in the DNA—the concept of a stressed Jupiter—or the DNA may be damaged in a way that inhibits production of the molecules that shut down the cell growth cycle.[73]

---

72 Please note that the date of diagnosis throughout the cases in this book is most often set at the 15th of a month; most survivors remember the month, but not the date; the 15th is a compromise that does not affect arc or transit measurements significantly at all in the scope of this work.

73 Trefil, pages 250–252.

There is every indication here that Ed could face a critical illness, probably in Plutonic body areas, the liver, the eyes (the Sun and Neptune), and/or the heart (Leo emphasis and Sun reference).[74]

Now for the timing, the pattern, the trigger: for the discovery date of his prostate cancer *SA Moon-Neptune had come exactly to square with the natal Pluto-Jupiter axis:* SA Moon was exactly square Pluto, and SA Neptune was exactly square Jupiter! This is extraordinary—but typically clear and dramatic—corroboration of initial cursory analysis.

SA Uranus at 16 Taurus was tightly applying to opposition with the natal Sun-Saturn conjunction. Additionally, SA Mars in the 6th was closing in on the square with natal Uranus.

The transits were almost too much to believe: transiting Pluto at 14 Libra—like SA Moon-Neptune—was also exactly square the Pluto-Jupiter opposition axis! And transiting Uranus was exactly conjoined with the natal Sun-Saturn conjunction!

Note also that transiting Saturn, the two weeks before diagnosis, had been conjoined with Moon-Neptune, the Moon ruling the Ascendant, corresponding to Ed's seeking help.

The "good guys" here—the Sun, Moon—versus the "bad guys"—Saturn, Uranus, Neptune, and Pluto—Ed saw it all. The early warning of this health crisis could have been anticipated years ahead of time.

The Solarscope for this case is also very productive and easy to visualize: the vital Jupiter-Pluto axis remains, of course, and so does the Neptune arc to that axis (the Moon is disqualified in the Solarscope because of the timing vagary); the Mars arc to square with Uranus remains too. But note the transiting position of Uranus at 16 Scorpio exactly conjunct the Sun-Saturn conjunction in the timed horoscope: this same natal conjunction and the Uranian transit, of course, would be brought *precisely to the Ascendant* in the Solarscope. The Solarscope would promise critical illness almost as well as the timed horoscope.

Early warning is indeed the key to prevention. With cancer, the lethal fear is metastasis (from the Greek, to change from one site to another). Early warning improves the probability that the localized problem has not metastasized (spread). Tests are always made to determine if a cancer

---

74 Ed has no liver problem (yet), but he does have myasthenia gravis, the major symptom of which is muscle fatigue, flaccid droopiness, double vision, and difficulty breathing. Antibodies that are normally formed to fight infection react instead against normal tissue. This is a rare disease (1 in 20,000 people).

has metastasized to other parts of the body, to a vital organ. If the cancer has spread beyond the site of its local occurrence, the condition is exceedingly dangerous and treatment is complicated. If the cancer has spread to the bones, the blood, or into the lymph system (a second circulatory system in the body that transports a fluid called lymph that helps to return water and proteins from the tissues to the blood; nodes or stations for the lymph are located throughout the body, most notably in the armpit and groin), *conditions are extremely serious.*

Cancer of the prostate tends to spread to the bladder and/or to the bones. Occasionally the diagnosis is made in the course of investigating progressive back pain. Bone scans are often used to determine if the malignancy has spread to the skeleton.[75]

Melanoma cancer of the skin is so very dangerous because the cells metastasize easily down through the skin and into the blood, which carries the cancer further.

Breast cancer is itself not lethal; it is the metastasizing that is. If breast cancer is caught early, before malignant cells have spread to the lymph nodes nearby, there is a ninety to ninety-five percent chance of a cure. Seventy-five percent of all women diagnosed with breast cancer *are* cured.[76]

Horoscope 21, Paul

Horoscope 21 shows a man whose cancer of the prostate did metastasize, where death was revealed to be imminent upon discovery of the cancer.

"Paul" had enormous pain in his hips, shoulders, and back. He thought he was severely arthritic. His pains got so he could hardly walk.

At a physical examination a year before his terminal diagnosis, Paul's PSA test had come in at 5, called "normal" by his doctor, but generally regarded on the high side for a man of 58 (norm would be between 2.2 and 4.0). The probability of cancer increases with a rising count between 4 and 22 and becomes highly likely over 22.[77]

---

75 Here is yet another instance of interrelationships in the body that call up interrelated astrological symbolisms. Saturn "rules" the bones and tumors; does involvement of Saturn within a cancer pattern in an organ suggest metastasis to the bone? See Case 21 that follows (page 91).

76 Mayo, Chapter 34, page 1165.

77 The Prostate Specific Antigen test has been available since the 1980s and is now administered to hundreds of thousands of men annually. The test measures the blood level of a protein produced by all prostate cells. After about age fifty, the prostate begins to enlarge and the increasing number of cells contributes to what is generally a steady but slight rise in the PSA count.

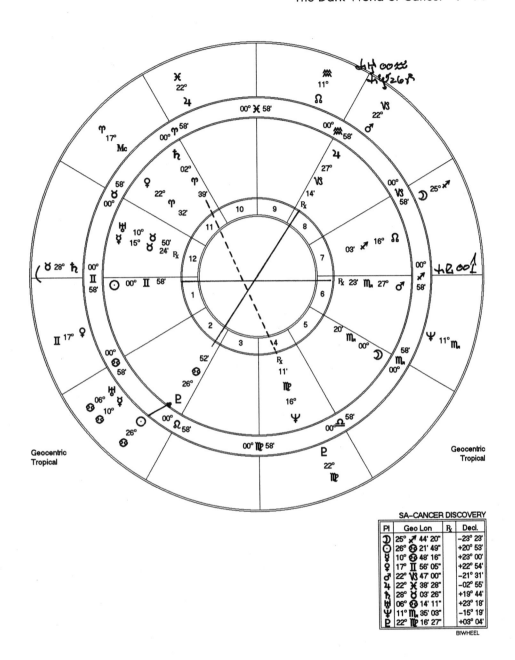

Paul's PSA was 1,836.

Paul's doctor gave him fourteen to twenty-four months to live. He was told to bring his affairs into order. The condition had gone too far for surgery. The cancer had metastasized everywhere in his bones. Part of his hip had broken off. He told me he felt that he would "break in two" at any moment, his bones were so brittle.

Paul could not get his birth time from the hospital or county office, but his Solarscope speaks volumes: note the natal Jupiter-Pluto opposition once again (see page 91), with Pluto ruling his Solar 6th. Mars is in Scorpio and opposes the Sun and Solar Ascendant. Uranus conjoins Mercury, ruler of the Ascendant, in the 12th House. Venus squares the Jupiter-Pluto axis, and Venus rules the 12th. There is every indication of a potential breakdown of liver function (and/or pancreas) and Pluto organs.

Additionally, we can note that Saturn and Neptune make a clear quindecile aspect (just add 15 to the Neptune position). This aspect alerts us to the bones, the skeleton, the knees, and also to the blood.

But the timing! See the arc of Sun and Solar Ascendant symbolism to exact conjunction with natal Pluto as transiting Uranus and Neptune conjoin Jupiter and oppose natal Pluto! Note transiting *Pluto at 00 Sagittarius exactly opposite the Sun!* And, finally, perhaps the metastasis dimension (to the bones) that is so fearsome: SA *Saturn* is closing in on the Sun and the Solar Ascendant.

There is simply no doubt whatsoever that early warning of this critical time could have been made for Paul several years in advance (the conspicuous Pluto transit and then the Sun-to-Pluto arc, with the accompanying Uranus-Neptune transit). He could have insisted on going beyond a moderately high PSA, to a biopsy, to know conclusively what was behind all his aches and pains, before metastasis occurred throughout his entire body.

But there's more here: Paul started a radiation therapy program backed up with drugs. *He was cured!* Within two months, his PSA registered .7 and three months later .02! Bone scans were excellent, showing a regression the likes of which had never been seen before by the doctors.

Paul is very religious. Upon diagnosis, he had become involved with a national network of prayer power. He attributes his cure to these thousands and thousands of prayers delivered up for him over a period of time.

I am emphasizing prostate cancer cases at the beginning of our study of timing for several reasons: the symbology deals with the outermost, slowest moving, and often most dramatic planet, Pluto; I had detected the involvement of Pluto often in prostate cases—and cancer in general as we shall see; Pluto and the prostate gland have much to do with sexuality, and sexuality, in turn, with hormones and the aging process. The region finds itself at the fundamental first Chakra. It seemed a fundamental starting place in my study for an orderly build up of deduction, tests, and results. Through Ed Kaps, I learned of a prostate survivors support group nearby and they participated with me grandly in my initial research program; giving me some sixty case histories.

There is another reason, which may surprise you: the prevalence of prostate cancer in men outpaces the incidence of breast cancer in women by thirty-three percent! Each year in this country, more than 317,000 men are found to have cancer in the prostate gland. Approximately one out of every ten men will develop prostate cancer during his lifetime.[78]

Prostate cancer causes more than 41,000 deaths annually. Tennis great Bobby Riggs died of prostate cancer (age seventy-seven); so did actors Telly Savalas (seventy), Bill Bixby (fifty-nine), and Don Ameche (eighty-five); musician Frank Zappa at fifty-two; French Premier Francois Mitterrand (seventy-nine); the Ayatullah Khomeini (eighty-nine), Timothy Leary (seventy-five) to name those reported by *TIME* magazine recently. One man dies of prostate cancer every thirteen minutes.[79]

Senator Dole has survived prostate cancer; so have Sidney Poitier, Jerry Lewis, Robert Goulet, Senator Jesse Helms, Mayor Marion Barry of Washington D.C., King Hussein of Jordan, financier Michael Milken, and so many others.

Doctors like to say that every man dies *with* prostate cancer, not necessarily *from* it. The organ is practically vestigial after the life period of procreation (see below). It is a disease of the older male; it is more prevalent among blacks than among whites, and it is inherited within families. As more and more men live longer and longer and escape heart disease or stroke, the more men will die from undetected or ignored cancer of the prostate.

---

78 Breast cancer in women metastasizes more readily than prostate cancer, so more women die from breast cancer: in 1997, 44,300 women are expected to die from the disease (the annual average); the national toll for men is growing, with some 41,400 deaths expected in 1997. TIME, April 1, 1996, page 60.

79 Bostwick, page xxi.

The prostate is a sex gland found only in men located inside the lower abdomen at the base of the penis, just below the bladder and in front of the rectum. Normally, the prostate is about an inch and one half in diameter—roughly the size of a golf ball.

The prostate wraps completely around the urethra, the tube that empties urine from the bladder through the penis. The prostate supplies fluid to the semen to regulate its acidity and to protect sperm as it travels through the acid environment of the female reproductive tract. The prostate acts as a valve that allows sperm or urine to flow in the right direction at the right time.

Nerves that run alongside the prostate are responsible for directing bloodflow to make the penis become hard during an erection. Surgery (and radiation and chemistry) on the prostate threatens these nerves dramatically, and losing the capability of an erection is a very real concern in treating prostate cancer. Therapies work with delicate probabilities.

Because of the threat to erectile capability, men tend not to want to learn about a prostate condition. Not enough men over forty routinely get a PSA test (the doctors digital examination through the rectum discloses only perhaps fifty percent of the gland to his touch). Denial and fear are difficult hurdles to early detection.

One of the key symptoms is frequent sleep interruption for urination during the night; the urgency to urinate; dribbling before and after urination; incomplete voiding of the bladder.

A client of mine just last week showed natal Pluto squared by Uranus, SA Saturn coming to square his Ascendant at the same time as transiting Neptune would conjoin his Saturn and transiting Saturn itself would square his natal Saturn! This is a real threat. I asked him how often he got up from bed to urinate during the night. He did not answer, "Oh, once or twice," which is normal; instead, he said emphatically, "Every two hours." He made an appointment with his urologist immediately after our consultation; this would be an early warning for a difficult time sixteen months from now, not at all too soon.

Horoscope 22, Daniel D. Rostenkowski

Horoscope 22 (see chart on page 96) belongs to Daniel D. Rostenkowski, long-time Democratic Congressman from Illinois.

The Solar Arcs and transits are for the exact day of his operation for prostate cancer. Note that SA Mars-Saturn were opposed natal Neptune (ruling the 6th), which is square to Venus in *Scorpio,* with Venus ruling his Ascendant; *SA Pluto* was opposed Jupiter-Uranus (Pluto again; Jupiter again!), and SA Moon was applying to natal Pluto!

There is a heavy omen here through the Aries Point: while the AP= Uranus, corroborating Rostenkowski's rebellious and brazen congressional image (the tough guy from Chicago) and Sun/Mars and Sun/ Node (the rough, tough people's hero), *the AP also equals Saturn/Pluto, the high potential for loss, pain, scandal.*

We look for the transit triggers, and they are there: transiting Saturn at 7 Aries was square to Mercury (ruler of the 12th) and the Sun; transiting Uranus at 3 Aquarius was square the Moon, ruler of the Midheaven, and *transiting Neptune was exactly on Rostenkowski's fourth cusp, opposing his Midheaven!*[80]

These configurations hardly need further explanation. It was a critical time for Rostenkowski's career. The key angular measure, of course, is transiting Neptune on the fourth cusp opposing the Midheaven: "a very important time of life; there can be the sense of ego disappearance; the identity somehow gets lost in situations through disregard." On this day, Rostenkowski entered the penitentiary for a prison term of seventeen months for two charges of government financial and mail fraud. He was operated on in the prison hospital for his newly diagnosed cancer of the prostate.

---

80 Additionally transiting Pluto at 0 Sagittarius was at the midpoint of Sun/Ascendant, usually the sense of "fated events," but here an attack through Pluto symbolism upon the health (the Sun and the Ascendant).

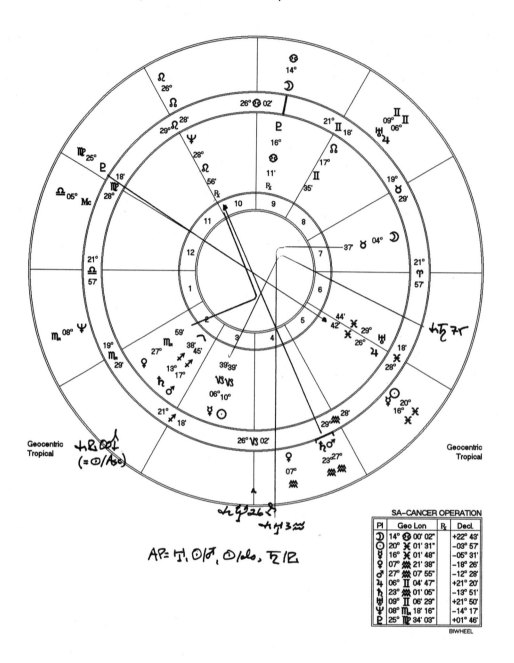

Horoscope 22, Daniel D. Rostenkowski

Inner Chart
January 2, 1928, 2:00 A.M. CDT
Chicago, IL
87W39 — 41N51

Outer Ring — Cancer Operation
SA: July 22, 1996

SA-CANCER OPERATION			
Pl	Geo Lon	Rx	Decl.
☽	14° ♋ 00' 02"		+22° 43'
☉	20° ♓ 01' 31"		−03° 57'
☿	16° ♓ 01' 48"		−05° 31'
♀	07° ♒ 21' 38"		−18° 26'
♂	27° ♒ 07' 55"		−12° 28'
♃	06° ♊ 04' 47"		+21° 20'
♄	23° ♒ 01' 05"		−13° 51'
♅	09° ♊ 06' 29"		+21° 50'
♆	08° ♏ 18' 16"		−14° 17'
♇	25° ♍ 34' 03"		+01° 46'

BIWHEEL

Horoscope 23, Male

Horoscope 23 shows still another differentiation of the basic prostate cancer profile—or simply "cancer" profile, as we shall see. Natally, the horoscope shows a diagnostic signal of Saturn conjunct Pluto, both retrograde. Mars is sesquiquadrate (135 degrees) from its position in Scorpio to the Saturn-Pluto conjunction, and Mars is conjunct Mercury, ruler of the 12th. The Mars-Mercury sense is channeled very strongly into the sense of Saturn-Pluto.

From this pattern alone, we know we can *anticipate* a physical breakdown in terms of Plutonic parts, the knees, the stomach, the skin. Additionally we see Neptune, ruling the 6th, squaring the Sun (over the signline). As well, this introduces concerns about the eyes, the heart, the lower back.

In February 1992, this gentleman of seventy-eight was diagnosed with prostate cancer. Notice that transiting Pluto (again!) at 22 Scorpio was conjunct natal Mercury, ruler of the 12th; transiting Uranus and Neptune were at 16 Capricorn opposed the Midheaven (and had just been squaring the Ascendant), and transiting Saturn at 8 Aquarius was conjunct natal Uranus.

The backdrop Solar Arc measurement that gives the dire dimension of this time is SA Ascendant=Saturn-Pluto! [The Solar Arc for this time— SP-SA Sun minus natal Sun gives 78 degrees 12 minutes, added to the Ascendant gives 91 Libra 35 or 1 Capricorn 35.]

This man opted for surgery, as opposed to radiated seed implants or chemotherapy, and has been cancer-free for five years.

Another client at eighty who had colon cancer (transiting Pluto square his Sun-Saturn conjunction in the 12th, etc.) fourteen years ago, has just been told he has prostate cancer (transiting Uranus-Neptune exactly opposite his Sun-Saturn conjunction). Prostate cancers are usually slow growing, but do vary in speed; at eighty, my client has opted *not* to have the operation at this time. This is the attitude of "watchful waiting."

Our final example of prostate cancer, Horoscope 24—I have some fifty others, *all* echoes of the same themes we are learning to see—is a Solarscope, but it shows how very, very helpful astrology still can be in establishing early warning of critical illness. The repetition of these cases here helps to build our confidence in what we see.

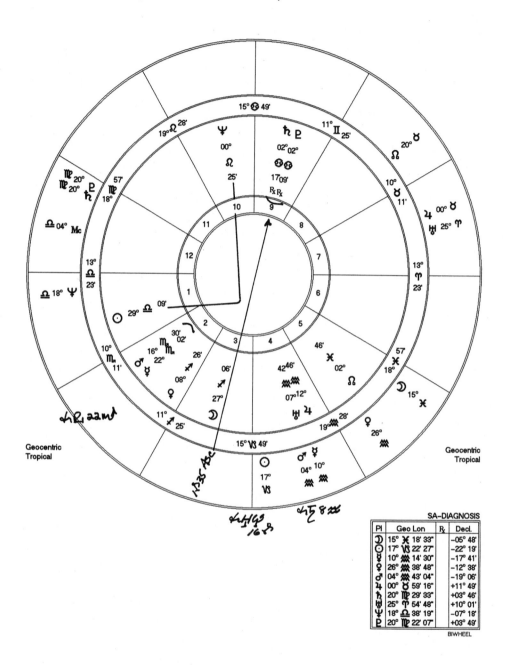

Solarscope 23, Male ☉
Outer Ring — Cancer Diagnosis
SA: February 15, 1992

Horoscope 24, Male

In this solarscope, there is no emphasis on Pluto natally, but the natal Sun is in Scorpio and is squared by Uranus. The Saturn-Neptune conjunction is opposed by Uranus. We can feel emphasis of Scorpio disease potential and the heart.

In consultation with this man within the past few years, we would have instinctively noted the date of transiting Pluto's conjunction with the Sun, ruler of the Solar Midheaven, February 1993. Studying the transit positions at that time would reveal that transiting Saturn would be conjoining natal Uranus. This is an important month indeed, a major shift in this man's life perspective.

When we would draw the Solar Arcs to this month of February 1993, we would see SA Uranus square natal Neptune-Saturn, SA Mercury conjoined Uranus, and most subtly SA Jupiter squaring the Sun, i.e., augmenting its condition in Scorpio (increasing cell growth during its application), *now triggered by transiting Pluto in exact conjunction with the Sun!*

We get all of this from the Solarscope. Clearly, we could have looked ahead and seen the month of February 1993 as critical. This man's prostate cancer was diagnosed at that time.

Final Note: While cancer of the prostate is a disease of matured males, it is reaching epidemic proportions *because males are living longer.* Every medical information source urges all men over forty to get annual PSA tests so that the relative score relationship will track formation of the disease with the earliest possible warning. The PSA test can indicate the presence of prostate cancer as much as five years earlier than diagnosis by other means, like the digital rectal exam.[81]

If we watch carefully the progress of transiting Uranus and Neptune through Aquarius in opposition relationship with Pluto in Leo in the horoscopes of all born between 1940 and 1957, we can be alerted to transit trigger signals that can appear 1996 through 2010, when these men are in their fifties.

---

81 *Fortune* magazine, May 13, 1996; "Taking on Cancer" by Andy Grove. Additionally: The PSA records the size of any tumor; the larger the tumor, the more often it extends outside the prostate gland to other parts of the body to begin metastasizing.

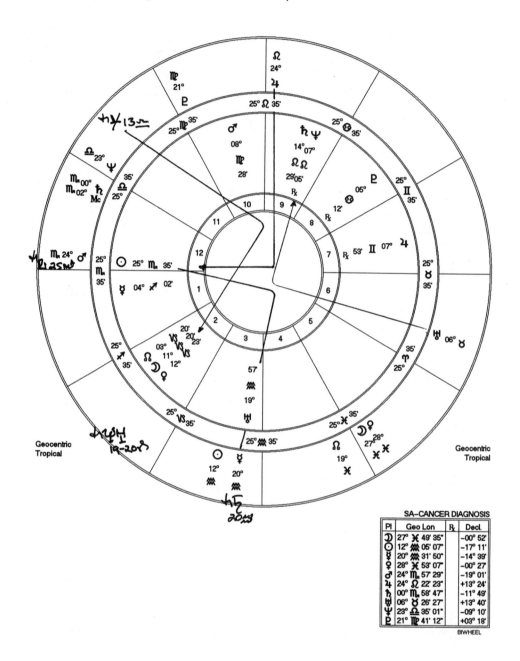

Solarscope 24, Male ☉
Outer Ring — Cancer Diagnosis
SA: February 15, 1993

Testicular Cancer

Cancer of the testicle(s) is most well defined in males between fifteen and thirty-four years of age and occurs four times more frequently among whites than among blacks. It is associated significantly with boys born with an undescended testicle (eleven to fifteen percent will develop testicular cancer; a surgical procedure is now prescribed for the condition quickly after birth).[82]

There are some 5,000 new case of this cancer in the United Sates annually. A tumor in the testicle is almost always malignant; while most testicular cancers can be cured by a combination of radiation and chemotherapy, early warning is essential; metastasis is lethal.

Horoscope 25, Scott Hamilton

Scott Hamilton, men's singles figure skating Olympic champion, 1984 in Sarejevo, Yugoslavia, was diagnosed with testicular cancer in March 1997.[83] With the skill we are building in seeing patterns for critical illness, this Horoscope 25 becomes startlingly clear: Pluto and Mercury strongly conjoin the Sun (Mercury rules the 12th and is in mutual reception with the Sun) and this cluster is opposed by the Moon, ruler of the Midheaven (an angular statement). Mars squares this opposition axis widely. This suggests potential heart concerns (delayed certainly by the top conditioning procedures of an athlete), stomach concerns, and Plutonic concerns, especially.

Uranus conjuncts Venus, ruler of the Ascendant, in Leo. This is another heart reference.

Neptune is conjoined Jupiter. This conjunction is over the signline and Neptune rules the 6th; medically, we can *feel* perhaps something awry in cell division, in blood transport. We check Saturn and see that it is semi-square Neptune.

The midpoint analysis discloses Pluto=Sun/Moon, an extremely powerful drive signature, disruptive to get ahead, etc., but in health matters it reiterates the Moon opposition with Mercury-Sun-Pluto. This is very, very strong. Hamilton was born with stomach problems and had to be fed through a tube; his growth was stunted (5'3" as an adult).

---

82 Rosenfeld, 354.

83 Hamilton was adopted; his birth certificate supports the birth time.

The AP=Moon/Neptune, Sun/Node/ Mercury/Neptune, Jupiter/ Pluto, and Saturn/Midheaven represents a tremendous string of statements about public presence and achievement. We see the Moon, ruler of the Midheaven, in *quindecile* with Uranus (conjunct Ascendant ruler Venus), an obsession with "making it," proving the self.

Any time transit or Solar Arc Pluto conjoins or squares an angle, life perspective almost invariably changes, often involving death concerns within the extended family, major job adjustments, parental adjustments in the early home (when the contact occurs in the first eighteen years of life), separations, etc. It signifies a life-milestone.

Measure the distance between Hamilton's natal Pluto and his Ascendant—that's our objective here: bring the Pluto emphasis into an angular relationship, preferably at the Ascendant, the center of the health concerns (and note that the Ascendant is in this case square the Midheaven).

The measurement is 38 degrees; Hamilton is a Summer birth, the Solar Arc will be slow, requiring thirty-nine years to reflect the arc passage of 38 degrees (see page 79). Hamilton would be thirty-nine on his birthday in 1997. The transit record for mid-1997 shows transiting Saturn at 10 Aries in April 1997, conjunct Hamilton's seventh cusp, *opposing his Ascendant and squaring his Midheaven!*

This means that Hamilton's development would be defined by SA Pluto=Ascendant with transiting Saturn opposed Ascendant in the Spring of 1997. Is there any doubt whatsoever that these are markers of a powerful change in Hamilton's life? Could these markers have been seen two years earlier, three years earlier? Could we have included in our understanding of future development a challenge to health, following the diagnostic guidelines in his natal horoscope? Could astrology have presented early warning of critical illness?

Of course, the answer is "Yes" to all these questions, emphatically. Hamilton's testicular cancer was announced on March 18, 1997.[84] Television interviews with him reveal that he had "carried" the mass for some two years (transiting Pluto square Mercury, ruler of the 12th, transiting Saturn square Saturn) and the massed tumor, through metastasis had grown to the size of "a small canteloupe" lodged in his intestines (Mercury). More about this horoscope appears on page 206.

---

84 The exact Solar Arc measurement of Pluto to that date was 9 Pluto 44.

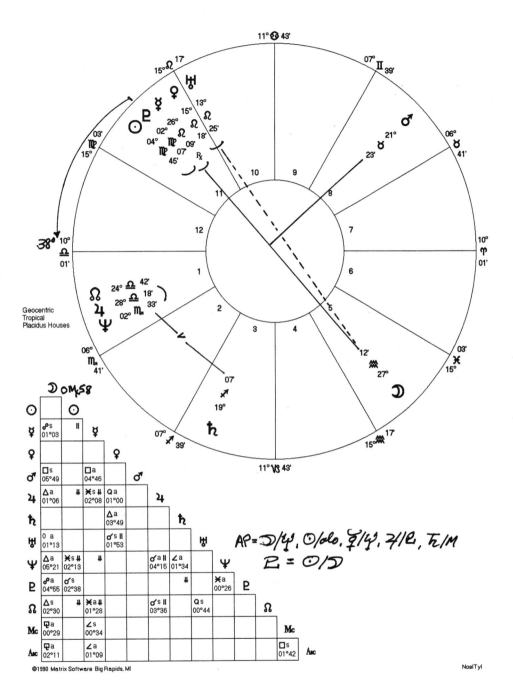

Horoscope 25, Scott Hamilton
August 28, 1958, 9:00 A.M. EST
Toledo, OH
83W33 — 41N39

Horoscope 26, AdZe MiXXe

Astrologer AdZe MiXXe died on the second of July 1997 of testicular cancer. I did not know MiXXe; I learned of his death on the internet.

His birth data help us all meet this unusual man: the Sun-Moon blend and the Ascendant, with Mars opposed the Moon, the axis squared by Uranus, with Mercury peregrine at the Aries Point, all promise a reaching out to people as a dominant thrust of energy, working overtime with well-developed aesthetic, artistic, and eventually "soft" ways of doing things—spiritual and avant garde ways—to gain unusual personal recognition. The going is tough in the developmental years (Saturn retrograde conjunct Neptune retrograde; Saturn ruling the 10th; the Moon ruling the 4th, squared by Mars; Uranus retrograde in the 4th), with much anger and bitterness building up, and the body's system is threatened with breakdown, perhaps sooner than later (Ascendant= Mars/Saturn; Saturn-Neptune both retrograde opposed Venus, ruler of the 7th). The significators of all four angles are highly stressed, as are the Angles themselves.

I think it is clear that Neptune is key here, and I feel AdZe would agree with me. Opposing the Ascendant, Neptune makes the closest aspect in the horoscope (along with the Moon square the Midheaven). This Neptune rules the 12th and disposes the 12th House Sun in Pisces. AdZe was caught up with the unconventional, with things Neptunian, meditative, New Age spiritual.

AdZe's friends tell the story of his unusual name: it came to him during a meditation within a dream, a dream about being a Viking in a past lifetime. It was dramatically corroborated later, in real life, when he met a stranger who recognized him by this peculiar name, embraced him in recognition from a past life, and was able to tell AdZe details about that past life...as a Viking named AdZe. It was a life-changing experience.

AdZe's horoscope shows arcs and transits that tell us much about his perilous disease. At death, we see SA Sun almost precisely opposed Saturn; SA Saturn in the 8th applying to the square with his natal Sun; and transiting Saturn conjoining his Ascendant. Transiting Jupiter was opposing natal Pluto exactly, the only contact with a testicular reference. As we have learned, the Jupiter component is a clear alert-significator for cancerous growth.

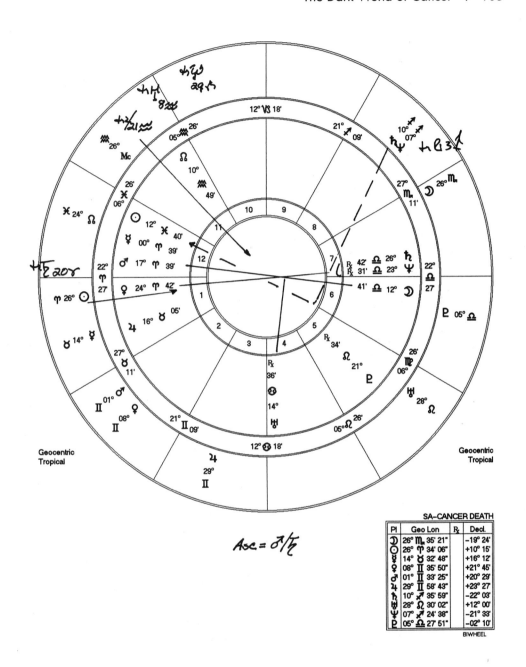

Asc = ♂/♄

PI	Geo Lon	℞	Decl.
☽	26° ♏ 35' 21"		−19° 24'
☉	26° ♈ 34' 06"		+10° 15'
☿	14° ♉ 32' 48"		+16° 12'
♀	08° ♊ 35' 50"		+21° 45'
♂	01° ♊ 33' 25"		+20° 29'
♃	29° ♊ 58' 43"		+23° 27
♄	10° ♐ 35' 59"		−22° 03'
♅	28° ♌ 30' 02"		+12° 00'
♆	07° ♐ 24' 38"		−21° 33'
♇	05° ♎ 27' 51"		−02° 10'

SA–CANCER DEATH

BIWHEEL

Horoscope 26, AdZe MiXXe

Inner Chart
March 3, 1953, 8:10 A.M. EST
Philadelphia, PA
75W09 — 39N57

Outer Ring — Cancer Death
SA: July. 2, 1997

I wondered why this crisis time had not been anticipated in the horoscope, i.e., a warning seen and followed. The crisis—and, more importantly—the build-up were clear, even if the Plutonic nature of the problem was not so prevalent as in our other cases. If it had been anticipated, with medical diagnosis, treatment, and the high rate of cure with testicular cancer, this "death" chart would simply have been a challenge of life reorganization professionally (Saturn rules the 10th; the Sun, the 5th), perhaps with teaching activities and/or writing (note SA Jupiter square Mercury, ruler of the 3rd, and the 6th).

I inspected the arc positions: note that SA Sun was opposed *Neptune* three years (degrees) earlier; in 1994, early in the year, transiting *Neptune* was at 22 Capricorn, exactly square MiXXe's Ascendant; transiting Saturn was just beginning to conjoin his Sun. *This* was the key time. What had happened *then?* Would that have been the time when the disease was detected? Was there some chance of misdiagnosis (the Neptune component that is so prevalent here (natally as well, in conjunction with Saturn in the 7th, Neptune ruling the 12th)?

A colleague of MiXXe's received word directly from the beneficiary and executrix of the estate that "AdZe had symptoms since *late Winter 1994* (i.e., early 1994), which he ignored, and then refused to consult with any but alternative health workers." This was firm corroboration of AdZe's Neptunian personality and belief system and, as well, our paradigm for the occurrence of critical disease.

MiXXe's medical diagnosis and surgery took place so late, in Summer 1996 with transiting Neptune square natal Saturn. The malignancy had metastasized to his intestines (Mercury peregrine, ruling the 6th, receiving the square arc from Jupiter). MiXXe would be dead in one year.

Women of course do not have a prostate gland or testicles, but women born with Pluto-specific profiles like those we have been studying, within the larger emerging profile of critical illness, have high probability of systemic breakdown as well, of course.

Horoscope 27, Male/Female

Horoscope 27 is the Solarscope for *two* people! It is the test *un*timed horoscope for General Schwarzkopf, brought forward from 18b, page 81, AND the Solarscope for the lady of Horoscope 16 (see page 65). The General and my client were born on the same day, two hours and 19 minutes apart in real time, separated by six times zones. Their Solarscope—presuming we did not know their birthtimes—*would be the same*. Indeed, *everyone* born on that date, August 22, 1934 in either earth hemisphere, without extreme polar latitude disorientation, *will have the same Solarscope!*

Remember: we have seen that the Solarscope can be eloquent in its portrayal of profiles of personality, somatic and systemic weakness, and critical illness. I estimate that we lose approximately thirty percent in accuracy *away* from the timed natal horoscope—yet even this lesser chart is of significant help in the work we do.

The shared Solarscope here means that *everyone* born on August 22, 1934 anywhere in the world will (should) have faced important challenge in the Spring of 1994! As daunting as that sounds, that is astrological reality; we astrologers are simply not accustomed to thinking that way. But what are *generational influences*, anyway, but world populations born under special long-lasting celestial conjunctions! Practically everyone involved in the leadership of World War II, on all sides, had the conjunction of Neptune and Pluto in Gemini in their natal horoscope!

In the case here, *each person will have transiting Pluto exactly square the natal Sun and the Solarscope Ascendant and transiting Neptune-Uranus opposed natal Mars-Pluto*. For Schwarzkopf, we saw the diagnosis of critical illness. But what happened to his date-twin?

Look back for a moment to the lady's timed horoscope on page 65: note that she has Scorpio on her Ascendant and her 12th House; the Neptune-Uranus transit opposed her natal Mars-Pluto would certainly put focus on the sickness profile, and the Pluto transit square her Sun set at the Solarscope Ascendant would corroborate the situation strongly.

Did this woman have a health crisis with her gynecological organs or her colon (Pluto) or her stomach or breasts (Mars-Pluto in Cancer)? No. She was under great, great stress, under a psychologist's and a psychiatrist's care and medicated, within a bewildering and dramatic divorce proceeding.

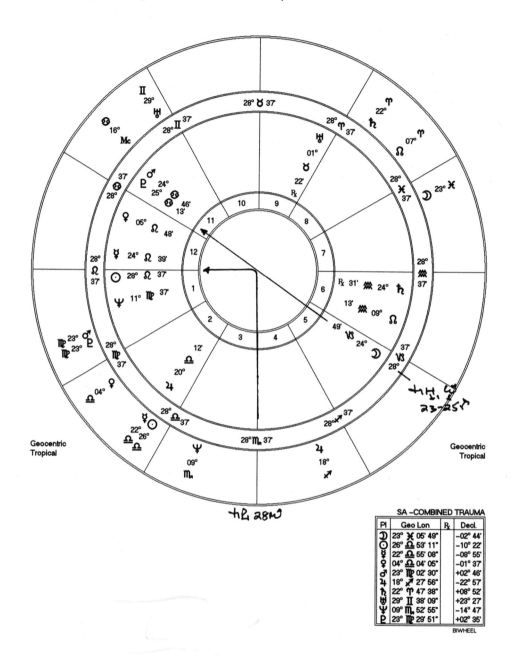

Solarscope 27, Male/Female ☉
Inner Chart: August 22, 1934
Outer Ring — Parallel Traumas, SA: March 15, 1994

This reality reminds us that any aspect (natal, arc or transit) to the Ascendant *is also an aspect to the Descendant.* [85]

We must not shy away from the generational or date-time generalities of astrology; we must refine them as well as we can with respect to gender, sociometric level, sociocultural backdrop, inherited factors, and individual exigency. But the fact remains that the potentials are there; the expectations are there. Understanding and adapting and interpreting communication within an individual frame of reality comprise the astrologer's art.

Colon Cancer
Horoscope 28, Female

Horoscope 28 shows a female born in 1929, just five years before General Schwarzkopf and his date twin, and many, many thousands of others. The time and location of her birth narrow down her individual space and time considerably, of course. The Sun-Moon blend suggests a need to work with the intangible, the inspirational, the ideal, to organize aesthetics in relation to some goal so that everything she does will have value.

The Aquarian Ascendant picks up this train of analytical deduction and suggests that this lady truly does "need a cause"; Uranus, ruler of the Ascendant, placed at the midpoint of Sun/Moon, states unequivocally that humanitarianism, the unusual, the avant-garde somehow will dominate this lady's life.

Jupiter barely in conjunction with the Sun, perhaps peregrine, i.e., poised to break away, to fly free, to build elsewhere, again suggests going beyond the profession (Jupiter rules the Midheaven). This lady is a communicator through and through, filled with visionary ideas (Mercury square with Neptune, co-ruler of her Ascendant, exactly opposed her Ascendant (recall MiXXe's horoscope Neptune, page 105); please note Mercury's final dispositorship of the horoscope (along with Saturn) and its quindecile with the Midheaven from the 3rd House.

---

85 Additionally, just as Schwarzkopf had SA Sun applying to his timed horoscope Midheaven, his date twin had SA Sun exactly semisquare her Midheaven and SA Moon=Sun/Jupiter at this time of crisis. For both, affects were ameliorated; the drastic was put off in degree. Schwarzkopf's operation was a success, there had been no metastasis, and his life was changed into a new direction. For the lady, her divorce worked out comfortably to her benefit and her life was dramatically changed into a new direction, location, level, and future.

The lady has had colon problems throughout her life; at this time, though, there was no outbreak in anything physically "Plutonic," i.e., the ovaries, for example, in parallel with Schwarzkopf's prostate. Why? We do not know; what is so eloquently shown in the General's case is not shown anywhere nearly as strongly in the lady's case.

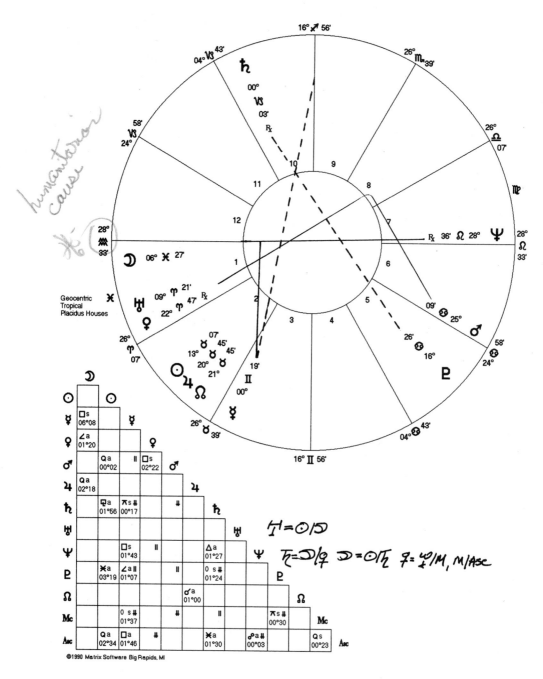

Horoscope 28, Female

While the communication dimensions are very strong, much developmental experience is suppressed here (northern hemisphere emphasis); a tremendous need for love emerges from a difficult homelife (note Mars, ruler of the self-worth 2nd, in an adjustment quincunx with the Ascendant; Saturn retrograde's rulership of the 11th House) and perhaps projection onto others to fulfill humanitarian service.

This stern, tight inner world is captured in the image of Saturn= Moon/Venus and Moon=Sun/Saturn; the overflowing aesthetics-love and sense of beauty and comfort dimensions are shown through Venus= Neptune/Midheaven and Midheaven/Ascendant.

For the inclination to critical illness, we must see the upper respiratory tract (Neptune square Mercury in Gemini) and Plutonic regions (the very powerful *quindecile* between Saturn, ruler of the 12th and Pluto; just add 15 to Saturn to come to opposition with Pluto, i.e., establishing the relationship as 165 degrees, the quindecile).

This is the horoscope of Audrey Hepburn, the much-loved movie star and indefatigable heroine—after her movie career—for food and medical programs for starving children in Africa. Hepburn died January 20, 1993 of cancer of the colon.[86]

Horoscope 28a (see page 112) presents the Solar Arc and Transit picture for Hepburn's death. We see SA Saturn just past the Ascendant. Could SA Saturn at the Ascendant have signaled the critical stage of her cancer? This would have occurred in July 1990 [31 Aquarius 07 minus 28 Aquarius 33 gives 2.34, i.e., two years and seven months earlier than the death mark date, July 1990]. With this backdrop, transiting Pluto was beginning to oppose Jupiter and transiting Neptune was beginning to oppose Pluto early in 1991.

Yet, even earlier, SA Jupiter was conjunct natal Pluto in August 1987. At that time, *transiting Pluto was exactly opposed Hepburn's Sun* and transiting Saturn was conjunct her Midheaven. This was time for definite alarm.

---

86 Hepburn had been born into a world of wealth and privilege, the daughter of a Dutch Baroness and a British international banker. In her earliest years she was painfully shy and insecure, using her imagination to create a substitute personal world as defense against quarrelling parents, divorced when she was six, against the outbreak of World War II (which consumed their lives), and the consequences of her estranged father becoming a Fascist and Hitler sympathizer. Music and dance were her sole joys.

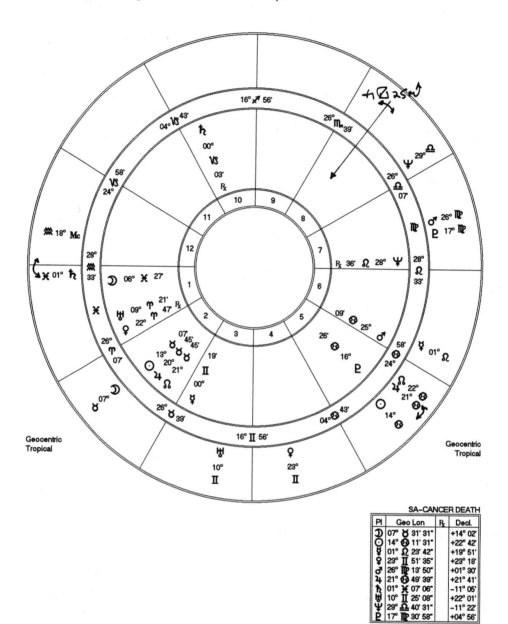

Horoscope 28a, Audrey Hepburn

Inner Chart
May 4, 1929, 3:00 A.M. GMD
Brussels, Belgium
04E20 — 50N50

Outer Ring — Cancer Death
SA: January 20, 1993

PI	Geo Lon	Rx	Decl.
☽	07° ♉ 31' 31"		+14° 02'
⊙	14° ♋ 11' 31"		+22° 42'
☿	01° ♌ 23' 42"		+19° 51'
♀	23° ♊ 51' 35"		+23° 18'
♂	26° ♍ 13' 50"		+01° 30'
♃	21° ♋ 49' 39"		+21° 41'
♄	01° ♓ 07' 06"		−11° 05'
♅	10° ♊ 25' 08"		+22° 01'
♆	29° ♎ 40' 31"		−11° 22'
♇	17° ♍ 30' 58"		+04° 56'

SA-CANCER DEATH

BIWHEEL

It is clear that these two time periods are key to the possible origination and/or development of her cancer: August 1987 and late 1990 to early 1991. She could have been warned then. Was she?

Cancers of the colon and the rectum run a very close second to cancer of the lung as the most prevalent form of cancer. Some 130,000 new cases are diagnosed each year. Dr. Isadore Rosenfeld states unequivocally, "Any unexplained change in bowel habits, such as alternating periods of constipation and diarrhea, abdominal pain, or the presence of blood in or on the stool, should be considered early signs of cancer of the lower intestinal tract until *proved* otherwise. Proper diagnosis at this time makes a cure possible."[87]

If there is a previous personal history of benign polyps, one must be rechecked very carefully at regular intervals throughout the rest of one's life. These polyps may be precursors of colon cancer, ten to fifteen years ahead of time. One is at an increased risk if there is a history of colon polyps among one's close relatives.

Horoscope #29, Male

Another example, Horoscope 29, is a male who was diagnosed with colon cancer in June 1994; the operation followed immediately. We see the key measurements of this crisis easily—which means that *the crisis could have been anticipated;* early warning *could* have been given.

Note SA Saturn conjoining the Midheaven; SA Venus conjoining the Ascendant (bringing the 12th House, ruled by Venus, to prominence at the health center at the Ascendant); SA Jupiter at 22 Cancer 49 square to natal Venus, ruler of the 12th; SA Ascendant conjunct Neptune; and SA Mars tightly square the Ascendant!

The trigger transits for this awesome SA backdrop were transiting Neptune square Venus, ruler of the 12th, and transiting Pluto opposed Mercury, ruler of the Ascendant, in the 12th!

There are more warning signs: the promise from the natal horoscope presents AP=Saturn(retrograde), opposed the Ascendant, and—you guessed it, or you've spotted it—*the quindecile between Saturn and Pluto,* ruler of the 6th (subtract 15 from Pluto to establish the aspect, i.e., in reference to the opposition with Saturn).

---

87 Rosenfeld, page 322.

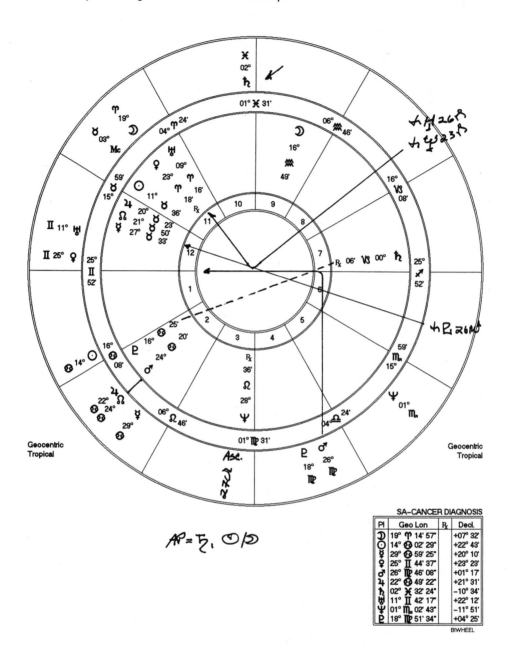

Horoscope 29, Male
Outer Ring — Cancer Diagnosis
SA: June 15, 1994

This is crisis. The patterns of crisis are clear—angularity, Pluto, Neptune, Saturn, 12th House, Ascendant—now surely becoming more and more familiar through the practice of some twenty cases so far in this book.

Initial Review of Early Warning Patterning

What we are seeing develop out of our preparation for cursory diagnosis is a scenario of planetary movements—developments—on two levels: Solar Arcs and Transits. What emerges is a distinct hierarchy of importance, which will be refined further in our study:

- Natal paths toward physical breakdown within the aging process are seen within stressed aspects between the outer planets—Pluto, Neptune, Uranus, and Saturn—and the inner planets—Sun, Moon, Venus, Mercury, Mars, and the Ascendant. Jupiter appears uninvolved, yet occasionally dramatically corroborative of cancerous conditions (of rampant cellular growth perhaps); the Secondary Progressed Moon seems insignificant as a key significator or reliable timing reference in relation to disease.

- We see the definite role of the *quindecile* aspect connoting intensity, even obsessive focus within development, perhaps the key link between anxiety dimensions in life and body reactions in response.

- Angular involvement is emphatically important, natally and in development through rulership or tenancy, especially with reference to the Ascendant.

- Midpoint pictures linking the Sun, Moon, Ascendant (or its ruler) with outer planets are critically helpful in cursory diagnosis; these pictures extend synthesis beyond the standard aspects between two planets.

- We see the importance of the 12th House, planets in the 12th and the planet ruling the 12th. The 6th House appears to be less prominent; a reinforcement of deduction if indicated.

- Finally, we see the adjunct significance of the Solarscope, which reflects any accentuation of the Sun and 12th House variables. When the Sun is not involved astrologically with a specific crisis complex, by transit or arc, the Solarscope falls off in reliability.

Now, let us focus on refining these and other specifics of the growing profile of critical illness.

General Infections
Horoscope 30, Female

Horoscope 30 shows a female with dramatically patterned measurements. The key aspect is Pluto, ruler of the 6th, quindecile Venus, the ruler of the 12th.[88] This promises an intense focus on potential systemic breakdown.

The Ascendant here is square the midpoint of Neptune/Pluto; this brings the health center of the horoscope into a tension construct of two outer planets. This contact introduces the idea of blood (Neptune) and of gynecological problems (Pluto). The mind easily thinks "infection" here, the blood carrying along poisoning agents that invade our system from the air, from food, from planets, from other people, and from animals.

Bacteria enter our body and create toxins (poisons) that damage specific cells in the tissues they have invaded; viruses, which can not reproduce themselves, enter our cells and take them over, instructing the cells to manufacture the parts the viruses need to multiply, and this process can eventually destroy the cell(s). The blood is the battlefield, and Neptune refers to the process (see page 42).

Studying this horoscope in terms of illness, we are alerted to infections, to easy infectability, if you will. A reinforcement of the Ascendant= Neptune/Pluto picture might well be the Jupiter square with the Sun; as original ruler of Pisces, Jupiter carried with it much symbolism to do with the blood because of the liver's role in regulating composition of the blood.

An additional backup comes from the midpoint picture Saturn= Mercury/Venus: Saturn (classically "debilitated" here by retrogradation, the conjunction with Mars, and the occurrence in Cancer) is brought into connection with the rulers of this woman's Ascendant and 12th House, through the midpoint equation.

Then there is Pluto=Sun/Midheaven which, in illness-scan of the horoscope, becomes significant because Pluto is related to the Sun (the life giver) and an angle. We then come back to the quindecile between Pluto and Venus, ruler of the 12th.

---

88 I urge astrologers to take this aspect seriously (see page 9). That it is new to our "tool kit" does not mean that it is faddish, discardable, superfluous; it is not embarrassing not to have known about this aspect earlier. It was there, of course, but it has just resurfaced in the last three years. I have tested it in well over 500 cases, in person, and perhaps 200 other cases historically and through presentations made to astrologers in twelve countries. The quindecile is vitally important.

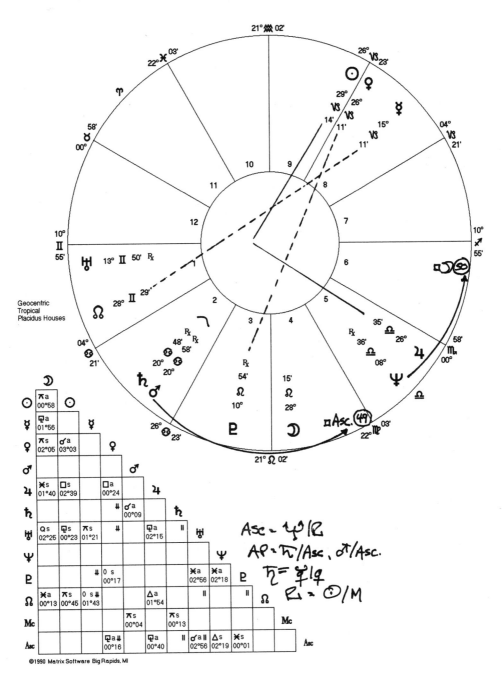

Horoscope 30, Female

We see Venus (in its conjunction with the Sun) square to Jupiter as well, and this suggests the potential of a family history of diabetes (see page 19). Indeed, this lady's father contracted diabetes late in life, her great-grandfather died of diabetes, and two younger cousins have diabetes. She herself now is pursuing tests and watchful waiting.

Additionally the Mars-Saturn conjunction in Cancer brings into question the stomach, the abdomen. After her child was born, this lady suffered intense abdominal pains for a protracted period of time.

A final note: Mercury is *peregrine,* not making a Ptolemaic aspect in the horoscope. I have found that, *when the Ascendant ruler is peregrine,* the responsiveness of the Ascendant in terms of illness concerns or responses is heightened.

Now, our question—in consultation with this client, say in 1993, when she was forty-seven years old—would be about arcs and transits about to form in her near future. In our horoscope preparation, we would have arced the natal Mars-Saturn conjunction ahead some 49 degrees to *a square with the Ascendant,* a vitally important time of alert, of course (simply note the square position to the Ascendant, i.e., 10–11 Virgo, and measure the number of degrees to that point from the natal Mars-Saturn conjunction that is so dramatically poised in the horoscope: 49–50 degrees/years of age).[89]

Similarly, our experience and instinct *that more than one major measurement will probably be present at a critical time* suggest adding *that same arc* to other planetary positions to see if there is a "companion" arc at that same time. There is: 50 degrees added to natal *Neptune* gives 58 Libra or 28 Scorpio, *square the Moon.*

When we check the ephemeris for the trigger transits at that time, i.e., 1995–1996, when the lady was fifty-eight years old, we find transiting Neptune exactly conjunct natal Venus (within the quindecile with Pluto) in April 1995 and transiting Uranus conjunct the Sun! Transiting Saturn is square the Ascendant in January 1995. [And before that, transiting Pluto had been square the Midheaven throughout 1992 and then squaring the Moon throughout 1994, the probable beginnings of difficulties that could manifest in the future.]

We make a careful arc-transit drawing of the time ahead, Spring 1995, and we are perfectly fortified to give warning about possible critical illness, the importance of seeing a physician for a checkup.

---

89 The eye learns this quick arcing with experience: it becomes easy to see 50 degrees added to Mars-Saturn at 20 Cancer giving 70 Cancer or 10 Virgo.

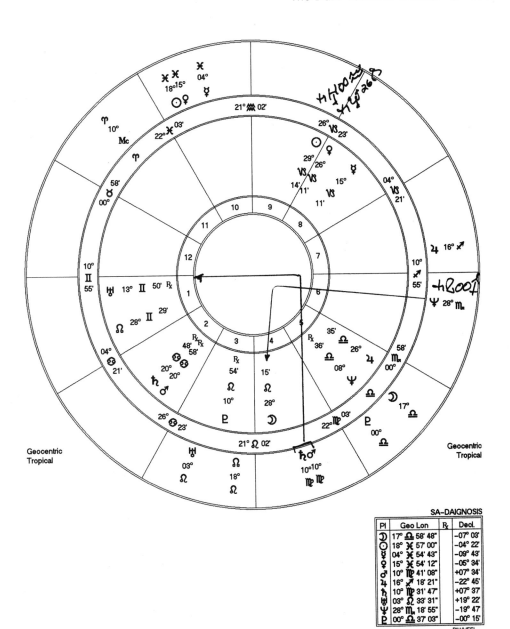

Horoscope 30a, Female
Outer Ring — Diagnosis
SA: April 15, 1995

SA-DAIGNOSIS

Pl	Geo Lon	Rx	Decl.
☽	17° ♎ 58' 48"		–07° 03'
☉	18° ♓ 57' 00"		–04° 22'
☿	04° ♓ 54' 43"		–09° 43'
♀	15° ♓ 54' 12"		–05° 34'
♂	10° ♍ 41' 08"		+07° 34'
♃	16° ♐ 18' 21"		–22° 45'
♄	10° ♍ 31' 47"		+07° 37
♅	03° ♌ 33' 31"		+19° 22'
♆	28° ♏ 18' 55"		–19° 47'
♇	00° ♎ 37' 03"		–00° 15'

BIWHEEL

Horoscope 30a is the horoscope drawn for April 15, 1995, showing everything discussed above. It is unavoidably clear. Our eyes are getting used to seeing these things; we are learning confidence with these techniques.[90]

This lady had taken on all kinds of strange symptoms, yet no one could find anything wrong with her! After nine months of fevers (which had begun in Spring 1994 with the *first* transiting square of Saturn to the Ascendant, when the major arcs were forming within one degree of partile!), in April 1995, one determined doctor suspected a hidden tumor in the gynecological area and operated in July.

The surgeon found a strange but benign tumor (Neptune) and removed it. A month later, he reopened the scar and removed a cyst that had been hidden behind the tumor. It was full of poisons (Neptune) but not malignant. Our lady with the infections recovered completely.

Horoscope 31, Male

We have seen two cases of leukemia early on in our study (see Case 9, page 47, and Case 10, page 48). Here is another, Case 31, that is extremely clearly defined.

Leukemias are cancers of the body's blood-forming tissues, including the bone marrow and the lymph system. These cancers bring about the formation of a tremendously high amount of white blood cells, the cells normally used to fight infections in the body. When their numbers—especially unhealthy white cells—become so high, they interfere rather than help with the functions of the vital organs. Eventually, they overwhelm the production of healthy blood cells, red and white.

Since the white cells include a grand number of unhealthy cells, the body's ability to fight infections deteriorates. With the production of red cells blocked, the body's organs do not receive enough oxygen. Without successful treatment leukemia is fatal.[91]

This group of malignancies ranks about 10th in occurrence in the United States, with some 30,000 new cases reported annually. It accounts for about forty-five percent of children's cancers. There is slightly more

---

90 The Solarscope for this same period would also indicate the critical time. Any arc or aspect of importance to the Sun will always be registered in the Solarscope as arc or aspect to the Sun and Solar Ascendant. In this case, transiting Neptune and Uranus were conjoining Venus, Sun, and Ascendant of the solarscope.

91 Mayo, page 964.

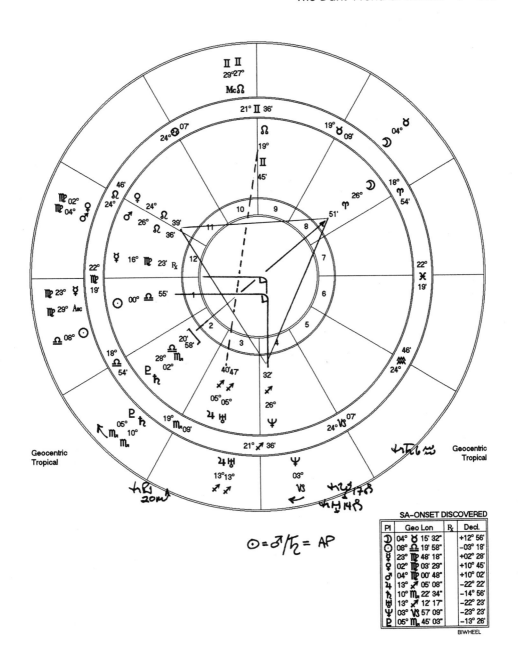

Horoscope 31, Male
Outer Ring — Onset Discovered
SA: April 15, 1991

leukemia among whites than black, among Jews than other whites, and among more women than men. There is no definite evidence of any familial predisposition to leukemia.[92]

Front-line research is pursuing leukemia as a viral infection. In the laboratory, we are able to induce leukemia in animals by infecting them with certain viruses. The hope is that variations of certain viruses will soon permit the manufacture of vaccines to prevent more common types of leukemia.

In Horoscope 31, this little boy—eight years old when diagnosed—has Neptune angular and square the Sun in the Ascendant (and Neptune is also square the Ascendant). Neptune is the significator for the blood; the Sun rules the 12th.

The Sun is at the Aries Point and, in this position, is at the midpoint of Mars/Saturn (See Sun=Mars/Saturn in Case 9, page 47; and the cases on pages 35, 143, 160, and 168), suggesting a breakdown in physical well being.

The ominous conjunction of natal Saturn and Pluto opposes the Moon. The conjunction of Jupiter and Uranus (intensified cell development?) is quindecile the Midheaven angle. Mercury is retrograde and peregrine in the 12th, ruling the Ascendant and the Midheaven; while this suggests many things characterologically, within the health profile, it suggests an underlying level of potential breakdown.[93]

The breakdown occurred in April 1991. Perhaps true to the promise of the symbol Neptune, we can not find any pertinent arc or transit to correspond with the time of diagnosis, no astrological symptom (except perhaps SA Mars square Jupiter). However, *three years earlier in 1988,* we can see that *SA Pluto conjoined Saturn* and *SA Neptune was exactly square the Sun,* with transiting Saturn and Uranus square the Sun. That was the birth time of this leukemia.

The young boy endured two full years of chemotherapy, and then the cancer went into remission for four years. He was knocked down once again in May of 1997 when the condition returned (with a bone marrow transplant) with transiting Pluto at 5 Sagittarius exactly conjunct Jupiter-Uranus and transiting Neptune square Pluto.

---

92 Rosenfeld, pages 344–345.

93 Leukemia can develop insidiously—a Neptunian trait, of course! In about a third of the cases, there are *no symptoms at the time of diagnosis!* These cases are detected when routine blood tests give abnormal results. Mayo, page 964.

Stomach Cancer
Horoscope 32, Female

Horoscope 32 (see page 124) is a female whose susceptibility to gynecological and/or stomach difficulties is extremely clear-cut, as is the activation time of critical illness.

Note the square between natal Jupiter and the natal Moon in Cancer, ruling the 12th House.[94] And note once again, the quindecile between Pluto in Cancer in the 12th and Saturn retrograde, ruling the 6th. These are dire portents for problems with the stomach; yes, for stomach cancer.

Midpoint pictures support this analysis: Pluto=Moon/Saturn links the planets in quindecile with the 12th House and the organ significator, the Moon; Ascendant=Neptune/Pluto (the same picture as for number 30 (see pages 117)), and the quindecile between Mars and Uranus involves the Descendant and the Midheaven through the Mars opposition with the Midheaven. The angles are tense.

When transiting Neptune came to 24–25 Capricorn opposing natal Pluto, with SA Uranus square natal Jupiter, this lady was diagnosed and had surgery for Mesotheioma, cancer of the lining of the stomach wall.

We can ask when this condition might have begun to form, when the earliest possible warning could have been given. Note that SA Neptune was just over Mars and, earlier, just over the fourth cusp opposed the Midheaven. At the same time that Neptune=Midheaven occurred (four years earlier in the Summer–Fall of 1992), *transiting Saturn was at 18 Aquarius exactly opposed the Ascendant.*

---

94 Throughout the research I have conducted in the field of critical illness, I have finally weaned myself of "Jupiter the benefic." Indeed, astrology recognizes the high-probability reward cycle of the Jupiter transit, but, in concerns of the body, it is extraordinary how Jupiter "rarely seems to help"; how Jupiter somehow appears to corroborate augmentation of difficulty, perhaps cell growth, as we have discussed frequently in this study.

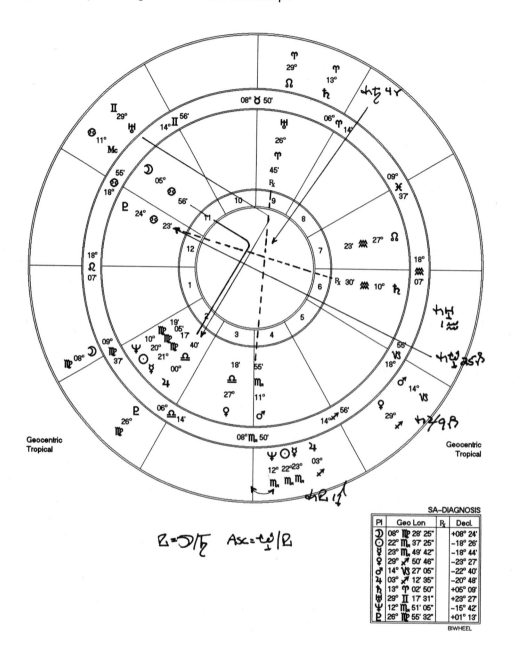

Horoscope 32, Female
Outer Ring — Diagnosis
SA: October 15, 1996

Bone Cancer
Horoscope 33, Carl Sagan

The celebrated astronomer Carl Sagan's horoscope provides yet another conclusive test for our profiling of critical illness.

Sagan's Sun-Moon blend promises a tremendous philosophy and idealism, a twin thrust to understand why things are as they are. To plumb the depths of research and understand things were his *raison d'etre*. This is always so clearly developed in those who are born with the Sun in Scorpio and the Moon in Sagittarius: evangelist Billy Graham, astrology researcher Michel Gauquelin (horoscope, page 237), and television and newspaper personality Larry King (who has conducted over 30,000 interviews in his career; horoscope, page 182), each in his own way showing this need to control by knowing, to have opinions respected, come hell or high water!

Sagan was also destined to be a public figure (AP=Midheaven/ Ascendant), always proving a point (AP=Jupiter/Saturn). His high-energy drive and sense of authority were well known (Sun=Mars/Pluto) and Mars=Uranus/Pluto (even to the point of fanaticism). He was his profession; his profession was he: Venus, ruler of the Ascendant, was quindecile Uranus, ruler of the Midheaven.

Sagan undoubtedly had difficulty with relationships, so energetic, so highly charged were his opinionation and his search for truth (Uranus square Pluto, ruler of the 7th). Friendship was well down the list of what Sagan was about.

But the health-scan of the horoscope reveals threats to that energetic thrust into life: note that Saturn is square the Sun and Venus, the life-giver and the Ascendant ruler respectively, and Saturn is also square the Ascendant. Neptune is conjunct Mars, ruler of the 12th. Neptune is sesquiquadrate Uranus; Uranus, squared by Pluto, is itself in the 12th.

All of us have such aspects and rulership networks *to one degree of intensity and specificity or another;* that is part of astrology foretelling the aging process for everyone, the breakdown of our systems and our body. *WHEN* this can be sharply tapped in time, *THAT* is what this book is about; *THAT* is what astrology can contribute to the process of early warning, the process that buys more life time.

Any seasoned astrologer looking at this horoscope in 1996 would *know* instantly that Sagan was to absorb the transit of Uranus at his

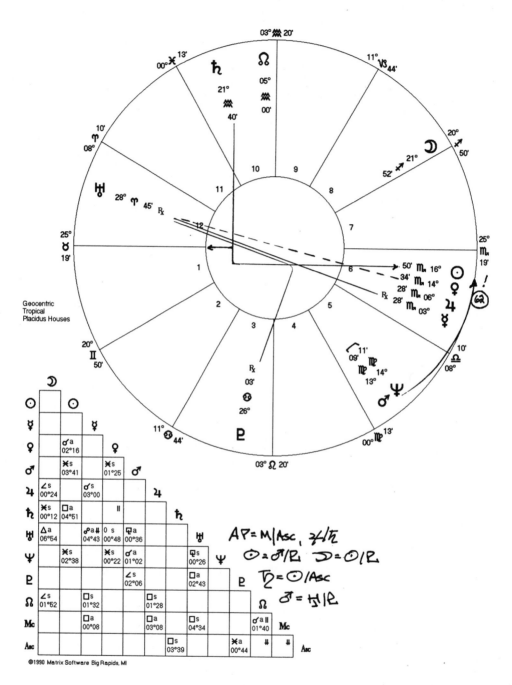

Horoscope 33, Carl Sagan
November 9, 1934, 5:05 P.M. EST
New York, NY
74W00 — 40N43

Midheaven late in December 1996. Checking the ephemeris would then reveal that, *at the same time,* transiting Neptune would be at 26 Capricorn *exactly opposite natal Pluto.* Two dramatic major transits would be recorded. This time late in 1996 would be a key, key time in Sagan's life. He would be just past his sixty-second birthday.

Sixty-two years—a sextile plus 2—added to Neptune-Mars will arc Neptune-Mars (Mars ruling the 12th) to 16–15 Scorpio, *conjunct the natal Sun!*

In just a short moment of study, we discover SA Mars-Neptune=Sun, with transiting Uranus conjunct the Midheaven and transiting Neptune opposed Pluto and squared Uranus in the 12th. What would you have said to Dr. Sagan sitting in your office, say, two years earlier?

Sagan died on December 20, 1996; the cause of death was confused in various press reports, but the consensus pointed to bone cancer.

There are 206 bones in the human body to which the muscles are attached and within which the organs are located. The bones are living, changing tissues that produce blood cells (Neptune) and act as storehouse for the minerals calcium and phosphate.

Disease can affect the bone; osteoporosis is relatively common; one out of every four women over forty-five years of age and nine of every ten over seventy-five have varying degrees of osteoporosis, which gradually depletes the store of calcium in the bones.[95] Any disease of the bones results from a failure of the function of the skeleton, ruled by Saturn.

In Sagan's horoscope, *Saturn squares the Sun and the Ascendant.* The other measurements we have studied above create a pedestal for this difficult link with the Sun.[96]

Looking back into the years preceding his death, we can suggest other key times when a health alert could have been given to Sagan: for example, transiting Uranus was opposed natal Pluto (which natally squares natal Uranus in the 12th, as we have seen) in Spring 1994, with transiting Saturn at the same time opposing natal Mars-Neptune. And what about Sagan's second Saturn return in January–March 1993?[97]

---

95 Mayo, page 894. Men start with more minerals in bone reserve so osteoporosis (from the Greek, bone passages), the loss of bone density, shows up later in life and to a lesser degree than in women.

96 Additionally, at death, transiting Saturn was at 1 Aries, conjunct the Aries point and at the midpoint of Sagan's Midheaven and the Ascendant.

97 Of course, in consultation, one would check the conditions of the 1st Saturn return in mid-1963, a critical time for Sagan then as well, with tr. Neptune conjunct his Sun at the same time!

Cancer Cases not-so-specific, Astrologically

All the cases in this book so far could very easily be replaced by as many other cases that would be as strongly articulated astrologically. These clear cases represent the horoscopic norm behind critical illness. They help us learn the patterns of the breakdown of health. But there are horoscopes where crisis is clear but the specific bodily reference is not. Astrology can still be extremely helpful, of course; after all, I repeat again and again, *the astrologer's objective can not yet be to make a reliable medical diagnosis but, rather, it is to offer a definitively reliable timely referral.*

With sophistication in seeing patterns, we gain a skill also with less dramatically demarcated horoscopes. But, still there are unknowns, vague areas, unsure areas, inexplicable happenings.

For example, please look again at colon cancer case 29 (page 114). The crisis was monumentally clear, as you will recall. The natal Saturn quindecile with Pluto ruler of the 6th and the transit of Pluto to opposition with Mercury, ruler of the Ascendant, delineate the colon reference within the crisis. And yes, it could well have been the prostate gland in this man of sixty-five. As yet, we can not break down the Pluto/Scorpio symbolism more specifically. Why the colon was damaged instead of the prostate could simply be a result of eating habits throughout life, i.e., referencing Mercury (eating disorders, diet), which is squared natally by Neptune and opposed by transiting Pluto at the time of crisis.

Six months after the operation on his colon in June 1994, this gentleman was still not feeling right. Seven months later in July 1996 he had another CT SCAN: there was no problem anymore in his colon, but there *was* a tumor underneath the colon in the pelvic area. Chemotherapy followed and was very effective, until, in November 1996, the doctors discovered a spot in the man's liver. The spot was/is cancerous, and he is under radiation and chemotherapy.

I can not "find" the liver (Jupiter) prominently highlighted in this horoscope, neither natally nor in arcs or transits (except for the wide square from Neptune). There is no clear explanation for this cancer going further, at that time.

However, there *is* travail indicated ahead: *in an already debilitated system,* we can expect a strong response from the indications of the transit conjunction of Mars and Saturn in April 1998 at 22 Aries; it will be conjunct this gentleman's Venus, ruler of his 12th, already besieged in crisis past.

These trauma are difficult for astrologers too. We see so much; we continue to see more; we don't see enough. People learn to look to us for a miracle: "Since you have seen it coming, tell me when it will be cured, when will it be gone? What will make it right?" It is one thing for the astrologer to sound the alarm and make the referral; and it is quite another thing to go on after that when the system does not return to health and strength. The role of counselor in this issue is more with the doctor with his or her vast empirical resources than it is with the astrologer.

Kidney Cancer
Horoscope 34, Joan Negus

Horoscope 34 (page 131) shows the horoscope of Joan Negus, a prominent astrologer and teacher for many years. Joan was diagnosed with Kidney cancer in January 1997.

Each of us has two kidneys. Their primary function, a complex one, is to remove excess fluid and waste material from the blood. Although other organs such as the skin (through perspiration), the lungs (through exhalation), and the intestine also remove fluids, the kidneys, working with the urinary tract, are by far the most important organ for fluid excretion.

The blood that leaves the kidneys contains salts, protein, sugar, calcium, and other substances vital to maintaining normal body function. Injury, poisons, tumors, or infections in *other* parts of the body can cause kidney damage, usually best and first detected through urinalysis.[98]

Kidney cancer ranks twelfth in the malignancy occurrence in the United States health profile, with about 18,000 new cases every year. It is twice as common in men as in women, and, in either event, usually occurs after the age of sixty.

Cigarettes seem to be the most important risk factor for cancer of the kidney. Smokers are twice as likely to develop it as are nonsmokers, and it is estimated that thirty percent of these cancers in men and twenty-four percent in women are directly caused by tobacco.[99]

Joan's natal horoscope shows Saturn retrograde quindecile to Pluto in the 12th House. This measurement alone, which we have been seeing over and over again within natal patterns toward debilitation, seems to be a beacon for physical trauma, especially when related to (the outer

---

98 Mayo, 826–827.
99 Rosenfeld, 339.

planet(s) and/or) the 12th House or its ruler. There is no escaping this observation.

This Saturn retrograde is opposed Jupiter (which you do see emerging through my research as apparent significator of accelerated cell growth and tumor formation), and Jupiter is in the 12th House. The Moon, the ruler of the 12th House, *is square the axis of Jupiter-Saturn.* This "picture" often carries with it a hypersensitivity psychologically and systemically.

The 3rd House Moon in Libra is also opposed by Uranus. While all of this intensifies Joan's profile as the effective communicator that she is (with Mercury in Leo peregrine as well; with the Moon exactly quindecile the Midheaven), proving points, establishing a personally dramatic position with her adoring public, we can see the complex as highly tense in the profile of potential illness, critical illness: potentially a Grand Cross of squared opposition axes (Moon-Uranus, Jupiter-Saturn), with strong focus into the 12th House.

The kidneys work with the blood. The blood is symbolized by Neptune. In Joan's horoscope, *SA Neptune came to exact square with the 12th House Sun (and Ascendant) in January 1997.*

At the same time, looking for a companion arc to this very difficult one that threatens to wipe out identity to one degree or another, in one way or another, we see that *SA Saturn arced out of its difficult natal complex to 10 Pisces 58, precisely square natal Mars.* The relationship between Saturn and Mars (especially the square) very often carries with it life-and-death decision-making demands.[100]

Joan is one of the rare exceptions to part of the Neptune observation, i.e., the loss of identity somehow when arcing or transiting conjunct or square an angle (or Sun or Moon). She received astrology's highest award, The Regulus, at the United Astrology Congress of 1995, in the Spring when transiting Neptune *and* Uranus were square to her Midheaven. Perhaps the Uranus symbolism lessened the correspondence of ego loss that is indisputably applicable to this Neptune transit.

Perhaps SA Neptune square the Sun in the 12th House building throughout 1996, could be ameliorated somehow by intervention of

---

100 The escape artist Harry Houdini (March 24, 1874) had Mars square the opposition of Saturn-Uranus; I find this image helpful when working with the Mars-Saturn relationship. Reinhold Ebertin observed this same life-and-death image within Mars-Saturn contacts, the challenging meeting of extremes.

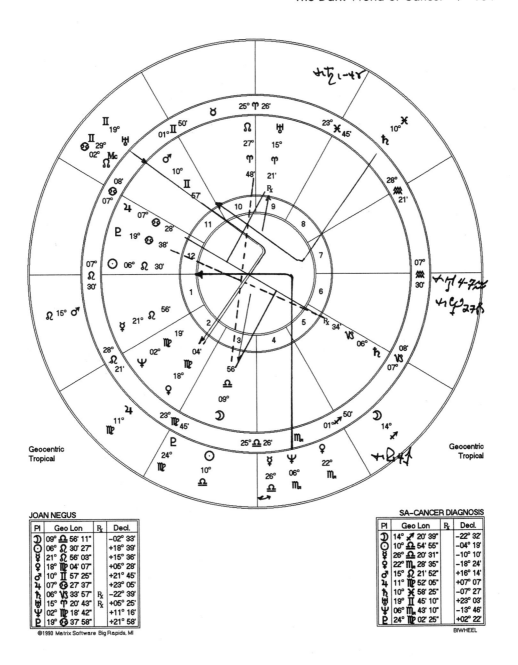

JOAN NEGUS

Pl	Geo Lon	Rx	Decl.
☽	09° ♎ 56' 11"		-02° 33'
☉	06° ♌ 30' 27"		+18° 39'
☿	21° ♌ 56' 03"		+15° 36'
♀	18° ♍ 04' 07"		+05° 28'
♂	10° ♊ 57' 25"		+21° 45'
♃	07° ⊕ 27' 37"		+23° 05'
♄	06° ♑ 33' 57"	Rx	-22° 39'
♅	15° ♈ 20' 43"	Rx	+05° 25'
♆	02° ♍ 18' 42"		+11° 16'
♇	19° ⊕ 37' 58"		+21° 58'

©1990 Matrix Software Big Rapids, MI

SA-CANCER DIAGNOSIS

Pl	Geo Lon	Rx	Decl.
☽	14° ♐ 20' 39"		-22° 32'
☉	10° ♎ 54' 55"		-04° 19'
☿	26° ♎ 20' 31"		-10° 10'
♀	22° ♏ 28' 35"		-18° 24'
♂	15° ♌ 21' 52"		+16° 14'
♃	11° ♍ 52' 05"		+07° 07'
♄	10° ♓ 58' 25"		-07° 27'
♅	19° ♊ 45' 10"		+23° 03'
♆	06° ♏ 43' 10"		-13° 46'
♇	24° ♍ 02' 25"		+02° 22'

BIWHEEL

Horoscope 34, Joan Negus

Inner Chart
July 30, 1930, 6:04 A.M. EDT
Trenton, NJ
74W45 — 40N13

Outer Ring — Cancer Diagnosis
SA: January 15, 1997

another aspect pattern. But we see SA Saturn=Mars building *at the same time;* transiting Uranus opposing the Sun *at the same time;* and yet another Solar Arc contact, *SA Uranus square to natal Venus at the same time.*[101]

All of this is undeniably a serious state of affairs on the level of critical health; all of this could be seen ahead of time.[102]

In Joan's natal horoscope, the planet Venus is not stressed in any way.[103] We are hard pressed within the diagnostic structure at present in astrology to specify a weakness in the kidneys, unless we were to see Venus in wide square with Mars. But, in the developed picture with *the arc of Uranus to the square with her Venus,* we *do* see in the build-up of that measurement (along with the others simultaneously) a specific kidney (bladder, perhaps lower back) concern. Does that arc indeed call in the wide Mars-Venus natal square?

We could also be guided to a kidney concern *by the dominating arc of Neptune exactly square the Sun in the twelfth House, ruling the Ascendant:* since Neptune rules the blood. Perhaps this condition could have been illuminated a year earlier in January 1996, when SA/SP Sun conjoined the Moon, ruler of the 12th. The condition faces yet a strong challenge with the angular transit by Uranus opposed the Sun and then opposed the Ascendant in August and December 1997.[104]

---

101 Fascinatingly, when Joan Negus received her Regulus Award in the Spring of 1995 with transiting Uranus and Neptune squaring her Midheaven, *SA Uranus was precisely square (exactly partile) with her natal Venus, ruler of the kidneys,* lower back, bladder, etc. There is simply no doubt that, at this major time of her professional life, a dire circumstance was forming simultaneously within her health breakdown profile.

102 At exactly this moment in writing this paragraph, I received a telephone call from someone versed in astrology. She complained of a year of sluggishness, upset, feeling terrible. She asked me if that could have anything to do with the build-up of the Pluto contact with her Sun (I had mentioned this period of time to her a year ago in another conversation). I explained the extremely important warning this aspect was giving to her for a new "body-perspective," the need to check everything out. She complained specifically and at length about "toxins in her body," her feeling of toxicity. I suggested what we know, that Neptune "rules" toxins, a poisonous state. She replied, "I have Neptune conjunct my Sun!", i.e., absorbing the Pluto transit as well! She is now going to a doctor for complete tests; the warning given is probably early enough.

103 Venus does square the midpoint of Mercury/Uranus (Venus=Mercury/Uranus), but this simply adds a sense of artistry to her thinking process, an echo of the Mercury-Mars quintile and the Venus-Jupiter quintile.

104 One week after this manuscript was completed, on September 20, 1997 at 9:12 A.M., Joan Negus died.

A client of mine for many, many years, now semi-retired, recently was suddenly taken to the hospital in critical condition from kidney failure, "out of the blue." This man has been ultra-sensitive and careful about his health for years. Our consultation a year ago did not register any warnings at all about health. The one measurement we had seen did not seem to be threatening since it contacted his Midheaven, and he was extremely successful and retired; we were thinking almost exclusively in business terms. I was complacent about the SA Neptune=Midheaven (semisquare) signature, coming out of natal Neptune conjunct his Moon in the 6th, that conjunction opposing Venus in his 12th, Neptune ruling his Ascendant.

In the light of what we know now about the patterning of critical illness, I appear remiss for not having sounded the alarm. It will never happen again if I can help it. We must be vigilant with what we know; we must recognize the inexorability of the aging process, the weaknesses indicated in the natal horoscope, and the triggers of change seen through arcs and transits *in spite of healthy, positive, comfortable, successful realities.* We must have the courage to see.

Pancreatic Cancer
Horoscope 35, Marcello Mastroianni

This is the horoscope of Marcello Mastroianni (page 135), the celebrated international movie actor in some 120 films (eleven with actress Sophia Loren), winning many awards, including three Oscar nominations in Hollywood and two best actor awards at the Cannes film Festival. The portrait is extraordinarily focused within three aspect patterns:

1. First, look at Uranus: Uranus opposes Mercury in its own sign, ruler of the 7th; Uranus makes crucial quindecile aspects with the Sun and the Moon (brought into orb through its conjunction with the Sun).

2. At the same time, Uranus squares the Ascendant.

3. The Sun and Moon are conjunct in Libra and make no other Ptolemaic aspect in the horoscope. The Moon is at the Aries Point. The Sun and the Moon are a peregrine "island," running wild with the horoscope, i.e., creating, attracting, needing unrestrained public popularity. This is reinforced by the Aries Point equalling Pluto/Ascendant, the square between Jupiter and Mercury, ruler of the 7th, and the opposition of Mars-in-Aquarius with Neptune (anytime Mars is strongly articulated with Neptune, a measure of charisma, of magnetism can be expected).

With the Uranian focus "attacking the Sun and Moon and the Ascendant and with Pluto, ruler of the 12th, peregrine, the suave, comedic leading man with an unflappable public image could very well face very serious issues in the health profile (and in relationships).

These indications are also seen through the images Saturn=Jupiter/Uranus, which adds temperance to the runaway personality powers, and *Saturn=Neptune/Pluto, which is an image of depression, grief, weakness, torment* we have already noted (see pages 31–32 and 33).

Note that Saturn is also peregrine and is semisquare Mercury, again modifying the lofty professional thrust (and undermining successful relationship; Mercury rules the 7th). *Saturn in Scorpio* almost always carries with it complicated, somber, deeply organized tightly structured purpose and ambition; here undoubtedly related to early home circumstances and young development conditions (Mastroianni's father was a carpenter who put the boy to work in his shop at an early age; during World War II, Marcello was in a German forced labor camp in the Italian Alps, escaped to Venice, and lived near poverty until the war ended).

So our initial orientation of this horoscope sees a social skyrocket pulled down by some depressive, controling influences, which surely have to do with patterns taken on in the early home life that affected Mastroianni's *self-worth profile* strongly (parental ruler Mars opposed by Neptune; parental ruler Venus conjunct Node-Neptune in the 8th; Saturn ruling the 2nd House of self-worth along with Uranus, so powerfully tense in this horoscope).

Again and again, we see two worlds here: the outer world potentials of beauty, charm, and popularity; the formative and underlying inner world, surely tight, tending to depression and self-torment while motivating great self-proving achievement.

A final observation in our orientation to the natal horoscope is key here: Jupiter is rising at the Ascendant, in its own sign. It is another suggestion of personal exuberance; square to Mercury (articulate, voluble, charming) and squared by Uranus (usually material luck, rising up to be counted). But it must also be seen as a depository of the tensions focused through Uranus and its ties.

We must remember that Jupiter—even in its own sign—is not always the classic "benefic" accent in analyses. Difficulty in life so very, very often registers not from too little of something but from too much, certainly a

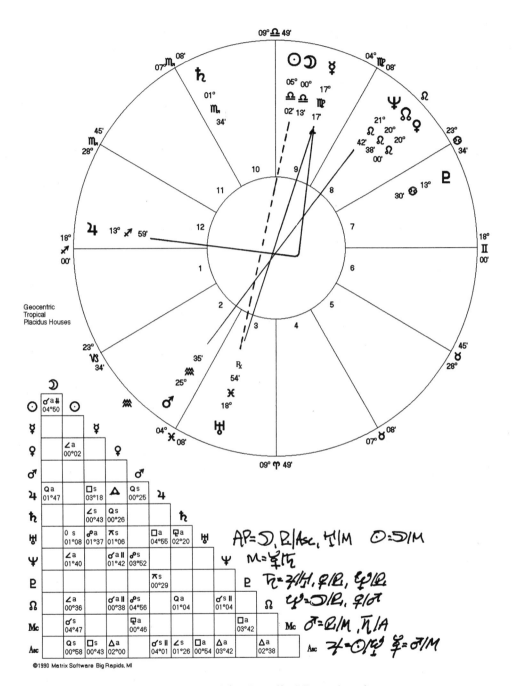

Horoscope 35, Marcello Mastroianni
September 28, 1924, 12:15 P.M. CET
Frosinone, Italy
13E19 — 41N38

Jupiterian concept. With the idea of excess, comes the idea of the vitally important developmental dynamic of overcompensation. This theme within the split world we detect here is undoubtedly very important.[105]

Now, on the basis of the hypothetical split world of tensions here, with the deserved suspicions about the symbol Jupiter in terms of critical health crisis, and with Jupiter in the 12th, ruling and positioned at the Ascendant, one would have to be alerted to potential dysfunction of the liver, the liver and the pancreas. Again and again, we see two worlds here: the outer world potentials of beauty, charm, and popularity; the formative and underlying inner world, surely tight, tending to depression and self-torment while motivating great self-proving achievement.

- With experience and confidence, this vulnerability could be seen so swiftly at first glance at the horoscope: Uranus is highly tense with the Sun-Moon and the Ascendant and "feeds" that tension into Jupiter. Jupiter is at a key position. Pluto rules the 12th and is peregrine. Jupiter in the 12th symbolizes a warning. Within this stark structure of abbreviation, all the other patterns are working as we have just studied.

The objective here in caring for this horoscope, this man within the aging process in which we are all engaged, is not to be correct in order to glorify astrology or ourselves as astrologers. Rather, the objective is to be conscientiously inclusive in order to be comprehensively helpful to the client. "Mr. Mastroianni, I am not a medical doctor, but sometimes the horoscope speaks helpfully about the weak parts of the body, especially when it is under stress, emotional, vocational, etc. Has there ever been detected in you a difficulty with your liver; is there the incidence of diabetes perhaps in your family?" [See the Venus trine with Jupiter in the background (please see page 19).]

Chart 35a shows arc and transit build-up in Mastroianni's horoscope to the critical period of December 1996. This crisis could have been anticipated easily. How much would early warning have helped?

SA Saturn in the Ascendant opposes Pluto in Cancer, exactly, with Pluto peregrine and ruling the 12th. SA Neptune is just separating from

---

105 It is extremely important in analysis to note that any area of life activity that is overdone, that becomes excessive, is probably overcompensatory for some lack experienced, felt or imagined elsewhere. This approaches, for example, the realm where materialism substitutes for love (two levels of concern within the 2nd House).

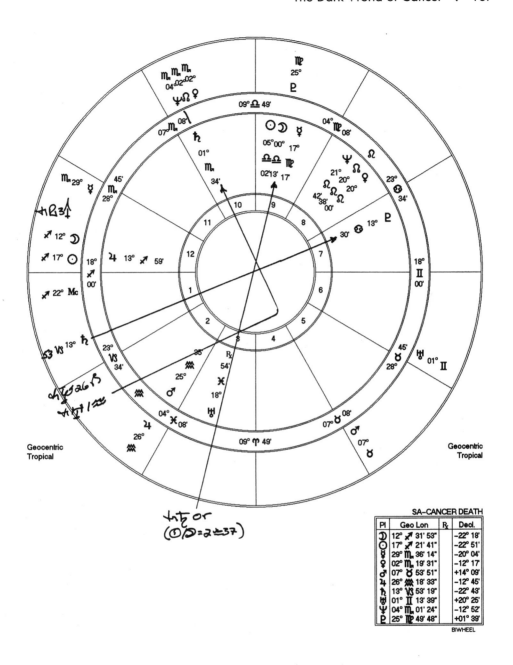

	SA–CANCER DEATH		
Pl	Geo Lon	Rx	Decl.
☽	12° ♐ 31' 53"		–22° 18'
☉	17° ♐ 21' 41"		–22° 51'
☿	29° ♏ 36' 14"		–20° 04'
♀	02° ♏ 19' 31"		–12° 17'
♂	07° ♉ 53' 51"		+14° 09'
♃	26° ♒ 18' 33"		–12° 45'
♄	13° ♑ 53' 19"		–22° 43'
♅	01° ♊ 13' 39"		+20° 25'
♆	04° ♏ 01' 24"		–12° 52'
♇	25° ♍ 49' 48"		+01° 39'

BIWHEEL

Horoscope 35a, Marcello Mastroianni

Inner Chart
September 28, 1924, 12:15 P.M. CET
Frosinone, Italy
13E19 — 41N38

Outer Ring — Cancer Death
SA: December 19, 1996

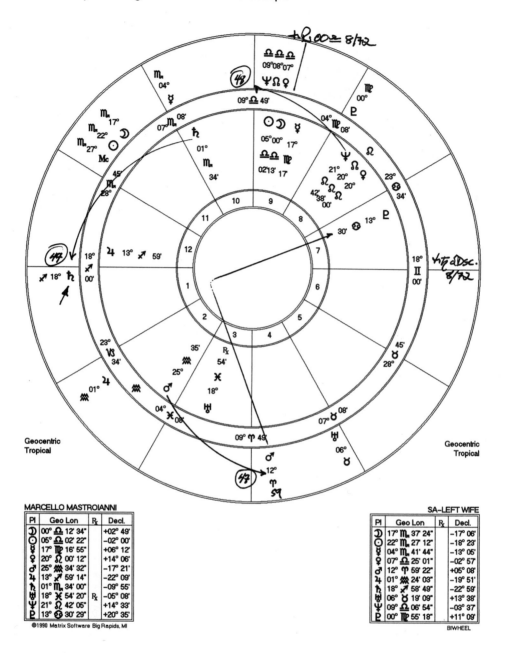

Geocentric
Tropical

Geocentric
Tropical

MARCELLO MASTROIANNI

Pl	Geo Lon	Rx	Decl.
☽	00° ♎ 12' 34"		+02° 49'
☉	05° ♎ 02' 22"		−02° 00'
☿	17° ♍ 16' 55"		+06° 12'
♀	20° ♌ 00' 12"		+14° 06'
♂	25° ♒ 34' 32"		−17° 21'
♃	13° ♐ 59' 14"		−22° 09'
♄	01° ♏ 34' 00"		−09° 55'
♅	18° ♓ 54' 20"	Rx	−05° 08'
♆	21° ♌ 42' 05"		+14° 33'
♇	13° ♋ 30' 29"		+20° 35'

SA–LEFT WIFE

Pl	Geo Lon	Rx	Decl.
☽	17° ♏ 37' 24"		−17° 06'
☉	22° ♏ 27' 12"		−18° 23'
☿	04° ♏ 41' 44"		−13° 05'
♀	07° ♎ 25' 01"		−02° 57'
♂	12° ♈ 59' 22"		+05° 08'
♃	01° ♒ 24' 03"		−19° 51'
♄	18° ♐ 58' 49"		−22° 59'
♅	06° ♉ 19' 09"		+13° 38'
♆	09° ♎ 06' 54"		−03° 37'
♇	00° ♍ 55' 18"		+11° 09'

BIWHEEL

Horoscope 35b, Marcello Mastroianni

Inner Chart
September 28, 1924, 12:15 P.M. CET
Frosinone, Italy
13E19 — 41N38

Outer Ring — Left Wife
SA: May 15, 1972

conjunction with natal Saturn, 2 degrees and 27 minutes (two years and five months) earlier, i.e., June 1994, with transiting Saturn then exactly squaring natal Jupiter; perhaps this was the key time of earliest serious system break-down, specifically the liver and pancreas (Jupiter) or when the condition focused itself. Leading up to this time—so clear to the astrologer—would have been the obvious time for warning, for medical checkup.

Dr. Cornell, in one of the few direct labeling statements in his encyclopedia, states: "the Pancreas is ruled by the Cancer and Virgo signs; Cancer of the Pancreas—Caused by the afflictions of Jupiter."[106] Here, we are led subtly to Jupiter; we observe the potential of the Uranus quindecile Sun-Moon with the Uranus opposition with Mercury, final dispositor of the horoscope in Virgo (diet), and we see the difficult Saturn=Pluto arc dramatically in place.

At the time of death, transiting Uranus was at 1 Aquarius exactly square Mastroianni's Saturn, and transiting Saturn at 0 Aries was precisely opposed his Moon.

Mastroianni died of pancreatic cancer on December 19, 1996.

I would like to spend another moment with Mastroianni's horoscope, away from the illness profile, and into the area of relationships where there was a critical break at mid-life.

Look back at chart 35, his natal horoscope with the aspect grid (page 135). The aspect grid shows us that the Sun makes a semisquare aspect with Neptune, with an orb of 1.40. Are there any other semisquare aspects natally? Yes: between the Sun and the Node (relationship, meeting, public), Mercury and Saturn, and *Saturn and the Ascendant* (opposing the Descendant).

Solar Arc theory projects for everyone the accumulated semisquare arc at age forty-four to forty-eight (the range allowing for fast Winter-birth arcs and slow Summer-birth arcs; see page 79): a time of developmental tension that is very important, often part of the so-called Mid-Life Crisis.

So, we know that at forty-five or so (the orb factor of the natal aspect) we will have Neptune=Sun (the sense of ego adjustment, loss, even "wipe-out," deception), Node=Sun (relationship), Mercury=Saturn (rela-tionship concerns, Mercury rules the 7th), and Saturn=Ascendant

---

106 Cornell is separating organ from function and disease, as we all would like to do, to make things cut-and-dried clear in medical astrology. In our explorations in this book on critical illness, we are following planets and planetary contact much more than the planet and/or sign references that are the source of much confusion.

(tremendous difficult change). We can not help but see that Neptune, arced to the Sun, will then continue 3–4 degrees/years and conjoin the Midheaven (very serious); Saturn actually arcs to the Ascendant tightly two to three years *after* age forty-five. This is strong backdrop development suggesting that, at age forty-seven to forty-eight, Mastroianni will face extreme pressures that can change his life, his relationships, etc.

We check the ephemeris for that general time in his life, looking for major aspects (with the Sun, Moon, or an angle) and we find that *transiting Pluto will be at 00 Libra—precisely conjunct Mastroianni's Moon—in August 1972 and transiting Saturn will be precisely conjunct the seventh cusp (opposing the Ascendant) in August 1972...at the same time,* when Mastroianni is almost forty-eight years old.

Chart 35b shows this time in May 1972, the time of international scandal when Mastroianni left his wife of twenty-two years to live with celebrated actress Catherine Deneuve.

The Dynamics of Early Warning

With this case of pancreatic cancer as with many cases in this book, we are postulating an earlier time before the critical date of diagnosis or death when the disease *could have been anticipated*. When major arcs/transits press the debilitated system, changes occur. When the changes are in terms of a tumor beginning to form, a tumor beginning to grow, what time is left? Do tumors in different organs grow at different rates than others? How *practicable* is the advance warning time technique we are developing in this book?

Different cancers *do* grow at different speeds. In discussing tumor growth, doctors refer to a tumor's *doubling rate:* the time it takes for the number of cells in the tumor to increase by 100 percent. We can suspect that Jupiter plays a role in this observation.

Some tumors, such as certain lung cancers, double very rapidly. Others, like prostate cancers, grow relatively slowly, and years may pass before the cancer doubles enough times to cause any symptoms. But during that time, the tumor can be detected and the tumor can be treated, well before metastasis (see page 89), with extremely high probability of cure. Astrology can provide the warning, the catalyst for checkup that can save lives.

The potential for a tumor to spread to other tissues is related to three factors:

1. The size of volume of the tumor; the larger it is, the more likely to metastasize, to grow into neighboring tissues;

2. The degree of cell *differentiation*, the degree to which cancerous cells resemble the normal cells from which they arose; well-differentiated cancer cells, still resembling the original cells, are less likely to spread; poorly differentiated cells are more virulent;

3. The number of small blood vessels that nourish the tumor (microvessel density).[107]

The key question, then, is *when* does the cancer begin, *when* does it start to grow? The answer from medical experts to whom I have posed that question is that knowledge of a cancer in its earliest stages is dependent on the detection level of the diagnostic technique. How few cells banding together to form a tumor can the inspection technique detect...the bone scan, the mammogram, the MRI, and other diagnostic procedures?

When a tumor *is* removed or killed by radiation, there is still the worry—the watchful waiting—that a small number of cancer cells have escaped excision or radiation and that they have moved on in metastasis; the detection process at its level may not spot that low number of cells at this earliest stage. One thousand cells would be patently invisible; one trillion cells may be required to register as a tumor beginning. While some tumor cells can grow exponentially (and this is a complicated area of discussion since the body itself is fighting the cancer and there is significant cell loss in that struggle), when do the cancer cells grow enough to be detected?

While science can not answer the question directly, *astrology can dramatically define the time period of possible/probable development, including perhaps more often than not the earliest time for detection probability.*

---

107 Bostwick, page 24.

Thyroid Cancer
Horoscope 36, Richard Crenna

Horoscope 36 is the horoscope of motion picture actor Richard Crenna who was operated on for thyroid cancer, March 17, 1997.

The critical time in his life is clearly signalled in his horoscope. Look with confidence: SA Saturn conjoins the Midheaven; SA Uranus opposes the Sun; transiting Pluto is at 5 Sagittarius, separating from opposition with the Ascendant and applying to conjunction with the Sun. There is little doubt that this would be a critical time in Crenna's life, and *any critical time in an adult's life carries with it a challenge to the health system,* even in the most successful of times. This thesis becomes more and more liable with accumulating age. In March 1997, Crenna is approaching age seventy-one.

The thyroid gland (from the Greek, "shield shaped") is located at the base of the neck, wrapped around the trachea (windpipe). The thyroid helps to set the rate at which the body functions, by secreting the hormone thyroxine, whose actions control the pace of chemical activity in the body. The more thyroxine there is in the bloodstream (hyperthyroidism), the faster the body's chemical reactions occur. The increased speed affects appetite, heart rate, blood pressure, nervousness, and perspiration, swelling at the base of the neck, sleeplessness, irritability, and muscle weakness. Left untreated, hyperthyroidism is fatal.

Traditional astrology assigns the thyroid to the sign Taurus since the occurrence of the gland is specifically in the throat, so reference to the thyroid is added to the Venus archetype as ruler of Taurus. Yet, in addition, since the thyroid is operating as a *connecting link* between the pineal gland and the pituitary gland within the body, signaling the metabolic process, rulership is also given to Mercury. Empirically in my work with astrology, I find the Venus reference more reliable, but I watch as well any singularly developed Mercury signature.

There are only about 10,000 thyroid malignancies annually, and the tumor is usually slow-growing. Thyroid cancer affects twice as many women as men, any time between twenty-five and sixty-five years of age, normally.

Rosenfeld points out that, before 1950, infants and children were frequently treated with xrays for benign conditions of the head and neck, like inflamed tonsils and adenoids and acne, for example. Now, years later, many of these individuals are developing thyroid cancer. Excessive radiation is a clear cause of thyroid cancer.[108]

---

108 Rosenfeld, page 352.

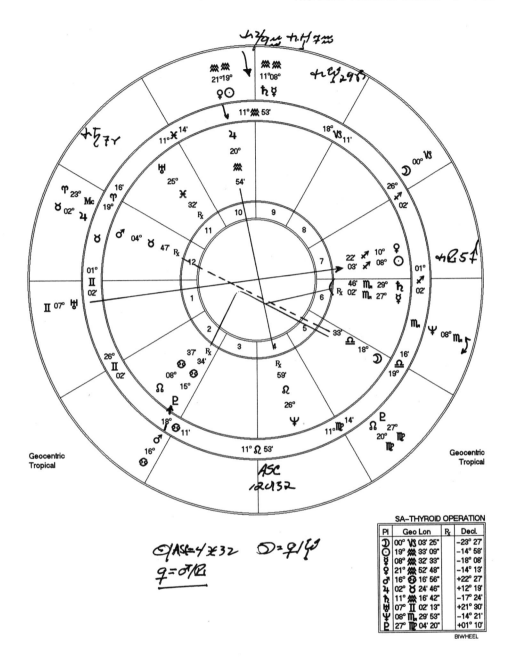

Horoscope 36, Richard Crenna

Inner Chart
November 30, 1926, 4:14 P.M. PST
Los Angeles, CA
118W15 — 34N03

Outer Ring — Thyroid Operation
SA: March 17, 1997

Natally, Crenna has Mercury retrograde conjoined with Saturn, the two squared the axis of Jupiter/Neptune. Mercury rules the Ascendant. This picture defines Mercury in strong developmental tension.

Venus is conjoined the Sun in the 7th and initially appears out of the picture. But Venus rules the 6th and is co-ruler of the 12th. In the 12th, Mars is in *Taurus*, retrograde, and *Mars makes a quindecile with the Moon*, and that Moon is squared by Pluto, co-ruler of the 6th. Much tension is focused in the 12th through Mars in Taurus.

Additionally Venus=Mars/Pluto! This picture links Venus with Mars in the 12th *quindecile* the Moon and Pluto *square* with the Moon. Suddenly Venus *is* active and vital within the overall portrait. The potential of a thyroid problem (Venus, Mercury; Taurus) is strongly indicated.

The critical measurements at the time of the cancer operation are dramatically clear as we have seen. But look further for an early-warning beacon: see SA Neptune at 8 Scorpio? When was SA Neptune opposed the 12th House focal-point Mars?

If we regress SA Neptune 3 degrees 45 minutes, we come to the opposition with Mars; this 3.45 translates to three years and nine months earlier, in July 1993. We check the ephemeris for vital transits and we find transiting Pluto at 23 Scorpio (26–23–26 Scorpio throughout 1993) applying to Mercury at the same time when transiting Jupiter, Uranus, and Neptune were squaring the Moon. This is undeniably a time of important warning of a possible health concern of big proportion.

With or without observation of systems or questioning about them; with or without suspicion of a thyroid problem or any other problem, the astrological measurements building in 1993 and culminating in 1997–98 could have been seen and led to the counsel for medical checkup.[109]

---

109 In this case, the SA Ascendant was at 12 Leo 32 in March 1997, i.e., an angle coming to an angle, a point of emphasis. Curiously the SA Ascendant does not seem significantly involved with critical illnesses, and is rarely included in these studies.

Breast Cancer

Cancer of the female breast used to be the leading killer-cancer nationally. Since the mid-1980s, it has been replaced at the top of the list by cancers of the lung and the colon and is presently, in the late 1990s, number three in overall cancer incidence (excluding skin cancer). There will be some 182,000 new cases of breast cancer diagnosed this year—seventy-eight percent of them in women fifty and older—and 46,000 will die from it.[110]

Statistics show that one in every eight women in the United States, more commonly white than black, and more frequently Jewish than any other ethnic group, will develop breast cancer.

The breast cancer rate begins to rise after age thirty. By fifty, age is a very definite risk factor, with chances increased by two or three times if one's mother or sister suffered from the disease. When one has cancer of one breast, cancer in the other breast is more likely than if no cancer had yet occurred.

We must repeat from the first section of this book: breast cancer itself is not lethal; it is the metastasizing that is. If breast cancer is caught early, before malignant cells have spread to the lymph nodes nearby, there is a ninety to ninety-five percent chance of a cure. Seventy-five percent of all women diagnosed with breast cancer *are* cured. Early warning is urgently critical to save lives.

From 1989 through 1992, the breast cancer death rate in the United States dropped five percent, which is the largest short-term decline since 1950. This is attributable to wide-range developments in research and technology, giving women more and more treatment options, as well as more and more refined prevention and screening methodologies and practices. Regular mammogram testing slashes breast cancer mortality rates thirty percent in women aged fifty and over.

The highest incidence of this disease is in the Untied States and other Western and industrialized countries; the lowest is in Asia, Africa, and Latin America. Since breast cancer rates in Japan, for example, are one-fifth the rates in the United States, many scientists now believe nutrition is key to breast cancer prevention. This could be related to Japan's high level of soy consumption: soy is rich in photoestrogens, plant hormones that have cancer-fighting properties.

---

110 Rosenfeld, page 327–332; *Modern Maturity* magazine, September–October 1995, page 82.

Horoscope 37, Betty Ford

Horoscope 37 shows Betty Ford, the wife of past president Gerald Ford. Mrs. Ford successfully stood up to her drug and alcohol problems and her fight with breast cancer and founded the Betty Ford Clinic in Palm Springs, California for the treatment of these serious conditions.

Here we see the Sun peregrine, in a fire sign, suggesting tremendous ego energies fighting for attention and fulfillment. Automatically, we have to sense and search out the potential occurrence of frustration to such energies during development, to assess the potential ravages of frustration and hurt.

The Moon position in Pisces tells us that such ego energies may be diluted somewhat; the need then would not be to trumpet one's excellence but, instead, to invigorate an ideal, to identify with it and explore it. Great sensitivity is often born in this combination; the energies can smolder, externalization can be difficult, and frustration can indeed abound. The Sun's position in the (behind-the-scenes) 8th House seems to open the door to this dilution through the Moon in the public 7th.

Our core hypothesis is reinforced by the conjunction of Saturn and Neptune, both retrograde, in the 11th (an enormous need for love), square to Mercury ruler of one arm of the parental axis.

Jupiter in the 10th, ruler of the other arm of the parental axis is square to the Mars-Moon opposition axis, the Moon ruling the 11th, the House of love received, hoped for, etc..

Betty Ford's potentials for public life are seen through the Moon in the 7th and the Aries Point's involvement with Pluto/Node, the Sun/Moon (a public relationship, a husband who is a public figure), and the Sun's square to the midpoint of Midheaven/Ascendant.

Two other midpoint pictures are important: Pluto=Neptune/Midheaven, "strange happenings touch the life, usually in the home"; and Sun=Neptune/Pluto, "a drain on the system through over-indulgences, rationalization winning over realism, and, as well, creative enterprise."

Note that Mercury rules the Ascendant and is squared tightly by Saturn-Neptune. This corresponds with a depressive state to one degree or another (here, to a strong degree as an extension of the other difficult measurements), that threatens debilitation of the health system (Mercury rules the Ascendant). The peregrine Sun clearly calls attention to the 12th, from the 8th.

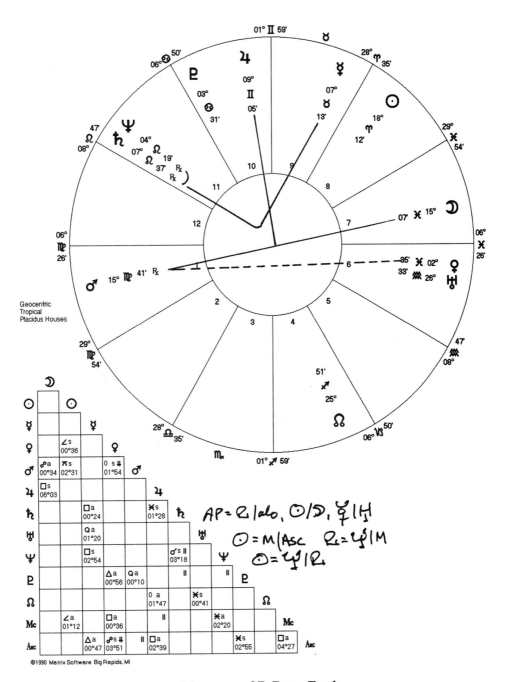

Horoscope 37, Betty Ford
April 8, 1918, 3:45 P.M. CWT
Chicago, IL
87W39 — 41N51

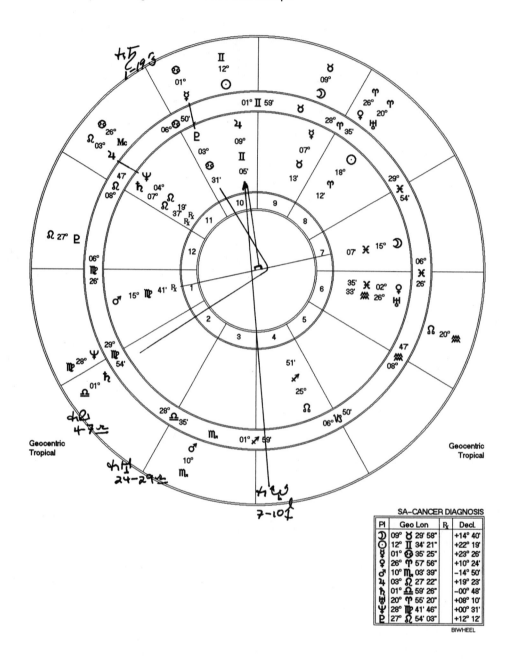

Horoscope 37a, Betty Ford

Inner Chart
April 8, 1918, 3:45 P.M. CWT
Chicago, IL
87W39 — 41N51

Outer Ring — Cancer Diagnosis
SA: June 1, 1974

	SA–CANCER DIAGNOSIS		
Pl	Geo Lon	Rx	Decl.
☽	09° ♉ 29' 58"		+14° 40'
☉	12° ♊ 34' 21"		+22° 19'
☿	01° ♋ 35' 25"		+23° 26'
♀	26° ♈ 57' 56"		+10° 24'
♂	10° ♏ 03' 39"		−14° 50'
♃	03° ♌ 27' 22"		+19° 23'
♄	01° ♎ 59' 26"		−00° 48'
♅	20° ♈ 55' 20"		+08° 10'
♆	26° ♍ 41' 46"		+00° 31'
♇	27° ♌ 54' 03"		+12° 12'

BIWHEEL

With Mercury in Taurus, one would expect a possible thyroid condition (see page 143); with Saturn-Neptune in Leo, we can anticipate a heart dysfunction should this signature or the Sun be challenged by strong arcs and transits.

When these strong arcs and transits did occur (see horoscope #37a) we see SA Jupiter=Neptune, SA Saturn=Pluto, with transiting Neptune opposing Jupiter and transiting Saturn squaring the Sun, and Betty Ford developed breast cancer. The horoscope does not suggest the breast as a potential weak part of the body. The health challenge is indeed indicated; the breast condition would have been detected in a thorough medical checkup.

Over and over and over again in cancer developments, *we are seeing strong Pluto conditions natally, in arcs, and in transits*—very often at all three measurement levels. This insight is becoming the prime core of our diagnostic/timing pattern. Mrs. Ford had transiting Pluto square its natal position.

As I have repeated often to this point in this study, our objective is not precise diagnosis to prove astrology a sacrosanct science. Astrology can not do this yet. And neither can psychology or theology, yet these disciplines are powerfully important considerations for the human condition in life.

Medical science *can* do the diagnosis most of the time, and, practically as reliably, *astrology can time the crisis* and expedite early warning. Astrology can work with the medical profession. To that end, in addition to the timing skill, astrology can explore its capabilities for cursory diagnosis, more often right than wrong.

When might the breast cancer have gotten started, been apparent at its earliest? When might a warning have been optimally valuable, most importantly given?

Notice that it would have been extremely obvious to us astrologers that transiting Neptune would be opposing natal Jupiter (which squares natally the Mars-Moon axis). Could this have suggested accelerated cell-division, tumor doubling?

In April 1973, checking that period in the ephemeris, we would immediately see transiting Uranus at 20–21 Libra, just past opposition with the Sun, which is peregrine and ruler of the 12th! *And transiting Neptune was square the Ascendant.*

One year earlier, in the periods January–March and October 1972, transiting Uranus was exactly opposed the Sun; transiting Saturn was conjunct natal Jupiter and squared the Moon.

1972

MONTH	MARS LONG	JUPITER LONG	SATURN LONG	URANUS LONG	NEPTUNE LONG	PLUTO LONG
JAN	03 ♈	22 ♐	00 ♊	18 ♎	04 ♐	02 ♎
FEB	24	29	00	18	05	02
MAR	13 ♉	04 ♑	00	18	05	01
APR	03 ♊	07	03	17	05	00
MAY	23	08	06	15	05	00
JUN	12 ♋	06	10	14	04	29 ♍
JUL	01 ♌	03	14	14	03	29
AUG	21	29 ♐	17	15	03	00 ♎
SEP	11 ♍	29	20	16	03	01
OCT	00 ♎	01 ♑	21	18	03	02
NOV	20	05	20	20	04	03
DEC	10 ♏	11	18	22	05	04

1973

MONTH	MARS LONG	JUPITER LONG	SATURN LONG	URANUS LONG	NEPTUNE LONG	PLUTO LONG
JAN	01 ♐	18 ♑	15 ♊	23 ♎	06 ♐	04 ♎
FEB	22	25	14	23	07	04
MAR	12 ♑	01 ♒	14	23	07	04
APR	04 ♒	07	16	21	07	03
MAY	25	11	18	20	07	02
JUN	17 ♓	12	22	19	06	02
JUL	07 ♈	11	26	19	05	02
AUG	24	07	00 ♋	19	05	02
SEP	07 ♉	03	03	21	05	03
OCT	08	02	05	22	05	04
NOV	29 ♈	04	05	24	06	06
DEC	25	08	03	26	07	06

Here we see the patterns we have learned to expect. Warning for a health checkup would have to have been given!

In the following seven horoscopes, let your eyes seek out with confidence the pattern we are developing, the extreme importance of Pluto, Neptune, and Saturn, reference to the 12th House and Ascendant, and, in breast cancer (though not as often nor as clearly as we would expect) the frequent dramatic occurrence of the Moon. Additionally, and by no means least, we must watch for the drama of focus promised by the natal *quindecile* aspect.

Horoscope 38, Female

This lady shows an orientation of suppression and defensiveness (northern hemisphere, eastern hemisphere exclusivity), response considerations in development that we know support (hasten?; see page 71) breakdowns within the aging process. Pluto is in the 12th, tightly square the Moon (in a female horoscope, almost assuredly a competitive tension with the mother; here reinforced by the Uranus square with the nodal axis).[111]

The Sun, ruler of the 12th, is conjoined with Neptune, ruler of the 7th, a difficult relationship pattern out of the early home tensions, i.e., more tension added to the system. The focus on tension in the sign Scorpio strongly suggests gynecological difficulty. Natal Saturn=Pluto/Ascendant: a high potential for great difficulty, involving the 12th holding Pluto, and the Ascendant, the core of health. The natal picture suggests gynecological difficulty first and breast concern (Moon) second.

For major transit activity, we know in late Summer 1996 transiting Pluto "will" be at 00 Sagittarius, exactly conjunct natal Moon and square its own natal position in the 12th. *At the same time,* we can check the ephemeris and see that transiting Uranus will be at 2 Aquarius, square the natal Sun.

When we draw the arcs for a full background picture in September 1996, everything comes into dramatic focus: *SA Neptune is exactly conjunct natal Saturn late in 1996.*

On September 10, 1996, this lady's breast cancer was diagnosed and surgical procedures were taken the next day.

A routine casting of a Solar Arc and Transit picture for the time "ahead in 1996" would have revealed all of this. The transit of Pluto, the arcs of Neptune and Saturn signaled a terribly important time, the Fall of 1996. Warning ahead of time would have been a clear judgment on the part of the astrologer.

Looking *ahead* from this time, we must note that SA Uranus will come to the Ascendant in Spring 1998 [look at the chart; figure these arcs out in your head!], as will SA Mars come to the Moon; and then, we see SA Jupiter activating the natal Moon-Pluto square early in 2002, with transiting Saturn conjunct the Midheaven.

---

111 See Tyl, *Synthesis & Counseling in Astrology,* pages 49–64 and 128.

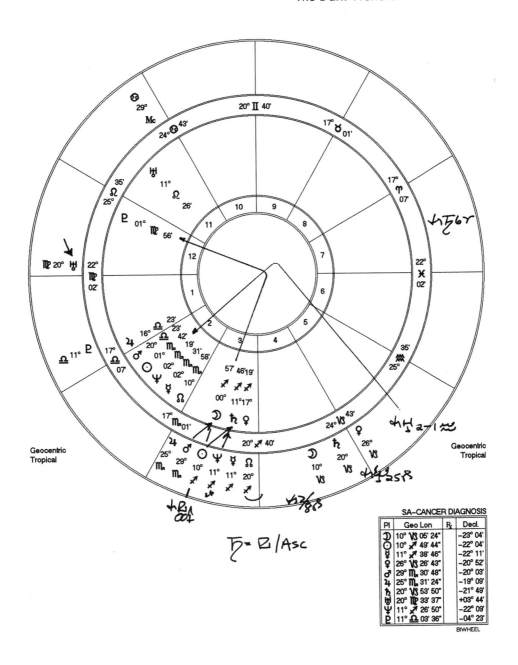

Horoscope 38, Female
Outer Chart —-Cancer Diagnosis
SA: September 10, 1996

PI	Geo Lon	Rx	Decl.
☽	10° ♑ 05' 24"		−23° 04'
☉	10° ♐ 49' 44"		−22° 04'
☿	11° ♐ 38' 46"		−22° 11'
♀	26° ♑ 26' 43"		−20° 52'
♂	29° ♏ 30' 48"		−20° 03'
♃	25° ♏ 31' 24"		−19° 09'
♄	20° ♑ 53' 50"		−21° 49'
♅	20° ♍ 33' 37"		+03° 44'
♆	11° ♐ 26' 50"		−22° 09'
♇	11° ♎ 03' 36"		−04° 23'

SA-CANCER DIAGNOSIS

BIWHEEL

Horoscope 39, Female

Horoscope 39 shows the conjunction of Jupiter and Pluto feeding into the Moon through an opposition. Immediately—rash as this judgment may seem, with reality continuously suggesting the diagnostic orientation of the horoscope to weaknesses in the body—we "feel" cancer potential, accelerated cell growth, possibly in the breast(s) (Moon). We check the 12th, ruled by Mercury: Mercury is opposed by Saturn retrograde. Mercury also rules the Ascendant and the Midheaven (two angles) and is final dispositor of the horoscope. This is an importantly telling measurement and a definite reference to critical illness—sooner or later in life. In other words, in this horoscope, we would track disease well through developments in relation to natal Mercury.

Note as well, the square between Pluto and Saturn retrograde *across the signline.*[112]

Additionally we see two quindeciles from Mars: one to Uranus and one to Pluto; and a quindecile between Neptune, ruler of the 6th, and the Sun. Please note that *every time we have seen a quindecile in any horoscope in this study,* especially involving Pluto, *it has been a crucial, telling statement about critical illness.*

The Solar Arc double-ring chart shows the planets positioned for the day of diagnosis of breast cancer.

Note that SA Neptune at 5 Sagittarius *opposes natal Mercury, ruler of the 12th, the Ascendant and the Midheaven.*

Now: look more closely at that SA Neptune; analyze its degree position backwards in time: we can see that five years earlier (back from August 1994), SA Neptune was conjunct natal Saturn AND—check this—SA Pluto, at the same time, was conjunct the Ascendant! It had to have been a key time. *At the same time,* transiting Pluto was opposed the Sun from June to September 1989. This is when watchful study with medical supervision would have been essential to catch the occurrence and growth of any breast cancer.

Additionally at the time of diagnosis in August 1994, transiting Pluto was at 25 Scorpio square its natal position and transiting Saturn was opposed the Ascendant. Whew!

---

112 These analyses accumulating in our study are not doomsday, negative "readings" of the horoscope. They are confident, seasoned, realistic direct assessments based upon the knowledge of the inevitable aging process and the astrology that accompanies life. Astrologers must build that composure, objectivity, and confidence.

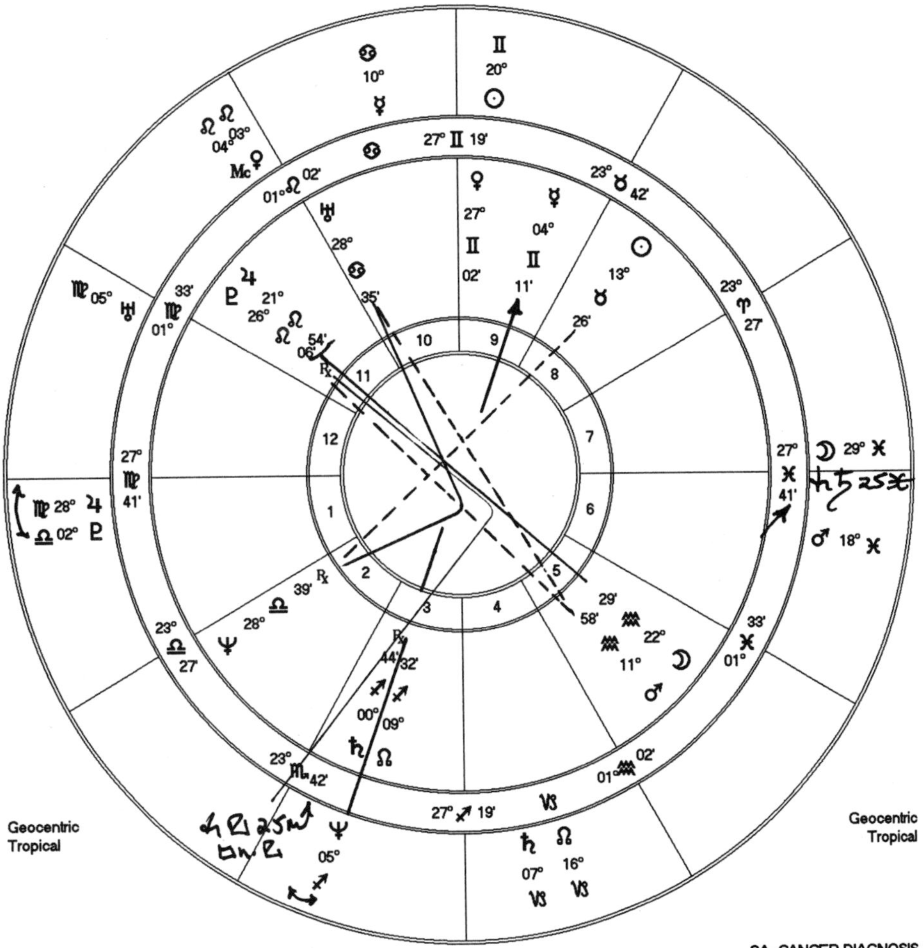

Geocentric
Tropical

Geocentric
Tropical

SA-CANCER DIAGNOSIS			
Pl	Geo Lon	Rx	Decl.
☽	29° ♓ 17' 14"		–00° 17'
☉	20° ♊ 14' 59"		+23° 05'
☿	10° ♋ 59' 27"		+22° 59'
♀	03° ♌ 51' 06"		+19° 18'
♂	18° ♓ 46' 15"		–04° 27'
♃	28° ♍ 42' 23"		+00° 31'
♄	07° ♑ 32' 45"		–23° 14'
♅	05° ♍ 23' 16"		+09° 32'
♆	05° ♐ 28' 08"		–21° 13'
♇	02° ♎ 54' 36"		–01° 09'

BIWHEEL

Horoscope 39, Female
Outer Ring — Cancer Diagnosis
SA: August 15, 1994

The cancer was diagnosed August 15; mastectomy and chemotherapy began the next day.

The cancer returned to the bones (Saturn) and was detected in July 1995. Transiting Pluto had moved into conjunction natal Saturn.

Horoscope 40, Female

The 12th House positions of Horoscope 40 suggest exuberant intellectual energy (Sun, Moon, Jupiter, and Ascendant in Sagittarius) somehow confined, the system having a hard time expressing it all (in spite of excited self presentation). This is reinforced by the quindecile between Mercury and Pluto, ruler of the 12th, by the square from Uranus in the communication 3rd, and the Eastern hemisphere orientation "defending" the Ascendant. [The retrogradation of all in the West confirms this Eastern orientation centered at the Ascendant and 12th House.]

Behind this hypothesis are considerations of the parental ruler Mars (ruler of the 4th) conjoined with Saturn in the 10th; with Venus, ruler of the parental 10th, peregrine. Saturn rules the self-worth 2nd.

From the Sagittarius, Jupiter, and Venus conditions, we would have to be aware of a possible liver (pancreas) weakness; the eyes (Uranus square both the Sun and the Moon); and the breasts, with the Moon central in this aspect scheme and square the midpoint of Mars/Pluto. Additionally, Uranus, while squaring the Moon and the Sun, is almost exactly square the midpoint of Moon/Ascendant.

Look at the arc positions for breast cancer diagnosis January 15, 1996, when this lady was one month past her 72nd birthday. SA Saturn was opposed natal Pluto ruler of the 12th. SA Mars had opposed Pluto four years earlier.

SA Moon was exactly opposed Neptune. Transiting Uranus was square natal Saturn. And, the clincher: *transiting Pluto was exactly conjunct Jupiter in the 12th*! This confluence of measurements is so startling, it would have been unavoidable within the astrologer's vision several years before. Warning could have been given.

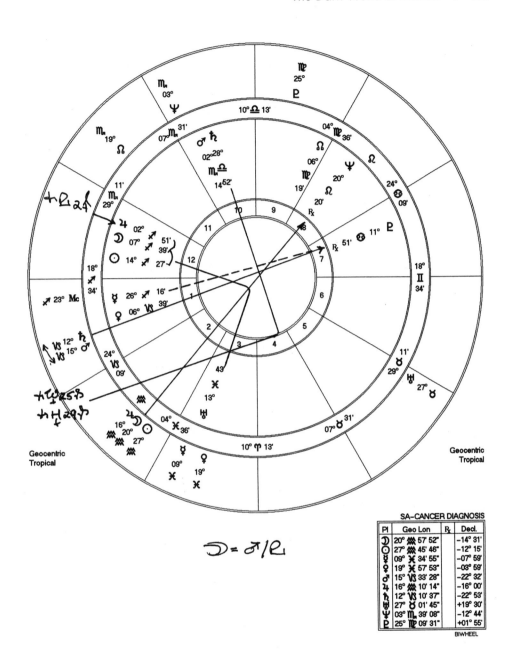

SA-CANCER DIAGNOSIS

Pl	Geo Lon	℞	Decl.
☽	20° ♒ 57' 52"		−14° 31'
☉	27° ♒ 45' 46"		−12° 15'
☿	09° ♓ 34' 55"		−07° 59'
♀	19° ♓ 57' 53"		−03° 59'
♂	15° ♑ 33' 28"		−22° 32'
♄	16° ♒ 10' 14"		−16° 00'
♃	12° ♑ 10' 37"		−22° 53'
♅	27° ♉ 01' 45"		+19° 30'
♆	03° ♏ 39' 08"		−12° 44'
♇	25° ♍ 09' 31"		+01° 55'

BIWHEEL

Horoscope 40, Female
Outer Ring — Cancer Diagnosis
SA: January 15, 1996

Horoscope 41, Female

Horoscope 41 is dominated by Saturn retrograde in the 10th opposing the Moon. Immediately we "feel" the incipient weakness in the lower back, the breasts (Libra Moon). Pluto is conjunct the Cancer Ascendant. Our "feel" is strengthened at the core health-center, holding, as well, Mars conjunct the Sun in Leo. Heart concern is introduced to the picture.

The 12th House is ruled by Mercury, and here Mercury is peregrine in Virgo; it is the final dispositor of the horoscope. Venus is also in Virgo and is conjunct Neptune. This combination strongly suggests concerns of the thyroid gland (see page 143). Jupiter is also peregrine and rules the 6th; the liver must be considered.

The tension in this horoscope is clearly focused on the opposition axis between Saturn and the Moon, on the conjunction of Pluto and the Ascendant, Mars-Sun, and Venus-Neptune. There is no square in the horoscope, not even to the angles; a rarity.

When SA Mercury, ruler of the 12th, came to 28 Libra, squaring natal Pluto and the Ascendant, transiting Neptune was square the Saturn-Moon axis. Cancer of the breast was diagnosed September 9, 1992. This lady's mother and sister had been diagnosed with breast cancer as well.

Horoscope 42, Female, born 1943

Horoscope 42 presents a very clear exercise in arc projection. The ruler of the 12th House is Pluto. Pluto here is in the 8th House. We know that SA Pluto (or transiting Pluto) *conjoining or squaring an angle is extremely important, usually a turning point in life.* When will natal Pluto arc to conjunction with the Midheaven?

The answer is 47 degrees or forty-eight years of age (25 degrees to finish Leo plus 22 degrees into Virgo gives 47 degrees; Spring birth (note late Pisces Sun), slowish arc, add one year of life after every thirty to compensate; see page 87). This was undoubtedly a major milestone time in this lady's life development and would be a key discussion point in the consultation, especially with transiting Neptune—back then—opposed Jupiter (ruler of the Ascendant) and transiting Saturn opposed Pluto (ruler of the 12th). Spring 1991: was there a health crisis then?

Now, when will continuing SA Pluto oppose the Sun, a key, key measurement as well? The distance is 6 degrees further, five years, i.e., 1996–97.

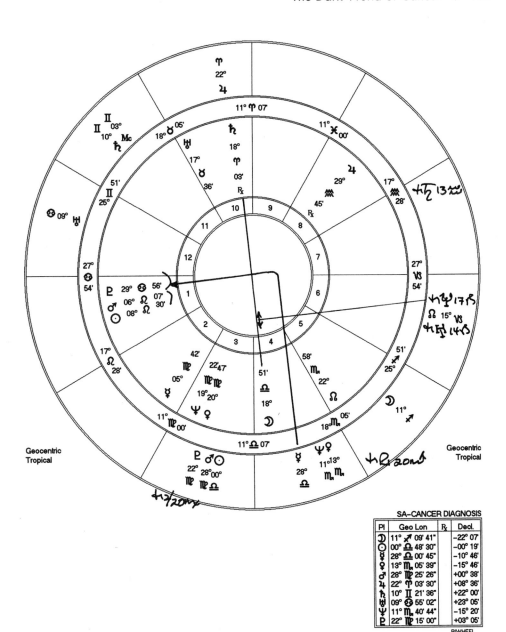

Horoscope 41, Female
Outer Ring — Cancer Diagnosis
SA: September 9, 1992

Pl	Geo Lon	Rx	Decl.
☽	11° ♐ 09' 41"		−22° 07'
☉	00° ♎ 48' 30"		−00° 19'
☿	28° ♎ 00' 45"		−10° 46'
♀	13° ♏ 05' 39"		−15° 46'
♂	28° ♍ 25' 26"		+00° 38'
♃	22° ♈ 03' 30"		+08° 36'
♄	10° ♊ 21' 36"		+22° 00'
♅	09° ♋ 55' 02"		+23° 05'
♆	11° ♏ 40' 44"		−15° 20'
♇	22° ♍ 15' 00"		+03° 05'

SA–CANCER DIAGNOSIS

BIWHEEL

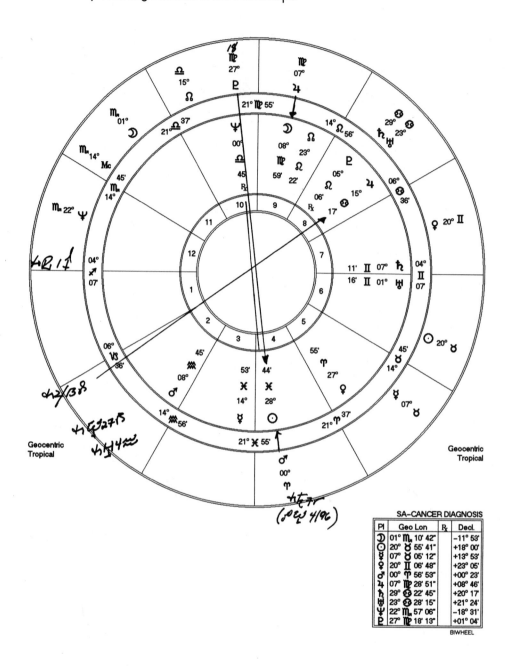

Horoscope 42, Female, born 1943
Outer Ring — Cancer Diagnosis
SA: July 15, 1996

Look at arcing Jupiter right behind arcing Pluto. Where would Jupiter be in 1996? While your computer does this work for you, the astrologer must be able to approximate visually in order to direct the computer to specific times of development for exact record of positions. Here we see that bringing natal Jupiter forward 53 degrees brings it to conjunction with the Moon in 1996!

Look at Mars late in the 2nd House. When will the arc come to opposition Neptune in the 10th? Fifty-two degrees/years (plus 1 for slow-arc): 1996.

1996						
	MARS	JUPITER	SATURN	URANUS	NEPTUNE	PLUTO
MONTH	LONG	LONG	LONG	LONG	LONG	LONG
JAN	24 ♑	29 ♐	19 ♓	29 ♑	25 ♑	02 ♐
FEB	19 ♒	06 ♑	22	01 ♒	26	03
MAR	11 ♓	12	25	03	27	03
APR	06 ♈	16	29	05	28	03
MAY	29	18	03 ♈	05	28	02
JUN	22 ♉	17	06	04	27	01
JUL	147 ♊	13	07	04	27	01
AUG	04 ♋	10	07	02	26	00
SEP	24	08	06	01	25	00
OCT	13 ♌	09	04	01	25	01
NOV	01 ♍	13	02	01	25	02
DEC	16	18	01	02	26	03

The ephemeris shows that—accompanying SA Pluto=Sun, SA Jupiter=Moon, SA Mars=Neptune—we have transiting Pluto at 1 Sagittarius *conjoining the Ascendant,* transiting Jupiter at 13 Capricorn opposing Jupiter; transiting Saturn opposing Neptune.

This lady was diagnosed with breast cancer in July 1996.

Horoscope 43, Female

In Horoscope 43, the conjunction of the Moon and Uranus is extremely important because of its angular position and its drawing in of Mars. In other words, the ruler of the Ascendant has pulled in the Moon, ruler of the 6th, and Mars; this is a tremendous focus of energy.

Then, we see the Sun opposed Mars retrograde **and** Saturn retrograde, ruler of the 12th. This tells us immediately that Sun=Mars/Saturn, an image that definitely carries with it the threat to the body or health, the breaking down under stress.

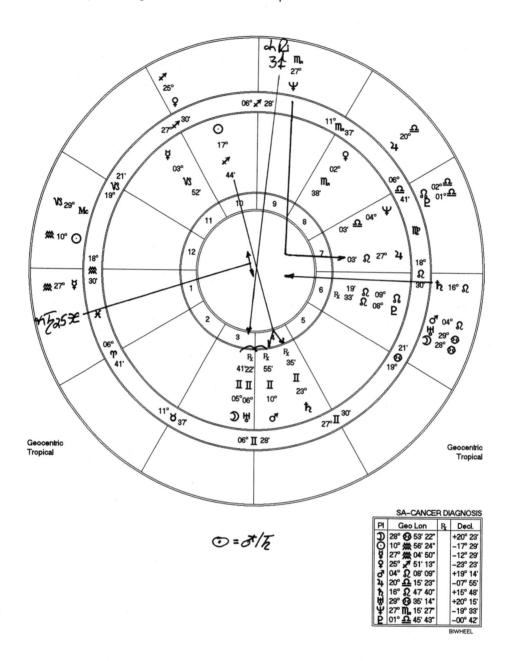

$$\odot = \eth / \hbar$$

SA–CANCER DIAGNOSIS			
Pl	Geo Lon	℞	Decl.
☽	28° ⊗ 53' 22"		+20° 23'
☉	10° ♒ 56' 24"		−17° 29'
☿	27° ♒ 04' 50"		−12° 29'
♀	25° ♐ 51' 13"		−23° 23'
♂	04° ♌ 08' 09"		+19° 14'
♃	20° ♎ 15' 23"		−07° 55'
♄	16° ♌ 47' 40"		+15° 48'
♅	29° ⊗ 35' 14"		+20° 15'
♆	27° ♏ 15' 27"		−19° 33'
♇	01° ♎ 45' 43"		−00° 42'

BIWHEEL

Horoscope 43, Female
Outer Ring: — Cancer Diagnosis
SA: March 15, 1996

Neptune is sesquiquadrate the Ascendant, another debilitating dimension within the health center at the Ascendant.

The tremendous accentuation on Gemini brings all Gemini health concerns to mind; the breasts would be a secondary concern here in our cursory diagnostic orientation through the Moon's involvement with the triple conjunction.

When this lady was diagnosed with breast cancer in March 1996, transiting Saturn was at 25 Pisces square the Sun-Saturn axis; transiting Pluto was opposing the Moon. In the background, SA Neptune (natally sesquiquadrate with the Ascendant) had come to square natal Jupiter exactly, dispositor of the Sun and Midheaven, angular in the 7th. *SA Saturn was opposing the Ascendant.*

This lady is "very sure" that she was born at 12 noon. However, if she were in fact born five minutes earlier (which is highly likely), the Ascendant would become 16 Aquarius 42, allowing SA Saturn to be exactly upon the horizon axis at cancer diagnosis, and the Midheaven would become 5 Sagittarius, bringing the natal Moon front and center on the Midheaven-IC axis.

Again, this astrological organization could have been seen ahead of time. Early warning was possible.

Horoscope 44, Female

Our final breast cancer patient, Horoscope 44, is of a seventy-four-year-old lady. I point out the age factor especially, since breast cancer occurs more in women after fifty and after menopause than earlier. Yet, women over fifty, as the literature reports, apparently pay less attention to prevention techniques (self-examination, mammography) than women under fifty. Case 44 is a clear portrait of critical illness.

Your eyes are accustomed to the pattern: Pluto opposes Mars, ruler of the Ascendant. That axis is squared by the Sun-Saturn conjunction in the 6th.

Uranus squares the Moon.

Saturn is quindecile the Ascendant. (Jupiter opposes the Ascendant, conjunct Mercury, ruler of the 6th.)

In these measurements, we lack reference to the 12th House, but looking further we do see the link among the key symbols: Neptune is the ruler of the 12th and *Neptune=Moon/Ascendant,* a very "draining"

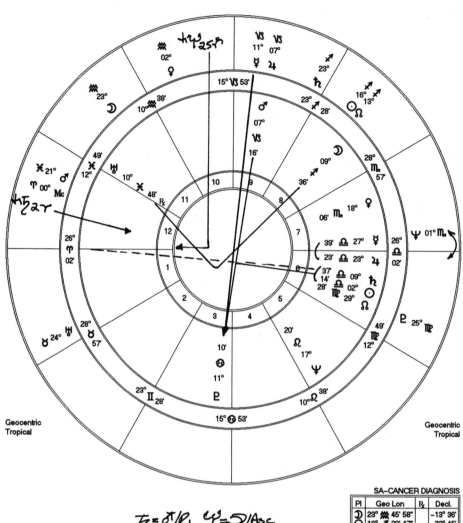

Horoscope 44, Female
Outer Ring — Cancer Diagnosis
SA: November 15, 1996

image; Moon=Sun/Neptune[113]; and Uranus=Sun/Neptune. The ruler of the 12th, the Moon and the Sun are all brought from one tension structure into another. This horoscope is riveted on these concerns.

When will they be crucially activated? When will the horoscope be crucially activated (weakened) and *call into prominence these difficult predispositions?*

One key arc catches our eye: SA Mercury to opposition with natal Pluto (the planet so very, very, very often involved with our predisposition to and early warning pattern for critical illness). *At the same time,* transiting Saturn would be exactly opposed the Sun in the 6th, and transiting Neptune would be exactly square the Ascendant. There is more here, and your eyes can find other signals, but this time in November 1996 loom dramatically as a key challenge to an aging system. There is simply no doubt about it.

The opportunity for early warning would be focused by a medical history throughout life development related to earlier arcs and transits brought into contact with the natal predisposition and then projected forward from a consultation time prior to the Fall of 1996.

Note SA Neptune would have crossed the 7th cusp (opposing the Ascendant) and Mercury (ruler of the 6th holding Sun-Saturn) five years earlier in 1991, at the same time—as you would see immediately in the ephemeris—as transiting Uranus was at 11 Capricorn opposing the difficult natal Pluto. Would this have been the key time to begin careful health checks in earnest?

Solarscope Review

Now, we must remember that any horoscope with a hard aspect to the Sun or to the ruler of the sign *before* the Sun's sign will translate helpfully through the Solarscope, the horoscope timed for 6:00 A.M. and given equal House development (Solar Houses) around the circle.

I have three cases of breast cancer before me that have no known birth time but do provide timing help.

Think these through, see them in your mind's eye: the first one has Jupiter-Pluto and the Sun in Leo in that order within the sign. This tells us that the suspicious Jupiter-Pluto conjunction in Leo *will be in the 12th House,* ruled by the Moon (Cancer), and the Sun in Leo will be on the

---

113 As well, this midpoint image very often signifies gynecological disorder.

Ascendant. When we draw that horoscope and cast the Solar Arcs for the date when breast cancer was diagnosed, we see that SA Saturn has come to conjunction with the Sun at the Solarscope Ascendant and transiting Uranus is opposed Pluto in the 12th. The measurements "fall in" because of the conspicuous involvement of the Sun and the activity within the Sun's sign in this horoscope.

Another: the Sun in 00 Virgo [immediately, the astrologer's mind anticipates the square involvement of transiting Pluto at 00 Sagittarius, early 1995, Fall 1996] with Pluto-Saturn, Mercury-Venus (two conjunctions) in Leo in the Solar 12th. At cancer diagnosis, transiting Pluto was at 1 Sagittarius, square the Sun and conjunct the Solarscope fourth cusp(!); SA Neptune was square Venus in the 12th, SA Uranus was conjunct Saturn in the 12th.

Another: Saturn in Aries *and the Sun in Aries* tells us that Saturn is in the 12th and that the 12th House has Pisces on its cusp in the Solarscope. At her second Saturn return, this lady developed breast cancer: transiting Saturn was conjunct Saturn and moving on to conjoin the Sun at the Ascendant while, *at the same time,* SA Mars was square the Sun and SA Uranus was exactly square Saturn, and transiting Neptune, ruler of the Solarscope 12th, was precisely opposed Pluto!

The Solarscope can definitely be helpful. Remember that, in the main, we are watching for planetary contact first, *the planets* arranging themselves and carrying into those arrangements the archetypal representations we have developed for them with reference to illness, sites in the body and functions in the body. Secondarily come emphases on other signs and House rulers.

For example, in our study of patterning we have seen Pluto begin as a specific signal within Prostate cancers. Then we saw Pluto continue its presence in patterns relating to cancer in other parts of the body. This focuses *Pluto as a component of a cancer signature.* And we take that further and note that Pluto is a component of critical illness generally.

Our objective through timed horoscopes, through Solarscopes, through planetary analysis, through full horoscope analysis, through predictive methodologies (specifically Solar Arcs and Transits) is to show *astrology's orientation within cursory diagnostics and astrology's powerful position within the timing patterns leading up to critical illness.*

Horoscope 45, Female

Horoscope 45 shows natally many planetary timing pressures for critical illness. In this case, *any* measurement coming into the natal complex would carry anxiety and fear with it and call for medical analysis. This is what happened. This is a horoscope of a rare cancer of the sinus.

Cornell in his *Encyclopedia* gives rulership of the sinuses to Scorpio, probably viewing them as a secondary alimentary organ, excreting air and mucus, metabolic residuals.

There is the confusion also of the four paired sinuses occurring in the head, above, below, and behind the eyes and nose, with the head "ruled" by Aries and Mars (also co-ruler of Scorpio).

In discussion with Ingrid Naiman, she and I differ from Cornell and agree that *Gemini and Mercury are the references of all air passages, all ducts.* Naiman adds this cogent insight, with an Eastern sensitivity: "Things stay still unless the 'wind' blows, unless the air moves. Without movement, things stagnate, and it is in stagnation that the seeds of disease begin to grow." Without the air (and its oxygen content), there is no nourishment and no vitality.

Astrologers refer to Gemini rulership as "the upper respiratory tract," which stops at the neck. We must extend that sensibility to include the sinuses (along with Mars references, say, Mars in Gemini under stress, or Mars in Aries). Here in this horoscope, the focus in Gemini is extremely clear in the 6th House, with the Moon in opposition in the 12th. Upper respiratory tract? Yes. And *Mars receives a quindecile from Neptune:* an orientation to the head and reminding us of the extension of Gemini symbolism? Yes.

Note as well that Mercury and Mars are the final dispositors of the horoscope. Mercury in Gemini is conjunct Uranus.

At the time of diagnosis, SA Pluto was exactly square natal Saturn and, *at the same time,* transiting Uranus was opposed the Sun and transiting Saturn (also in the 12th House) was opposed natal Saturn and...and a major signal indeed: *transiting Neptune was at 5 Capricorn conjunct this lady's Ascendant.*

If we did not have a timed horoscope for this birth, we could construct the Solarscope show here as 45a. The development of tension is seen dramatically at the Ascendant and in the 12th House from SA Pluto and transiting Saturn and Uranus.

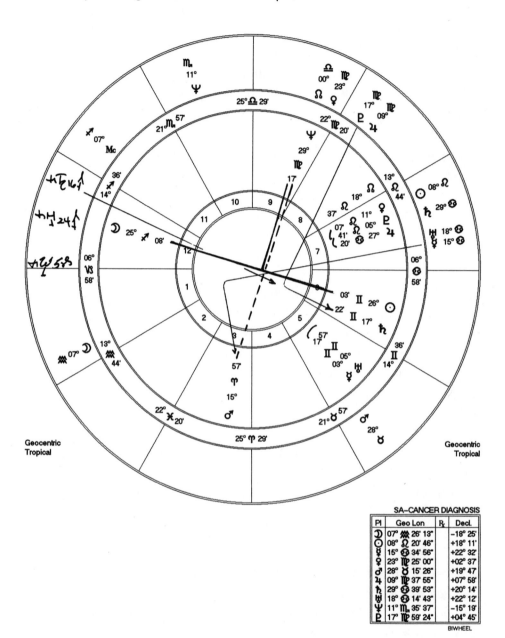

SA–CANCER DIAGNOSIS			
Pl	Geo Lon	Rx	Decl.
☽	07° ♒ 26' 13"		–18° 25'
☉	08° ♌ 20' 46"		+18° 11'
☿	15° ♋ 34' 56"		+22° 32'
♀	23° ♍ 25' 00"		+02° 37'
♂	28° ♉ 15' 26"		+19° 47'
♃	09° ♍ 37' 55"		+07° 58'
♄	29° ♋ 39' 53"		+20° 14'
♅	18° ♋ 14' 43"		+22° 12'
♆	11° ♏ 35' 37"		–15° 19'
♇	17° ♍ 59' 24"		+04° 45'

BIWHEEL

Horoscope 45, Female
Outer Ring — Cancer Diagnosis
SA: October 15, 1987

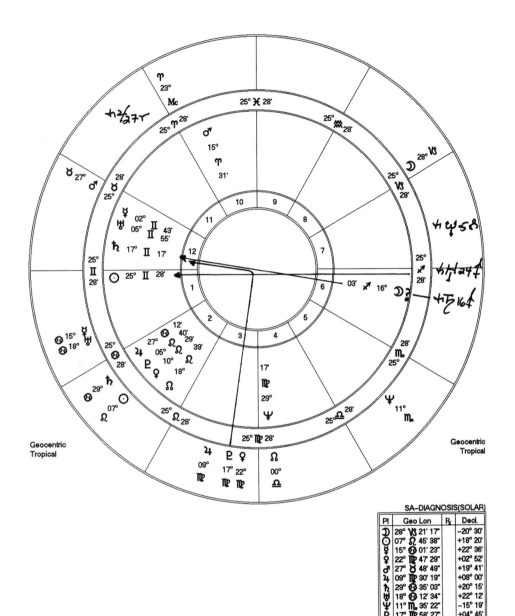

Solarscope 45a, Female ☉
Outer Ring — Diagnosis
SA: October 15, 1987

	SA-DIAGNOSIS(SOLAR)		
Pl	Geo Lon	℞	Decl.
☽	28° ♑ 21' 17"		−20° 30'
☉	07° ♌ 45' 38"		+18° 20'
☿	15° ♋ 01' 23"		+22° 36'
♀	22° ♍ 47' 29"		+02° 52'
♂	27° ♉ 48' 49"		+19° 41'
♃	09° ♍ 30' 19"		+08° 00'
♄	29° ♋ 35' 03"		+20° 15'
♅	18° ♋ 12' 34"		+22° 12'
♆	11° ♏ 35' 22"		−15° 19'
♇	17° ♍ 58' 27"		+04° 45'

BIWHEEL

Final Review of Early Warning Patterning

We can now refine and add to our "First Review of Early Warning Patterning" studied on page 115. The cases presented to this point in our study support the following observations:

Operations Orientation

- *The astrologer creates a general overview synthesis of the horoscope:* hemisphere emphasis, Sun-Moon blend, dominant aspect patterns, rulership networks (with major attention to the angular Grand Cross of Houses and the Succedent Grand Cross suggesting identity formation through early homelife development and issues of self-worth, love, and relationships).

- *Specific keys are noted and assimilated in the general synthesis;* a scenario of personal development, updated in specifics and level through dialogue with the client and appreciation of the client's reality experience: Saturn retrograde, involvement with the Nodal Axis, peregrination, the Aries Point, key midpoint pictures, especially involving Sun/Moon.

- *Specific focal areas of developmental tension within the horoscope are clearly defined and translated symbolically to potential weak spots in the body.*

Early Warning Patterning

(presented in hierarchical format)

- SA or Transiting Pluto promises pointed systemic breakdown: as an agent in symbolic development and/or as a reflector from the natal position, especially in relation to the Ascendant, Midheaven, Sun, Moon, or 12th House through its significator.

- SA or Transiting Neptune promises general systemic weakness as agent or reflector, especially in relation to the Ascendant, Midheaven, Sun, Moon, or 12th House significator.

- SA Saturn promises a threatening rearrangement of reality as agent or reflector, especially in relation to key horoscopic positions; Transiting Saturn appears as a reliable time marker, its slowness allowing for the relative gradualism of disease development.

- SA or Transiting Uranus accentuates change, reinforces other observations made through Pluto, Neptune, and Saturn, especially in relation to the Angles, the Sun, Moon or 12th House significator.

- SA Mars operates as a secondary level of Pluto.

- Transit delineation gains strength dramatically through the background Arc development; Arc development supports the transit trigger.

- SA Jupiter, Transiting Jupiter, and SA Ascendant appear infrequently engaged.

Then, with a predisposition established, we can look for a timing pattern that meets our research criteria. With grace and care, we must press for medical consultation for a "checkup"; we must give warning.

In our analysis of the horoscope, we are able to detect to a respectable degree a generality of potential disease occurrence, of physical breakdown within the aging process. Through client discussion, we are able to learn a personal health history through the key development years to clarify the maturing analysis. From the astrology, we are able to refine deductions to the reality being lived by the client.

Life and Sensibility Centers

The Heart
Horoscope 46, Bill

This man had a heart attack "out of the blue"! Horoscope 46 shows "Bill's" peregrine Sun in Leo, the final dispositor of the horoscope, dominating the whole behavioral concept in Leonine terms. But there is little *obvious* tension with the Sun in the natal horoscope, and there is *no developmental contact* with the Sun at the time of the heart attack! This is another case that shows a critical occurrence perhaps not registering immediately analytically, until we press our pattern of critical pressures strongly upon the horoscope and its defining measurements. We see after-the-fact what we must learn to see before-the-fact.

Indeed, natal Sun squares Mars/Saturn (Sun=Mars/Saturn) and this midpoint picture registers—natally or in arcs, whenever the Sun moves into that position—as a possible threat to the body or health, breaking down under stress and strain. But does it promise heart attack? We do not know; but *it does register as a weakness within the system; it suggests a critical problem.*

I believe that that means *everyone* with Sun strongly configured with Mars and/or Saturn is absorbing a debilitation to the cardiovascular system. Here, because the Sun is peregrine, it does not appear pronounced—but that *peregrination,* especially in a fire sign, may be pronouncement enough!

Natal Saturn-retrograde is opposed the Mercury-Neptune-Venus conjunction in the 4th House, and an astrologer will have to discuss in great depth the tensions in the early homelife (the Saturn retrograde phenomenon, Neptune ruling the 10th and placed in the 4th, Mercury in the 4th, ruling the 4th, in its own sign). These tensions undoubtedly undermined Bill's tendencies to run away with self-aggrandizement, his nascent king complex. Did they also undermine the strength of his heart?

Saturn opposes the Sun/Moon midpoint (Saturn=Sun/Moon) and, opposing Mercury tightly, promises a withdrawal from hurt, depression, introversion, inner tightness; note that Mercury rules the 12th as well as the 4th. There will be a difficult time with relationships (Saturn rules the 7th; Sun/Moon symbolism); a depressed sense of inner pain, perhaps underachievement, being let down.

The Ascendant=Sun/Uranus: this picture always promises sudden excitement, sudden events.

Bill suffered the withdrawal of friends and their funds from a business venture. He felt crucially let down. And then it came: *a heart attack on December 22, 1990.* SA Uranus had moved to conjunction with the Ascendant. Just think of all the pressures brought to bear on this man then; how would his being hold up; *what ways were routined throughout his development to cope with the tensions?*[114]

Uranus=Ascendant does not a heart attack "make." I have lived through this arc, with dire Uranian, Saturnian, and Neptunian transits to my Sun in 10 Capricorn 1989-91, and my heart is fine; my wife is just coming through the same arc, and her heart is fine too. There were/are other challenges, indeed, in our lives. We must remember that *it is the systemic and personality reactions to the pressures represented by the critical*

---

114 Remember that any arc or transit to the Ascendant is an arc or transit *opposing the Descendant.* For example, we associate Uranian contacts with the Ascendant with considerations of divorce, i.e., the intensification of individuality (Uranus, Ascendant) within the responsibilities and dedication to relationship. Individuation threatens relationship or business partnership; separation or isolation can break the bond.

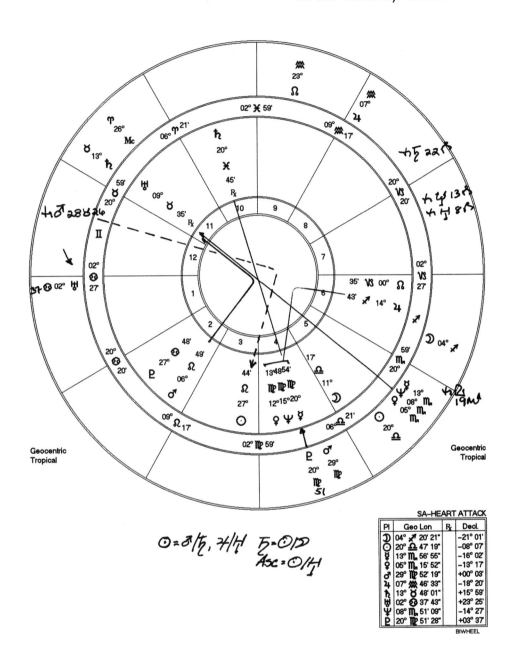

Horoscope 46, Bill
Outer Ring — Heart Attack
SA: December 22, 1990

arc or transit that tell the story of a heart attack, or any other manifestation. How the energies-to-be are fighting throughout the system, the degree to which the environment is cooperating, the past history of behaviors and how they respond to heavy challenge—*these* are the crucial considerations for evaluation.

There was, at the same time for Bill, the arc Pluto=Mercury, co-ruler of the 12th House, which *registered as well as SA Pluto opposed Saturn.* This arc Pluto=Saturn (or the reciprocal, Saturn=Pluto) does promise the pressures of extreme loss, potential self-destruction, hard, hard work. This IS a dire set of signals: Uranus=Ascendant with Pluto=Saturn.

Additionally, SA Neptune opposed natal Uranus suggesting a period of disorientation and great instability.

On the day of attack, transiting Mars was 40' of arc from precise square to Bill's Sun. But remember, Mars is in this position (squaring, conjoining or opposing the natal Sun) approximately every five and one-half months, many times already in this man's life. With the fearful background of three powerful arcs, though, involving the Ascendant, was that Mars transit this time *enough to signify attack upon the heart?*

Indeed, we do not have answers as specifically as we would like. But we are learning the procedure of analysis, the weighing of variables, and the development of deductions throughout time to anticipate critical illness. For sure, *a warning could have been given to Bill,* say, two years ahead of time: "A tremendous development time is building now over the next two years; it's going to take its toll on just about everything that defines who you are, Bill....These plans we've been talking about...etc. are going to come to a focus, critically perhaps by the end of 1990.

"Look at it this way: it's like the champion meeting the challenger: you've got to be *in top physical condition to do your best!* When was the last time you got checked out medically? Did that include an electrocardiogram?....What? You haven't had a physical lately!? Under all this pressure that's building here, it's a good idea to be in top form; please make an appointment and call me with the results. OK? It will pay off, I promise."

During a heart attack, or *myocardial infarction* (muscle-heart tissue dying/dead because of deprivation of oxygen), a blood clot forms and blocks the blood flow in one or more of the coronary arteries. Oxygen supply to the cells in a particular area is cut off. The person feels a profound squeezing pain in the chest, perspires profusely, usually experiences pains radiating to the left shoulder, arm, to the back and even to the jaw. It is a life-threatening emergency.[115]

Usually, the clot forms as a result of fatty deposits on the walls of the arteries which have narrowed the passageways for the blood. Delay in reaction is death, and delay does take thousands of lives a year. In the United States alone, at least 350,000 people die suddenly, or without much warning, from heart attacks each year; one person every eighty seconds, at least.

Isadore Rosenfeld, in his fine book *Modern Prevention—The New Medicine,* revives the work of San Francisco doctors Meyer Friedman and Ray Rosenman in the 1960s, which described the "coronary-prone" personality and labeled it "Type A." Now, this early study has entered our everyday language, but how often do we make note of it in our clients, the people we are trying to help through astrology. Rosenfeld himself remarks that "Cardiologists who agree in principle with this theory, including me, have, for the most part, paid no more than lip service to it over the years. We have our hands full just trying to get our patients to comply with more easily definable goals than changing their personality."[116]

The Type A personality is characteristically aggressive, ambitious, time conscious, angry and hostile, usually with higher blood pressure than the norm. Type As dominate conversations, pass every car on the road, take over every meeting, drum their fingers on the table nervously, swing their legs in restlessness, and rarely, rarely sit still or rest.

The Type B personality is characteristically more easy going, less competitive, less pressured, more philosophical, less aggressive, more contented, and—believe it or not—"no less successful than Type As."

Testing hundreds of *men* who had suffered heart attack, Freidman and Rosenman found through their psychological tests that the majority were Type As. So being "Type A" became an independent risk factor for coronary disease. Further tests of the theory in mid-1984—supported by a grant from the National Heart, Lung, and Blood Institute— strengthened the findings.

---

115 A heart attack is different from angina (a "choking" kind of pain) pains in the chest, usually brought on by emotional stress or over-exertion, in that the cut-off of the blood supply in angina is temporary. In a heart attack, the clot does not go away; the blood supply is definitively cut off, and the heart muscle affected begins to die. Mayo 661.

116 Rosenfeld, pages 208–212.

Additional discoveries showed that Type A men whose behavior patterns were modified (possible in seventy-five percent of the cases), *the heart-attack rate was reduced by fifty percent* (a better percentage than that which was affected in the cholesterol-lowering study). The correlation between Type A and heart attacks was confirmed.

The specific behavior patterns probably do apply to women also, according to Rosenfeld (there is a study showing that Type A women experience a higher incidence of stroke than their Type B counterparts).

Chronic stress is the presumed culprit. Since the time of earliest animals and humans, stress was combatted with adrenaline; it was nature's way of supporting the fight mechanism and protecting the animal (the human) life by using adrenaline's properties to constrict the blood vessels and to coagulate the blood in the case of injury, i.e., to stop the bleeding, to avoid fatal hemorrhage. In effect, the chronic supply of adrenaline is chronic constriction of the blood vessels, the set up for a heart attack.

Adrenaline is produced by two glands, each located on top of a kidney. The inner core of the gland produces two chemicals: epinephrine (adrenaline) and norepinephrine (non-adrenaline). When these chemicals are secreted into the blood stream they increase heart rate and blood pressure and affect other body functions. These hormones affect virtually every system in the body to some degree.

For astrology, Mars "rules" adrenaline. Mars is our planet of "attack," inflammation, agitation, excitement, passion, surgery, danger.

The man of Horoscope 46 *is* a type A personality. His friends abandoning him with their support funds apparently triggered his heart attack, i.e., played into his Type A personality practices, the debilitated system, the already troubled heart, with the Leonine energies running wild into frustration.

This case is presently an exception with regard to the measurement of the Venus relationship with Jupiter and its correlation with diabetes (see page 19)—one of two exceptions of Venus-Jupiter contact in this book: the man has no history yet of diabetes in his family and has only a slightly elevated level of cholesterol. One final note: there is no stressful aspect made with the Sun or the Moon; presently sixty-one years old, the man does not wear glasses.

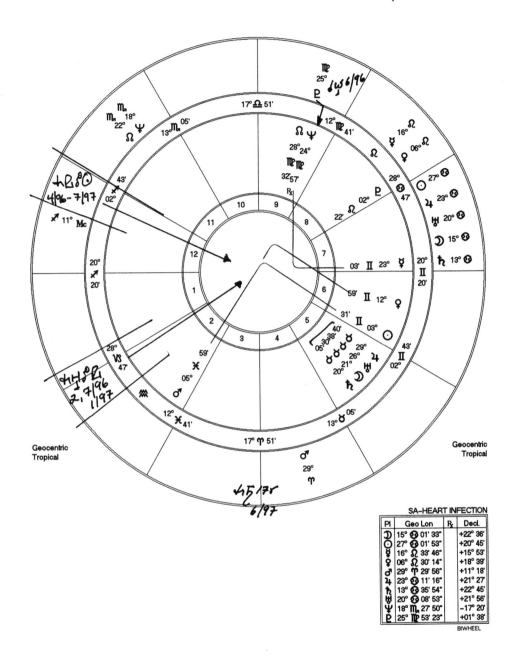

Horoscope 47, Bob Dylan

Inner Chart	Outer Ring — Heart Infection
May 24, 1941, 9:05 P.M. CST	SA: June 4, 1997
Duluth, MN	
92W06 — 46N47	

SA-HEART INFECTION			
Pl	Geo Lon	Rx	Decl.
☽	15° ♋ 01' 33"		+22° 36'
☉	27° ♋ 01' 53"		+20° 45'
☿	16° ♌ 33' 46"		+15° 53'
♀	06° ♌ 30' 14"		+18° 39'
♂	29° ♈ 29' 56"		+11° 18'
♃	23° ♋ 11' 16"		+21° 27'
♄	13° ♋ 35' 54"		+22° 45'
♅	20° ♋ 08' 53"		+21° 56'
♆	18° ♏ 27' 50"		−17° 20'
♇	25° ♍ 53' 23"		+01° 38'

BIWHEEL

Horoscope 47, Bob Dylan

Horoscope 47 belongs to Bob Dylan, the celebrated folk-rock singer and composer most popular in the 1960s, a cult hero still today.

The Sun-Moon blend of Dylan's horoscope suggests quite a world of thoughts, learning, and communication, all in some aesthetic form (Sun in Gemini, Moon in Taurus, Sagittarian Ascendant). "What is learned is channeled into making things what they are supposed to be." And then, this image is complicated by the conjunction of Saturn and the Moon, and the Moon and Uranus: here is the rebellion and the championing of the underdog. All of this is supported in creative communication by the trine with Neptune, ruler of the communication 3rd, which is square to Mercury in Gemini on the horizon (at the 7th cusp). The bottom line here, in my opinion, is that Dylan is a depressed idealist.

This begins to suggest that Dylan is a Type B personality, or a suppressed Type A, or a Type A who has moved closer to B in the last twenty years. (Remember: the type A-B classification theme is a spectrum, not an either-or polarity; one can be closer to one than the other, most people are, rather than totally at one end.) Perhaps the Uranus-Jupiter (ruler of the Ascendant) rebellion has given way to the Saturn-Moon withdrawal. Mars (adrenaline for the personality) reflects this possibility: *square to the Sun* but diluted in Pisces.

People can change; I'm sure I spent most of my life as a Type A and, in the past dozen years or so, have eased much closer to Type B. So the question becomes: how much damage was done during the Type A years?

This kind of observation is essential for the analytic astrologer. The planets are simply guidelines, only guidelines to our client's individual experience in reality. The horoscope is reflected in the individual's reality. This is the orientation of the artist analyst.

Dylan was hospitalized in June 1997; the hospital announcement on June 4 said that he was there for a "mysterious heart infection," that was severe and dangerous.

The Solar Arc of *Pluto* had just crossed natal Neptune (infections, blood). *Transiting Pluto was exactly opposite the Sun* and transiting Uranus was opposite *Pluto*. Was the condition incubating for a year, from when SA Pluto conjoined Neptune precisely (June 1996) and transiting Pluto made its first contact opposed the Sun (April 1996) and transiting Uranus made its first opposition contact with Pluto (February and July 1996)? I think Dylan was suffering for a year and did not know why.

The key trigger here seems to be transiting Saturn exactly conjunct the fourth cusp in June 1997, at the time of hospitalization. All our operational guidelines presented on page 170 have been followed and corroborated.

Horoscope 48, Jayj Jacobs

Horoscope 48 belongs to Jayj Jacobs, a nationally prominent astrologer, a co-founder of AFAN (the international Association for Astrological Networking) and astrology's legal "point" man for many years in the nationwide campaign for fairness under the law.

The Sun-Moon blend shows Jayj's rich blend of individualistic innovation and receptivity to others. There is great intuition and even influences from other realms that blend the real and the unreal, the practical and the theoretical, the scientific and the poetic, and certainly support some artistic talent. Introspection drives the personality, working with a strong sense of philanthropy, of people-service (Ascendant=Saturn/Midheaven, working with others in a serious understanding; AP=Moon/Midheaven, a public professional position; Midheaven and Ascendant rulers conjoined).[117]

Pluto opposes the Sun-Mercury-Mars triple conjunction; this suggests a strong rebellion motif in development; it also brings immediately to mind a potential weakness within the heart, at some time or other in the aging process. Jayj had a heart attack—"without any sign or warning"— on February 21, 1997 and underwent successful triple bypass surgery on February 25.[118]

Jupiter, ruler of the 12th and the Ascendant, is conjunct Venus, and this immediately brings to mind the risk of diabetes. Jayj's father (the late astrologer Don "Moby Dick" Jacobs, whose scholarly rectification of Jesus's birth prevails in our literature) was diabetic and so is Jayj's sister. Jayj felt his own first symptoms early in 1995; he was diagnosed as diabetic in September 1995, when *Neptune* was at 23 Capricorn, *exactly on his natal Venus*, part of our diabetes signature (see page 19).

---

117 There is a clear image reflection here within the Sun-Moon blend of actor, philanthropist Paul Newman.

118 Additionally, we must not forget the strong aspect to the Sun or Moon correlating with eye disease or dysfunction: Jayj has worn glasses since he was fourteen years old, and his vision has continued to deteriorate in adulthood.

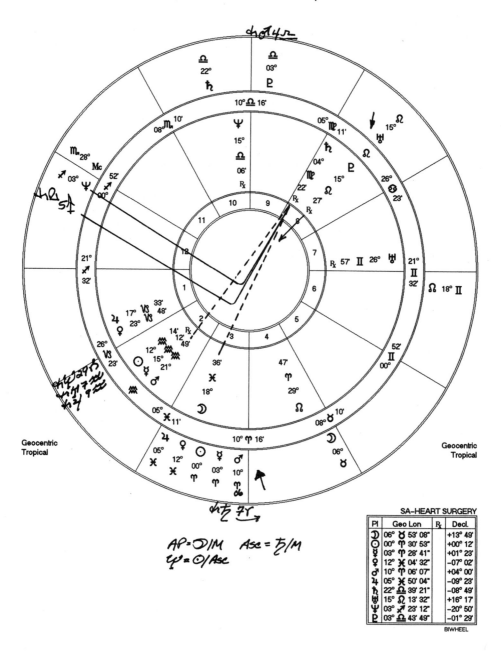

$AP = \mathfrak{D}/M$ $Asc = \mathfrak{h}/M$
$\Psi = \mathfrak{O}/Asc$

	SA–HEART SURGERY		
Pl	Geo Lon	Rx	Decl.
☽	06° ♉ 53' 08"		+13° 49'
☉	00° ♈ 30' 53"		+00° 12'
☿	03° ♈ 28' 41"		+01° 23'
♀	12° ♓ 04' 32"		−07° 02'
♂	10° ♈ 06' 07"		+04° 00'
♃	05° ♓ 50' 04"		−09° 23'
♄	22° ♎ 39' 21"		−08° 49'
♅	15° ♌ 13' 32"		+16° 17'
♆	03° ♐ 23' 12"		−20° 50'
♇	03° ♎ 43' 49"		−01° 29'

BIWHEEL

Horoscope 48, Jayj Jacobs

Inner Chart
February 1, 1949, 3:54 A.M. CST
Poplar Bluff, MO
90W23 — 36N45

Outer Ring — Heart Attack
SA: February 21, 1997

The sensitive Moon in Pisces is *quindecile* with Saturn retrograde. While this measurement plays into the difficult Neptune=Sun/Ascendant in suggesting the fight against feelings of being disregarded or unappreciated, it suggests strongly in the illness profile the vulnerability in the stomach, the importance of diet (along with Pluto opposite Mercury). Jayj had a pre-ulcer condition during college.

Jayj feels that he is a mid-spectrum Type A-B, living in the middle and easily capable of either extreme. Perhaps that is the retrogradation factor of Mercury (here perhaps a sense of control) conjoining Mars and opposed Pluto retrograde. Regardless, Mars is Mars, and when we arc Mars to seek out angular contact we see that it comes to the fourth cusp in a little less than 49 degrees, 48+. The exact Solar Arc Mars position on the day of Jayj's heart attack twenty days after his forty-eighth birthday is shown in the horoscope at 10 Aries 06, precisely conjunct the fourth cusp.

At the same time, SA Neptune in the 12th was squaring Saturn and *transiting Pluto* was squaring that Saturn, which is natally in the difficult quindecile with the Moon.[119]

I think that it is important to note that a warning prompt to look into the reality potential for a time of crisis could have been signaled by transiting Pluto at 00 Sagittarius in the Fall of 1996. That Pluto position was square Jayj's *Sun/Moon midpoint*, a vital position of synthesis in any horoscope. One would have then seen the related build-up of transiting Saturn over the fourth cusp early in 1997, with that coinciding with the major red-flag, SA Mars there as well.

Horoscope 49, Larry King

Horoscope 49 shows another heart attack that resulted in multiple by-pass surgery and excellent recovery. It is the horoscope of CNN world-news interviewer Larry King (*Larry King Live*); the commercials for his expertise and experience credit some 30,000 interviews managed in his professional career. The guests with whom he works on his nightly program broadcast throughout the world include the leaders of nations, governments, entertainment, social development, and scandal.

The Sun-Moon blend—similar to Carl Sagan's (see page 126) and Michel Gauquelin's (see page 237), as well as Billy Graham's and

---

119 Interestingly—and so characteristic of Jupiter behavior in my research—transiting Mars on the day of the heart attack was at 4 Libra exactly square Jupiter/Ascendant!

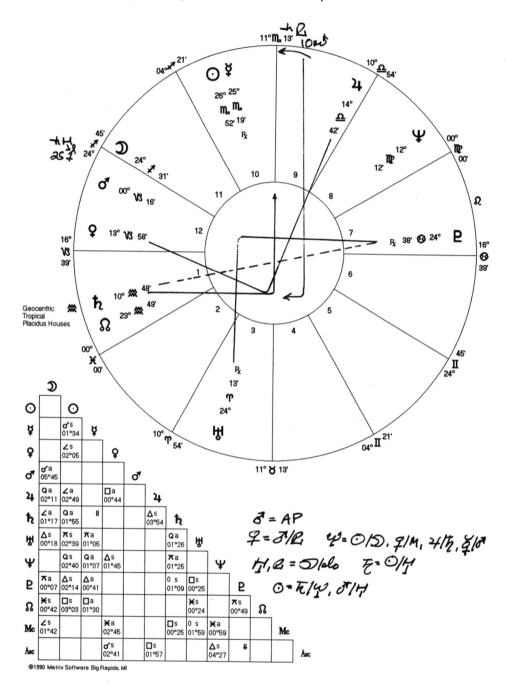

Geocentric
Tropical
Placidus Houses

©1990 Matrix Software Big Rapids, MI

Horoscope 49, Larry King
November 19, 1933, 10:38 A.M. EST
Brooklyn, NY
73W56 — 40N38

Picasso's—identifies a strong need-drive to understand *why things are as they are*, often in contraparallel to deep emotional stewing that threatens to mire personal developments with weighty emotional issues. Enormous relationship difficulties are indicated here: note the quindecile between Saturn and Pluto in the 7th House, Saturn ruling the Ascendant, Pluto ruling the Midheaven. We could suggest an obsession with relationships (professional and personal) to prove himself one-on-one.

This Pluto in the 7th is also squared by Uranus, co-ruler of the Ascendant, disposing of Saturn. There is no doubt about the relationship difficulty hypothesis (Larry King has been married seven times). Venus= Mars/Pluto suggests an adventuresomeness and passionate nature; Neptune equals Sun/Moon and promises many misunderstandings and even deception and discontent in relationships.

The Saturn-Pluto quindecile and the Uranus-Pluto square alert us to danger in the health profile, to come sooner or later. Danger with regard to the prostate is suggested strongly, as we have learned to see in the horoscope; to the knees (Saturn); the skin (Saturn); the bones, the skeleton (Saturn).

The Venus-Jupiter square suggests indeed the high probability of diabetes in the family history and as a real threat for him himself.

There are no other high tension aspects in the horoscope. Creativity abounds (Moon quintile Jupiter, Sun quintile Saturn and also Neptune, Mercury quintile Neptune, Saturn quintile Uranus) and is reinforced extraordinarily by the midpoint picture of *Uranus and Pluto equalling Moon/Node:* "Meeting exceptional people or experiencing unusual events through others; sudden attachments."[120]

The planet Saturn, ruler of the Ascendant, square the Midheaven, quindecile Pluto, semisquare the Moon, quincunx Neptune, positioned in the Ascendant and at the midpoint of Sun/Uranus (the fight against traditional ways of doing things promoting a rebellious way, causing many separations) is undoubtedly the dominating focal point of this horoscope.

Mars comes in "second," if you will: Mars is administratively powerful in Capricorn, of course, and here Mars is conjunct the Aries Point and perhaps is peregrine (a very wide conjunction with the driving Moon in

---

120 Again, a direct quote from the signature pictures included in the Appendix of Tyl, *Synthesis & Counseling in Astrology*, provided for 1,014 possible combinations.

Sagittarius), threatening to run away *with* power, *into* power. Power attracts, power sells. Note that Mars rules the communicating 3rd, holding the key Uranus which, besides the square with Pluto and quintile with Saturn, makes a trine with the Moon, ruler of the 7th. The public is the outlet for testing and accumulating personal power.

Let us go back to, say, early 1985, a hypothetical meeting between you and Larry King for a consultation. King would have been experiencing transiting Saturn on his Sun in the 10th House. Transiting Neptune would have just spent a year conjunct his Mars. This would have been an important career time for King; he is undoubtedly drawn out and drained. He is smoking heavily; his voice betrays the ravages of years of cigarettes; he is far and away into the Type A direction; he is tired of fighting. Is he breaking down?

There you are, early 1985; you look ahead in the Ephemeris to check the Pluto position that you know is building in early Scorpio. You see that transiting Pluto will come to King's Midheaven at the end of 1987, beginning its application in February-March 1987, i.e., within one degree orb. You note that, when transiting Pluto is at 10 Scorpio applying to the Midheaven, *it will be exactly square to King's critical Saturn,* February-March 1987.

1987						
	MARS	JUPITER	SATURN	URANUS	NEPTUNE	PLUTO
MONTH	LONG	LONG	LONG	LONG	LONG	LONG
JAN	25 ♓	18 ♓	15 ♐	24 ♐	06 ♑	09 ♏
FEB	16 ♈	23	18	25	07	10
MAR	06 ♉	00	20	26	08	10
APR	27	07 ♈	21	27	08	09
MAY	17 ♊	14	20	26	08	09
JUN	07 ♋	21	18	25	07	08
JUL	26	26	16	24	07	07
AUG	16 ♌	29	15	23	06	07
SEP	06 ♍	29	15	23	05	08
OCT	25	27	16	23	05	09
NOV	15 ♎	23	19	24	06	10
DEC	04 ♏	20	22	26	07	11

Pluto transiting the Midheaven: "An extremely important time of life: dramatic changes of perspective are practically assured; identity transformation is possible; job adjustment is major; professional developments are life-significant; a life milestone."

Pluto transiting square to Saturn: "the threat of loss; potential self-destruction; hard, hard work." With Saturn's rulership of the Ascendant and its position there, this is a very real attack on personal health, with dire portents.

At the same time, transiting Uranus will be conjunct King's Moon, in January-February 1987.

You need go no further, really: this is a critical time of tension build-up, of a threat to King's entire system, professional and physical: job (10th House, ruled by Pluto), relationships (7th House ruled by the Moon), and health (Saturn rules the Ascendant, natally in quindecile with Pluto; Uranus is co-ruler of the Ascendant). King is in trouble, building to a crisis point in February 1987. You could have warned him; you could have advised a reinspection of life style (behavioral modification) and a visit to medical authority.

King had a heart attack on February 24, 1987. His life changed. He gave up smoking. Ten years later, in 1997, he appears strong and fulfilled; he proudly tells of his grand recovery; he is newly married in Summer 1997 (SA Midheaven=Ascendant; perhaps finally a "fated attraction" lady (natal Pluto=Moon/Node). He now faces *SA Uranus=Mars throughout 1998*, applying throughout the last months of 1997 and most of 1998, exact in October, along with the transit of Mars-Saturn square Pluto (ruler of this 10th) in April and transiting Uranus square Saturn in March and December 1998. We see strong focus undeniably on a most challenging time in September–October 1997 through March–April 1998, in July, and then in October-December 1998.[121]

In this very clear case, we must note that the natal Sun is not involved with any stressful aspect (and yet King's heart breaks down and his vision is debilitated from early on in his life). Also, the Sun is not involved with the developmental measurements of his heart attack. Yet, despite these two jarring observations, we *know* the physical system is seriously debilitated and, depending on the observer's experience and medical expertise, focus *can* be put on the heart as the point of probable or possible collapse.

---

121 Key days are suggested by Tertiary Progressions (one Lunar Month equals one year of progressed life development): April 4 and May 23, 1998 are such days within this next phase of development. Additionally, we must note that SP Moon squares his Saturn in June and conjoins his fourth cusp, opposing the Midheaven, in July 1998. All the measurements suggest a time of great significance for King, for his relationship, and his profession.

Medical astrologer Ingrid Naiman teaches that someone running hard on adrenal energy does so at the expense of proper digestion of substance intake, and, as well, at the expense of many other functions of the body. What is left over from improper digestive (assimilative) function becomes a cause for clogging agents. A good example is cholesterol left over from food digestion (intake) and in relation to the amount of cholesterol produced by the liver itself. How many of us on-the-run, in fight or flight, in aggression or, indeed, in despair eat properly? What about the stressful situations of emotional panic, extreme exertion? These situations call upon the body over and over and over again to provide the energy in crisis fashion. How long can that process continue without breakdown?

A diseased heart or a congenital heart anomaly (or actual malformation) certainly sets up dire conditions for the attack response, but four points must be made most importantly: *stress is cumulative* in the process of living, the body functions holistically, there are many different kinds of heart attacks (heart problems), and we must know that the cause of a heart attack can originate *elsewhere* than at the heart site.

With cancer we "see" the tumor growing in a specific place, in an organ, on an organ (except for leukemia, cancer of the blood; and we fear its extension out of the prostate, out of the testicles, out of the lung, out of the breast—metastasis—into another organ, into the bone, into the general body system. With the heart attack, in the main, we "see" the general body condition working inefficiently, over working, under working, causing problem build up that blocks access to the heart, which is essential for nutrients for the whole of life. From the general, we affect the specific. From the specific, we jeopardize the whole.

Our common sense (based on a store of knowledge and observation we've packed away) speaks clearly when we observe, "Boy! If you keep going on this way, you're going to have a heart attack!"

Horoscope 50, Benjamin

Horoscope 50 belongs to a male physician, "Benjamin." At the end of our consultation, he asked me about his health! In that moment—in the midst of writing this book—our timing discoveries were being tested!

The tension aspects in this horoscope are immediately clear: Saturn retrograde is square Pluto in Leo, and Mercury in Leo, ruler of the Ascendant, is squared by Uranus retrograde.

The quindecile aspect between Neptune and Moon-Jupiter in conjunction in Aries in the 8th House (the strongly pressing need to be "numero uno") is not initially a health significator here; it involves Jupiter, ruler of the 4th and echoes Saturn retrograde *conjunct the Nodal axis*. Suggested is a parental complex/ego development situation taking place in the shadow of a most austere father and a powerfully influential mother. Neptune is also a corner of the much-needed(!) closed circuit of practical self-sufficiency that Benjamin adopted (the Earth Grand Trine) to defend himself in those hard developmental times. This Earth Grand Trine is a rare one, not involving the Sun or the Moon, i.e., operating in a separate context developmentally from the Sun-Moon blend, and it is keyed on, played out through, Neptune, ruler of the 7th; Benjamin, age fifty-seven at consultation time, has never been married.[122]

The tension aspects would immediately suggest the prostate and the heart, especially with Pluto in Leo, Mercury in Leo, Leo on the cusp of the 12th, and the Sun, ruler of the 12th in a sesquiquadrate aspect with Mars, also included within the Grand Trine. (I see Grand Trines as major defense mechanisms that siphon off developmental energy for self-protection rather than self-advancement. In that sense, the defense mechanism is a major tension aspect: energy is self-contained; it backs up in the system.)

Benjamin's horoscope is holistically tense, suppressed, and defensive, in spite of the deep reigning need to excel, to be number one (Moon in the 8th; retrogradation pattern to the west accentuates the defensiveness of the eastern hemisphere, guarding the Ascendant; the Neptune quindeciles and the Grand Trine symbolize tightness of containment). This is echoed by the midpoint picture Midheaven=Moon/Pluto, "a *one-sided* emotional intensity" and the tensely suppressed nerve processes and thinking patterns suggested by Uranus square Mercury in the 12th.[123]

Benjamin tape-recorded our consultation and has given me permission to use his case as a teaching example for my Certification Course for Astrologers. Here is precisely the dialogue that ensued between us when he said, "What about health?"

---

122 See Tyl, *Synthesis & Counseling in Astrology*, pages 284–302 for a thorough Grand Trine discussion.

123 For almost the entire consultation, Benjamin spoke with his hand almost covering his mouth; in a very hushed voice. It is also interesting that Benjamin had two of his fingers (Mercury, with reference to Gemini) cut off at mid-length during a workshop accident with his father.

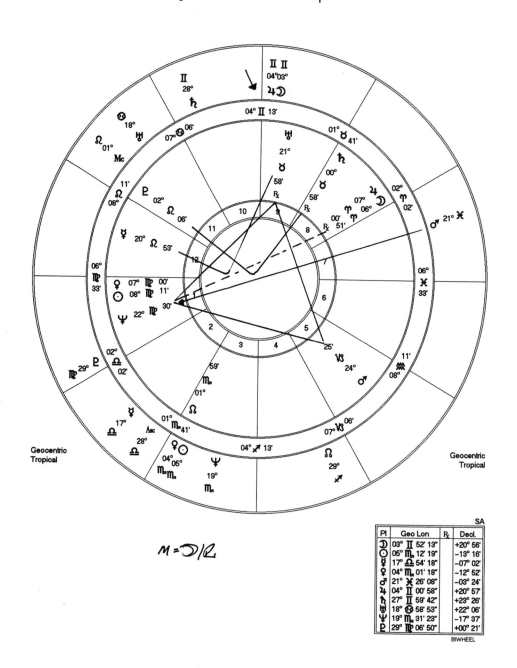

$M = \mathcal{D} / \mathcal{R}$

Pl	Geo Lon	Rx	Decl.
☽	03° ♊ 52' 13"		+20° 56'
☉	05° ♏ 12' 19"		−13° 16'
☿	17° ♎ 54' 18"		−07° 02'
♀	04° ♏ 01' 18"		−12° 52'
♂	21° ♓ 26' 08"		−03° 24'
♃	04° ♊ 00' 58"		+20° 57'
♄	27° ♊ 59' 42"		+23° 26'
♅	18° ♋ 58' 53"		+22° 06'
♆	19° ♏ 31' 23"		−17° 37'
♇	29° ♍ 06' 50"		+00° 21'

SA

BIWHEEL

Horoscope 50, Benjamin
Outer Ring
SA: September 1, 1997

NT: I always end with that, and I always say, 'I'm not a medical doctor...'

Ben: (interrupting me) But you *can* see where it's been and where it's going to go?

NT: That's it; yes. And I'm writing a book about this now. I did look to see if there were a critical time pressing now; there isn't. [Benjamin was under extremely positive, big-development measurements; note SA Jupiter-Moon conjunct his Midheaven, SA Uranus semisquare his Midheaven; then SP Moon conjunct his Midheaven; transiting Jupiter opposed his Moon and SA Midheaven=Pluto in July 1998.]

Ben: What do you see in the past?

NT: One second please...I'll do it exactly [already my eye had generalized certain measurements backward]; I want to be exact as I can be... [about forty-five seconds passed].

Here is what I did by hand in those forty-five seconds: I calculated the time in the past when the SA Sun had *opposed* natal Saturn retrograde (squared by Pluto natally), the major tension center in the horoscope; 5 Scorpio 12 minus 00 (Scorpio, opposite Taurus) 58 gives 4 degrees 14 minutes, which is roughly four years and three months back from the SA horoscope date of September 1, 1997. This translates to June 1993; and I noted quickly in the "Quick Glance" Transit Tables that no major transit would have triggered this arc in the Spring 1993, but it was an important time for sure.

Then I went forward in time, bringing SA Neptune to opposition with natal Uranus (21 Scorpio 58 minus 19 Scorpio 31 gives 2 degrees 27 minutes or two years and five months into the future, September 1999 to February 2000. I noted transiting Neptune opposed natal Pluto at the same time.

Needless to say, I was 'flying' with my mind, generalizing the computations in my head, checking them on paper, and abbreviating notations to guide the conversation.

NT: These measurements take me back to May of 1993 [I chose the midpoint of "Spring" 1993].

As far as the *future* health is concerned, there is an indication that I would have to check...(rechecking the transit) in two years and five months, which is the time leading into early 2000.

What I would ask a layman, Benjamin, is this [getting back onto the consultation track]: "Has there ever been detected in you a congenital heart anomaly, by stethoscope or electrocardiogram?" [He didn't respond at all.] So I ask *you*, is there anything there?

Ben: Yes.

NT: You're confirming that?

Ben: That's correct. I had a triple bypass a year ago June (1996).

NT: [As soon as Benjamin said June 1996, I recalled that, when I was rush-preparing the timeline a moment earlier, I had gone past that date—when transiting Saturn was exactly on the Moon—*in an effort to utilize the arc tensions already deduced from the natal horoscope and utilized in the hour-long consultation that had already corroborated much.*]
[I resumed strongly.] That triple bypass, I must suggest to you, that it (the problem) *really* was detectable or was forming, or happening three years *earlier*...a critical time in Spring of 1993. Is that tenable?

Ben: Yes. *I had a lot of chest pain then.*

NT: And before that [I persisted]—the time was 1991, in December, and June–October 1992 [I had glanced down again at the "Quick-Glance" Transit Tables while he had spoken to me, noting the transit of Pluto opposite Uranus]. *Those are critical times* [for the system breaking down] *and we would have seen the threat of ill health.*

Ben: Ohhhh, yes!

NT: What I've been able to test is that there is unfortunately in the future a high degree of probability of intensified anxiety about the heart situation peaking at the end of 1999, early 2000, and that means watching way ahead of that.

Ben: That would be expected; the technical lifetime of these new valves....

NT: But there's nothing about terminality here; that's not what astrology is all about. But warnings *are* possible.
I can't tell you how excited I am for all the positive stuff ahead of you! [Which we had discussed in detail.] That's the best medicine there is!

Thank you very much for this session today; I've enjoyed it very much; thank you for your faith.

Ben: Thank you.

Whew! The consultation had gone very well, lasted about an hour, and together we had gotten to the bottom of a lot of difficult developmental issues. The question about health, coming from a doctor, had challenged and touched me. I attacked the positions, the pattern, with confidence, persisted with the measurements, and gained the client's corroboration. Everything had "worked." I subsequently received quite a nice card of appreciation from Benjamin; and his remarkable eighty-year-old mother made an appointment with me the very next week.

The Heart and Extended Illnesses
Horoscope 51, David

"What about health?" The answer to that question by "David," Horoscope 51, would be "You name it; I've had it!" Indeed, now sixty-seven, David has been through everything, it seems, except lymphoma (cancer of the lymph glands, lymph fluid) and the brain. Most recently, David had five vertebrae fused in May 1993, open heart surgery in July 1993, prostate cancer (prostectomy) in February 1994, his right hip replaced in September 1994, and his left hip replaced in October 1995; he is now being treated for a spasmodic closure of his esophagus (a condition that has been with him since 1990).

"It all began," his wife, a nurse, reminded him, "when David contracted Rheumatic fever when he was eight years old."

Rheumatic fever occurs in children and young people, beginning with a severe throat infection from streptococcal bacteria. If the infection is not treated quickly and thoroughly, the infection can cause inflammation of the heart valves, arthritis migrating from one joint to another, raised red patches on the skin, and/or lumps under the skin, even invasion of the brain and random body movements. Abnormal heartbeat can be a reaction to scar tissue in the heart valves from the infection.[124]

Penicillin is essential for curing this infection. The antibiotic (discovered in 1928 and produced first only in 1940) has all but obliterated the disease in modern times. Yet there are still outbreaks, and

---

124 Mayo, pages 677–678.

one to two percent of schoolchildren in the United States have heart murmurs due to rheumatic fever, and as recently as 1975, half of all the recruits rejected by the armed forces in this country for cardiovascular reasons had rheumatic heart disease.[125]

David's horoscope shows a conspicuous southern hemisphere emphasis (above the horizon) suggesting practically axiomatically that life will be fashioned for him by others, by forces out of his control. This can approach the level of feeling victimized and/or working to fulfill oneself dramatically in the eyes of the world. In short, this is a weakness to the planetary orientation, especially with the dominating aspect of Saturn retrograde—a singleton in the North—opposing Pluto in the 10th House. This very difficult axis is squared (exacerbated) by Uranus.

Yet another powerful aspect suggests breakdown of the system: Mars in Aries, final dispositor of the horoscope (along with Mercury), is *quindecile* with the Ascendant. A definite attack on the health center (fevers, surgery, accidents).

Neptune is in the 12th and is exactly square to Mercury and Venus. Mercury rules the Ascendant receiving the quindecile from Mars, and the Midheaven, and is co-dispositor (with Mars) of the horoscope.

We "feel" the potential weaknesses of the entire horoscopic system. And there is more: note the midpoint (see aspect grid) of the Sun-Moon. This tells us that the Neptune debilitation of the Ascendant ruler (the exact square with Mercury) is *also square the midpoint of the Sun and the Moon.* We know that any planet so positioned will tend to "run away" with the horoscope. Here, with all the debilitating measurements considered—southern hemisphere emphasis, Saturn=Pluto, Mars QD Ascendant, Neptune=Mercury=Venus=Sun/Moon—we expect general systemic weakness, without any doubt whatsoever.

At eight years of age, David contracted Rheumatic fever: SA Mars was exactly conjunct Uranus (5 Aries plus 8 degrees/years) and—lo!—transiting Neptune was at 19 Virgo conjunct his Ascendant, transiting Saturn was at 13 Aries conjoining his Uranus, transiting Jupiter was at 00 Pisces opposed Neptune (and square the other mutable sensitive points), and transiting Mars on his birthday was at 18 Gemini conjunct his Midheaven!

---

125 Rosenfeld, page 188.

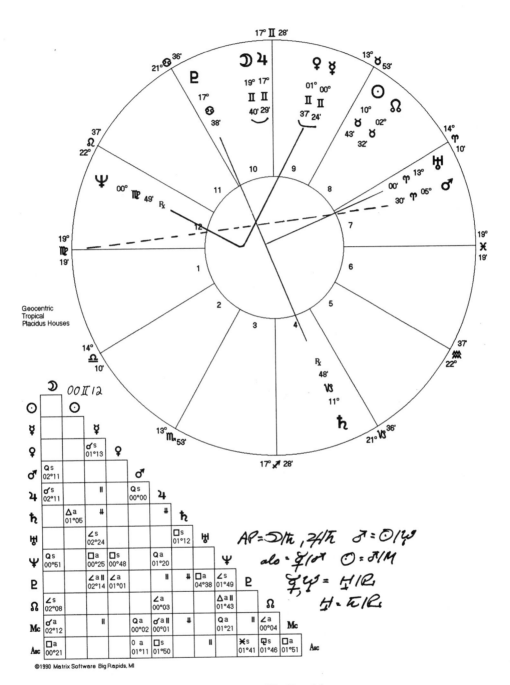

Horoscope 51, David
May 1, 1930, 3:20 P.M. CDT
Chicago, IL
87W39 — 41N51

This onset of lifelong weakness at eight years of age (1938, before the production of penicillin) corroborates our initial deductions in the horoscope. Rheumatic fever got to the heart, and this weakness shone throughout the rest of the system, just as the light of the sun shines upon every planet in our system to one degree of illumination or another.

Further corroborations gained in life development discussions with David—taking a more recent time-focus of difficulty—include the following:

- Lumbar fusion and then open heart surgery with transiting Saturn's first conjunction with the 12th House Neptune

- Prostate surgery with SA Sun opposed Saturn and transiting Saturn exactly opposed the 12th House Neptune for the final contact

- The right hip replacement with SA Pluto exactly conjunct the Ascendant and *transiting* Pluto square Neptune, opposing Sun/ Moon, with transiting Saturn exactly opposed the Ascendant

- And extreme concern and presently on-going tests for the long-time constrictions of the esophagus in Summer 1997 with SA Uranus conjunct the Midheaven and transiting Pluto still opposing Mercury, ruler of the Ascendant.

While this horoscope is a clear portrayal of a severely weakened health center, it is very complicated developmentally. I find it interesting and provocative to admit that astrology can see the weakened system and find many times when punctuation of the key pattern points corroborated real-life health crisis *but astrology is unable to enumerate or specify at times of crisis all the weak points of David's system*—and there are many more than are discussed here!

I resolve this for myself with the idea developed in part one of this study: as yet, astrology is not capable of reliable and complete medical diagnosis. We come close, admirably, but we are a medical diagnostic tool of only a little more than threshold reliability—yet faring better in the hands of medically sophisticated astrologers. What we are able to do among us all now is deduce the cursory diagnostics of the system AND *mark the pressure points within the time of the developmental (aging) process.* With these times marked, with early warning given, astrology can and does help to save lives.

David's case shows clearly the potential problems of the regenerative organs, specifically the prostate (see page 79); suggests the upper respiratory tract (Gemini; Mercury); and perhaps does promise the potential of a pervasive infection (Neptune square Mercury), if we develop Mars moving out of the quindecile with the Ascendant into a conjunction with Uranus by Solar Arc and *into square with the axis of Saturn-Pluto,* in childhood.

David's case does not suggest a heart problem *directly:* there is no attack upon the Sun in any way. There is no classic lower back reference except if we go to a secondary level of consideration for Venus under stress with Neptune, calling in symbology reference to lower back, kidneys, and the trachea (at the top of the esophagus, the windpipe).

We must always remember that early warning by definition is *before the fact of diagnosis.* After-the-fact analysis is all too easy; but I have worked diligently to present all examples here as time-honestly as I can: the examples all search for times before the fact, before diagnosis in order to prove the point of patterning.

Necessarily, the examples we learn from must work backwards from the reality of a condition's occurrence to hypothecate an early warning period. The intent is clear here; faith in the points being made and work with the system itself will establish astrology's empirical record.

Horoscope 52, Male

Here's another fine example of this point of discussion: the male shown here in Horoscope 52 has an extremely debilitated health center: Ascendant=Mercury, Neptune, Moon, a*nd Saturn/Pluto.*[126]

How is the health debilitated, by what weakness? Mercury (air, lungs), Neptune (weakened), Saturn/Pluto (depression, withdrawal). My experience supports the observation that *an addiction to smoking* is the answer to our question. Neptune, along with the Saturn/Pluto tie-in definitely becomes suppression of the nervous system (or the need to suppress it; people smoke urgently when they feel nervous or threatened; again, it is the phenomenon of constricting the blood vessels. Please recall page 175). Very clearly we see an echo of this deduction in the

---

126 It is helpful to read the Ascendant as "8" instead of 7 and a fraction. This man's birthtime is based upon personal statement, rounded off to the quarter-hour. It is very close, in my opinion, and eleven minutes later than the 6:15 A.M. time drawn here would put the Ascendant at 10 Leo, exactly at the target-center of these measurements.

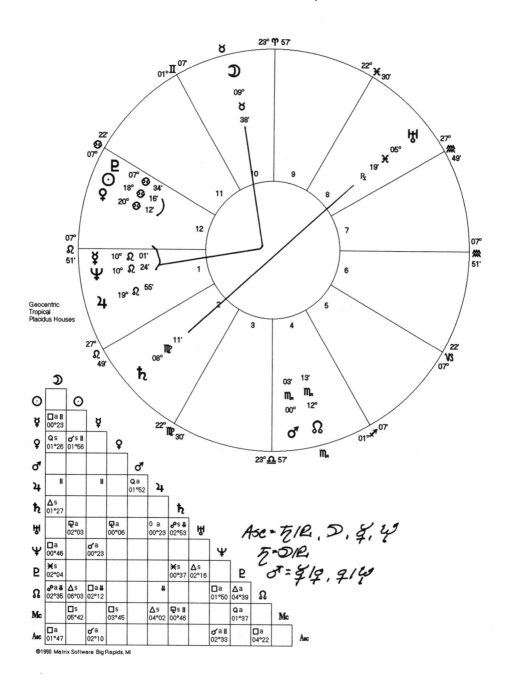

Geocentric
Tropical
Placidus Houses

©1990 Matrix Software, Big Rapids, MI

Horoscope 52, Male
July 11, 1920, 6:15 A.M. Zone -8:48
Vladivostok, USSR2
131E56 — 43N10

dominating Saturn-Uranus opposition, and that leads us to the sense of Uranus exacerbating (a fine word for Uranus) Jupiter (cell proliferation?) through the quindecile aspect between Uranus and Jupiter in the Ascendant.

The instant surmise, the instant suspicion is that this is a compulsive smoker running the risk of lung cancer and/or heart failure (Leo Ascendant; with the Sun in the 12th). Note as well that the powerful conjunction at the Ascendant, the focus of our deductions, is squared by the Moon, ruler of the 12th.

We can expect a mesomorphic (muscular, stocky) dramatically predisposed man, with great robust expression (Mars in Scorpio, *peregrine;* Leo Ascendant).

It is important to note that the Sun and Venus in conjunction are square to the Midheaven, which is ruled by Mars peregrine.

This man was a very powerful stage performer, actor/singer, who died of lung cancer from smoking. In the year or two before his death (October 10, 1985), knowing he was to die, he mounted a campaign to denounce smoking. The campaign was dramatically marked with videotape recordings (Mercury, Neptune) of his personal explanations about the addiction, to be shown after his death). This is the horoscope of Yul Brynner.[127]

Let's go back to two years before his death, to October 1983 (see Horoscope 52a, page 198).

Yul Brynner is sitting with you for a consultation. Your preparation has revealed the following dramatic measurements:

- SA Pluto exactly on Saturn

- SA Saturn exactly opposed the Moon and square Mercury-Neptune

- Transiting Pluto is conjunct Mars

- Transiting Saturn at 5 Scorpio is squaring the Ascendant group that month

- Transiting Jupiter and Uranus at 7 Sagittarius are square Saturn

127 Indeed, the Mercury-Neptune relationship in Leo at the Ascendant square with the Moon in Taurus in the 10th, Mercury ruling the communication 3rd, suggests the dramatically inspiring voice capability of the actor. Smoking stabilized the darkness of his voice. Yul Brynner, born July 11, 1920, at 6:15 according to personal statement; in Vladivostok, USSR2.

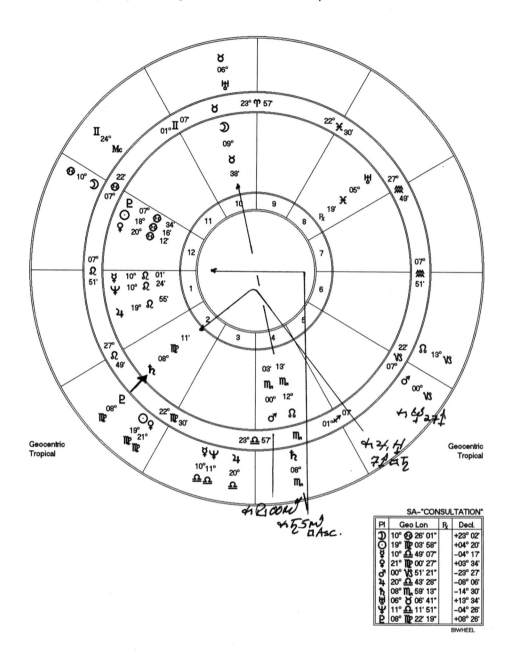

Horoscope 52a, Yul Brynner

Inner Chart
July 11, 1920, 6:15 A.M. Z08
Vladivostok, USSR2
131E56 — 43N10

Outer Ring — Consultation
SA: October 15, 1983

PI	Geo Lon	R	Decl.
☽	10° ⊗ 26' 01"		+23° 02'
☉	19° ♍ 03' 58"		+04° 20'
☿	10° ♎ 49' 07"		−04° 17'
♀	21° ♍ 00' 27"		+03° 34'
♂	00° ♑ 51' 21"		−23° 27'
♃	20° ♎ 43' 28"		−08° 06'
♄	08° ♏ 59' 13"		−14° 30'
♅	06° ♉ 06' 41"		+13° 34'
♆	11° ♎ 11' 51"		−04° 26'
♇	08° ♍ 22' 19"		+08° 26'

SA–"CONSULTATION"

BIWHEEL

1981

MONTH	MARS LONG	JUPITER LONG	SATURN LONG	URANUS LONG	NEPTUNE LONG	PLUTO LONG
JAN	01 ♒	10 ♎	10 ♎	28 ♏	23 ♐	24 ♎
FEB	25	10	10	00 ♐	24	24
MAR	17 ♓	09	08	00	25	24
APR	12 ♈	05	06	00	25	23
MAY	04 ♉	02	05	29 ♏	25	22
JUN	27	00	03	28	24	22
JUL	18 ♊	02	04	27	23	22
AUG	09 ♋	06	06	26	22	22
SEP	29	12	09	26	22	23
OCT	18 ♌	18	12	27	22	24
NOV	06 ♍	25	16	29	23	25
DEC	23	01 ♏	19	01 ♐	24	26

1982

MONTH	MARS LONG	JUPITER LONG	SATURN LONG	URANUS LONG	NEPTUNE LONG	PLUTO LONG
JAN	07 ♎	06 ♏	21 ♎	03 ♐	25 ♐	27 ♎
FEB	17	09	22	04	26	27
MAR	19	10	22	05	27	27
APR	10	08	20	04	27	26
MAY	01	05	17	04	27	25
JUN	03	01	16	02	26	24
JUL	13	11	16	01	25	24
AUG	29	02	17	01	25	24
SEP	17 ♏	06	20	01	24	25
OCT	08 ♐	12	23	02	24	26
NOV	00 ♑	18	27	03	25	27
DEC	16	25	00 ♏	05	26	28

1983

MONTH	MARS LONG	JUPITER LONG	SATURN LONG	URANUS LONG	NEPTUNE LONG	PLUTO LONG
JAN	17 ♑	01 ♐	03 ♏	07 ♐	27 ♐	29 ♎
FEB	11 ♓	07	04	08	28	00 ♏
MAR	03 ♈	10	04	09	29	29 ♎
APR	27	11	03	09	29	29
MAY	19 ♉	09	00	08	30	28
JUN	11 ♊	06	28 ♎	07	28	27
JUL	01 ♋	02	28	06	28	27
AUG	22	01	28	05	27	27
SEP	12 ♌	03	01 ♏	05	26	28
OCT	01 ♍	07	04	06	27	29
NOV	20	12	072	08	27	00 ♏
DEC	07 ♎	19	11	09	28	01

This is an incredible organization of measurements. Brynner is smoking incessantly as he sits before you. The predisposition is established; the timing pattern is revealed; warning must be given.

But it is probably too late. Two years before this consultation, say, in 1981, the astrologer would have to have seen these October 1983 measurements forming. The key at the end of 1981 would have been *transiting Saturn at 16–18 Libra square natal Sun in the 12th*. Looking ahead from that point would have revealed the arcs and accumulating transits. That might have been early warning enough.

The Brain: Stroke

The heart and the Sun are the micro and macro-energy sources for our life systems. Interruption of the flow of energy from either is the end of life. Twenty-percent of the heart's output of fresh blood and twenty percent of the heart's oxygen and glucose contents are *required by the brain*. Two major artery channels extend up the neck to distribute this blood throughout the brain. Any interruption of that flow (ischemia; *ihs-skee'-meea*)—even for a few seconds—causes upset in the brain's functions. Depending on what section of the brain is affected, there can be disturbance in vision, speech, even paralysis, loss of consciousness.[128]

If this disturbance lasts for more than a few minutes, the brain cells in the deprived area begin to die. Permanent damage, death take place.

The "brain attack" is called "stroke" (cerebrovascular disease). It is the most urgent human crisis; every second counts to restore oxygen service to the brain. The most common arterial disease that leads to a stroke, to ischemia, is atherosclerosis, a condition in which fatty deposits adhere to the walls of the arteries and gradually build into the center of the channel to block the flow of blood. A blood clot (thrombus) forms; cerebral thrombosis occurs; and the stroke is fact.

Stroke is the third leading cause of death throughout developed countries. Approximately 300,000+ Americans suffer a stroke each year. One-fourth to one-half of them die, and half the survivors have long-term disabilities. The risk for stroke doubles each decade after the age of thirty-five years. Five percent of the population older than sixty-five years has had a stroke.

---

128 A recent report in *Elle* magazine, September 1997, page 251: Dr. Susan Blumenthal: "a recent study suggests routine dental xrays can reveal an important indicator of the patient's vulnerability to stroke. Xrays can show calcium deposits in the carotid arteries [up through the neck to the brain], a sign of advanced atherosclerosis, a major cause of stroke."

Seventy percent of all strokes occur in persons with high blood pressure. Smoking, diabetes, and high blood cholesterol concentration also are distinct liabilities toward stroke.[129]

The incidence of stroke has been decreasing dramatically in the United States and in many other countries for the past forty years due to improved eating habits (except in Japan, where it is the number one cause of death, presumably because of the continuing high salt content of the diet).

A stroke is not a heart attack. It is a "brain attack", as we have seen, brought on by interrupted blood flow to the brain. The entirety of life function is threatened; the ultimate occurrence of stroke involves more and more the angles of the horoscope, the space/time orientation each of us has in life. While there are Neptune concerns (blood), Mars concerns (energy), and Mercury concerns (oxygen), there is no specific reference for stroke, as yet. While *specific* warning is impracticable through astrology, except through medical guidelines, personal history, and a certain degree of cursory deduction from the horoscope, *general warning* of critical challenge to the system *is* often possible. The general warning is prompted just as it is for the other somatic and systemic problems we have studied.

Horoscope 53, Joan McEvers

Horoscope 53 is the birth portrait of astrologer Joan McEvers, one of astrology's finest teachers and authors. Joan suffered and survived a stroke on September 4, 1995.

First, the natal horoscope shows Saturn square to the Sun-Neptune opposition axis and Mars square to the Moon-opposed-Mercury-Venus axis. Cursorily, we see this as a reinforced threat potential to the eyes *and* to the heart. This is furthered suggested by the quindecile between the Sun in the Ascendant and the Moon in Leo in the 6th: an intensely impassioned dedication to proving oneself, in the spirit of helping others, in public service, if you will. This is the suggestion of the workaholic for whom work performance is self-definition (intensified by the Mars square with the Moon; the projected personal idealism of the Mercury-Venus conjunction). Joan's eyes have the beginning of cataracts; the heart is presently without problem.

---

129 Mayo, pages 461–466; Rosenfeld, pages 274–289.

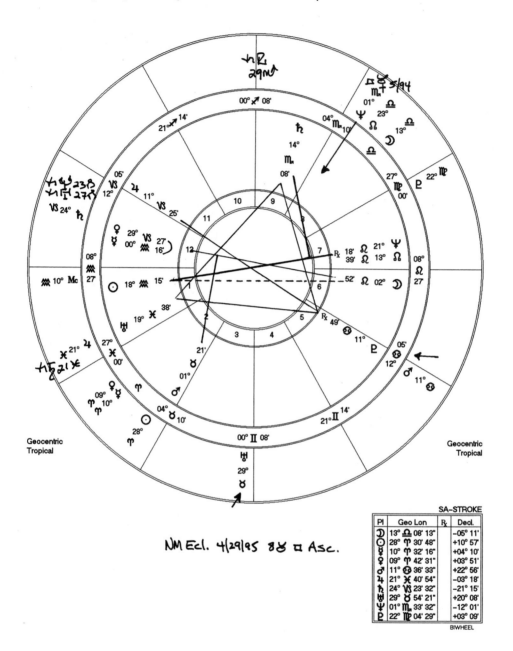

NM Ecl. 4/29/95 ♉♉ □ Asc.

Pl	Geo Lon	Rx	Decl.
☽	13° ♎ 08' 13"		–05° 11'
☉	28° ♈ 30' 48"		+10° 57'
☿	10° ♈ 32' 16"		+04° 10'
♀	09° ♈ 42' 31"		+03° 51'
♂	11° ♋ 36' 33"		+22° 56'
♃	21° ♓ 40' 54"		–03° 18'
♄	24° ♑ 23' 32"		–21° 15'
♅	29° ♉ 54' 21"		+20° 08'
♆	01° ♏ 33' 32"		–12° 01'
♇	22° ♍ 04' 29"		+03° 09'

SA–STROKE

BIWHEEL

Horoscope 53, Joan McEvers

Inner Chart
February 7, 1925, 6:34 A.M. CST
Chicago, IL
87W39 — 41N51

Outer Ring — Stroke
SA: September 4, 1995

The opposition between Jupiter and Pluto always keys the sense of extreme resourcefulness, but, as well, potential problems in the liver and in the regenerative organs within the process of growth and aging (reinforced by Saturn's position in Scorpio, ruling the 12th, and squaring the Sun in the Ascendant). None of these possible problems has as yet developed with Joan.

At the time of the stroke, *SA Mars* was exactly conjunct Pluto and opposed Jupiter; SA Neptune was exactly opposed Mars; SA Uranus was exactly conjunct the *angle* of the IC; transiting Saturn had just crossed Uranus, ruler of the Ascendant, and *transiting Pluto was exactly conjunct the angle of the Midheaven.*

This time period of critical astrological development was certainly to be seen a long time ahead. It would be a major time of life reorientation indeed; we would think for the best, for a final growth period begun in life at age seventy. The key of Uranus arcing to the fourth cusp would introduce (reveal) transiting Pluto conjunct the Midheaven *at the same time*. The Mars arc to Pluto then is exposed; the Neptune arc to Mars, and the optimism is modified.

But, let's look for a *specific* alert date, a warning time of the potential challenge to the life system, medical or otherwise. On April 29, 1995, four months before the stroke, for example, there was a New Moon eclipse at 8 Taurus square to Joan's Ascendant. This is a statement of emphasis, focusing, through the square, on the health center. The ephemeris would tell us that, at that same time, transiting Pluto was on the Midheaven, transiting Saturn was on Uranus, ruler of the Ascendant, and transiting Uranus was square Mercury. This *is* warning for a full checkup.

Now, a second type of stroke is called a cerebral hemorrhage: an artery leaks blood into the brain, causing compression and death of nerve tissue. The initial effect of a hemorrhagic stroke is often more severe than that of an ischemic stroke.

Horoscope 54, Franklin Delano Roosevelt

Franklin Delano Roosevelt (Horoscope 54) suffered a fatal cerebral hemorrhage on April 12, 1945.

The natal horoscope shows a considerable amount of developmental tension with regard to health: the Sun is squared by Saturn and by Jupiter-Neptune; Mercury, ruler of the Ascendant, is squared by Pluto; and the Ascendant is at the midpoint of Sun/Saturn, promising a threat to health. (See also page 31.)

Roosevelt was Assistant Secretary of the Navy, beginning in 1913, and with accumulating public prominence ran as Vice-President on the Democratic ticket in 1920. The ticket was defeated; nine months later in August 1921, he suffered a severe attack of polio and became partially paralyzed.

Poliomyelitis (also called infantile paralysis because ninety percent of those infected were/are children) was/is a viral infection (Neptune), entering the body through the mouth, invading the throat and digestive system and spreading throughout the lymphatic system and the bloodstream. The paralytic form begins when the virus goes from the bloodstream (Neptune) into the central nervous system (Mercury; Uranus). The virus then infects the nerve cells in the brain stem or spinal cord, which controls muscular activity.[130]

Roosevelt's horoscope shows the arc and transit development to the polio attack (deductions from this chart backward several months shows dramatically the defeat position in the 1920 election): *SA Neptune= Midheaven,* SA Pluto=Moon; transiting Neptune opposed the Sun, and transiting Jupiter-Saturn exactly conjunct the Ascendant. This was a system severely challenged, which could have been seen easily one year, two years before. The failure in the election bid was conclusively suggested by these measurements.

Like stroke, polio is difficult to guard against. Warning from physical symptoms and/or astrological patterns brings the individual into the care of doctors and the state of research at the time.

Now, horoscope 54a shows Roosevelt's situation on the date of his fatal hemorrhage. He was in ill health, probably from as long before as early 1942, at the height of the war effort, when SA Mars was at 27 Leo 18 exactly square natal Pluto and opposed natal Mercury, ruler of the

---

130 Mayo 485–486. Widespread vaccination of the Jonas Salk vaccine (1952–54) in modern times has all but eliminated polio.

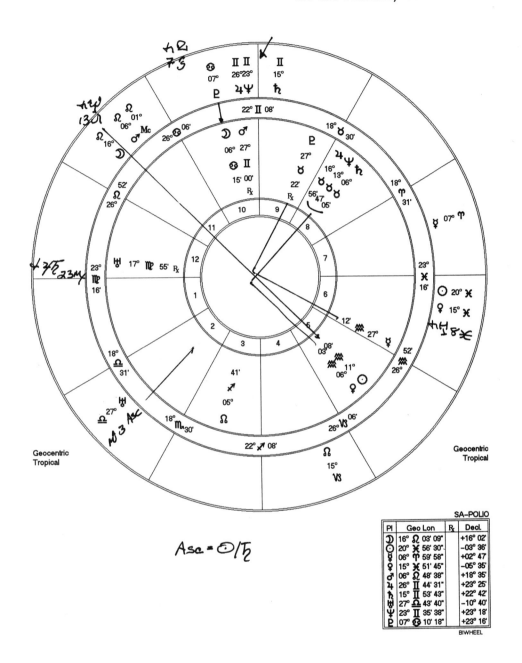

$Asc = ⊙/♄$

Horoscope 54, Franklin D. Roosevelt

Inner Chart	Outer Ring — Polio
January 30, 1882, 8:45 P.M. LMT	SA: August 15, 1921
Hyde Park, NY	
73W56 — 41N47	

Ascendant and Midheaven; SA Saturn was at 6 Cancer 23 exactly conjunct the Moon. The transits at that time showed transiting Pluto square Saturn and transiting Uranus conjunct Pluto. This was a terribly demanding time for Roosevelt, and it had significance not only in his world position with World War II (the 9th, foreign countries; the 11th the Allies; Mars, military attack) but on his personal health position as well.

At the time of cerebral hemorrhage, SA Ascendant was at 27 Scorpio, in opposition with Pluto and transiting Saturn was upon the Moon.

As I study stroke and cerebral hemorrhage, concerns of the brain and neurological explosion, Mercury and Uranus come more to the foreground than they have in studies of other disease conditions (except those dispositions that are pointedly Mercurial like asthma and other lung problems with reference to Gemini; intestines and diet, with reference to Virgo).

The Mercury factor often seems to become practically hypersentient in the timing patterns we are studying in this book. Look back to Horoscope 25 (page 103), the horoscope of Scott Hamilton. Mercury is squared by Mars within the Mercury opposition with the Moon. Mercury rules the 12th; Mercury is "heading into danger," if I may abbreviate, by arcing to conjunction with Pluto and the Sun.

SA Mercury came to conjunction with Pluto at five to six years of age (natal Pluto=Sun/Moon) when transiting Uranus was conjunct the Sun-Pluto conjunction: Scott was thought to have developed Cystic Fibrosis, a very dangerous inherited disease that affects both the respiratory and digestive systems (Mercury). It is the most common fatal *hereditary* disease in white children in the United States, affecting approximately one in every 2,000 infants. Only about half of the individuals with this disease live beyond the age of twenty-six.

The correct diagnosis was illuminated when Mercury arced to conjunction with the Sun at age eight: Scott had contracted Schwachman's Syndrome, a partial paralysis of the intestinal tract with concomitant lung complications (Mercury).[131]

Keep Mercury and Uranus especially in mind now, working with the brain, consciousness, sensibility.

---

131 Mayo, page 720.

132 Additionally: in Ralph Abernathy's horoscope (see page 38), natal Mercury is exactly square the Pluto-Ascendant opposition, and Uranus conjoins the Sun. At the time of his stroke (March 9, 1983), transiting Pluto was conjunct his Midheaven.

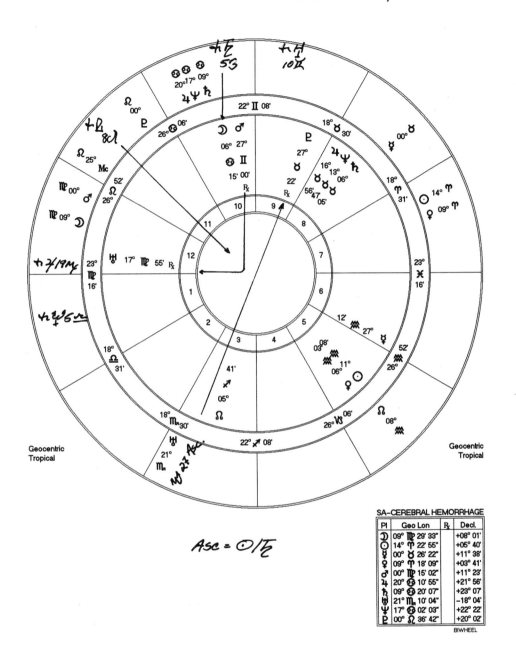

Asc = ⊙/ħ

SA—CEREBRAL HEMORRHAGE			
Pl	Geo Lon	Rx	Decl.
☽	09° ♍ 29' 33"		+08° 01'
⊙	14° ♈ 22' 55"		+05° 40'
☿	00° ♉ 26' 22"		+11° 38'
♀	09° ♈ 18' 09"		+03° 41'
♂	00° ♍ 15' 02"		+11° 23'
♃	20° ♋ 10' 55"		+21° 56'
♄	09° ♋ 20' 07"		+23° 07'
♅	21° ♏ 10' 04"		−18° 04'
♆	17° ♋ 02' 03"		+22° 22'
♇	00° ♌ 36' 42"		+20° 02'

BIWHEEL

Horoscope 54a, Franklin D. Roosevelt

Inner Chart
January 30, 1882, 8:45 P.M. LMT
Hyde Park, NY
73W56 — 41N47

Outer Ring — Cerebral Hemorrhage
SA: April 12, 1945

With Joan McEvers, (see horoscope on page 202), we see natal Mercury squared by Mars, opposed by the Moon, and in the 12th House, ruling an angle. Uranus is prominent natally because it is the ruler of her Ascendant, and key to a Water Grand Trine (that does not incorporate the Sun or the Moon, i.e., a behavioral construct of emotional sensibilities separated from the thrust of the Sun-Moon blend). This Uranus position calls strong attention to the health center symbolized by the Ascendant, a core focus of defenses. At the time of her stroke, as we see, the Uranus arc had developed to conjunction with her fourth cusp![132]

With Franklin Delano Roosevelt, Mercury is natally almost precisely squared by Pluto, and Mercury rules both the Ascendant and the Midheaven, and Mercury is in mutual reception with Uranus.

Horoscope 55, Marion March

Horoscope 55 is the horoscope of Marion March, astrology's leading lady for the last half of the twentieth century and Joan McEvers' writing partner for their series of best-selling teaching texts. Marion suffered and survived a stroke in December 1994 and, thereafter, a temporary but extremely dangerous collapse of her health system because of lung failure, December 12, 1996.

Marion's natal horoscope shows the predisposition to health weakness this way: the Ascendant ruler, Jupiter, is square with the axis of *Sun-Neptune* (hips, Jupiter-Sagittarius; the lungs in reflex action to Gemini; and Plutonic concerns through Jupiter's position in Scorpio). Uranus, the dispositor of the Sun, is square the Sagittarian Moon at the Sagittarian Ascendant, and itself *squares the Ascendant* (another reference to the hips-lungs suggestion).

Mars is square Pluto, ruler of the 12th (another reference to regions Plutonic), and Mercury (lungs) is *square the midpoint of Sun/Pluto (Mercury=Sun/Pluto)*. While this natal midpoint promises strong projection of thought and opinion (an echo of the reigning need of Moon in Sagittarius, to have one's opinions respected), it also links Mercury to the all-important symbols of the Sun (opposed Neptune) and Pluto (squared by Mars). Mercury is peregrine and will potentially run away with the horoscope; this midpoint picture, Mercury=Sun/Pluto, is extremely important.

---

132 Additionally: in Ralph Abernathy's horoscope (see page 38), natal Mercury is exactly square the Pluto-Ascendant opposition, and Uranus conjoins the Sun. At the time of his stroke (March 9, 1983), transiting Pluto was conjunct his Midheaven.

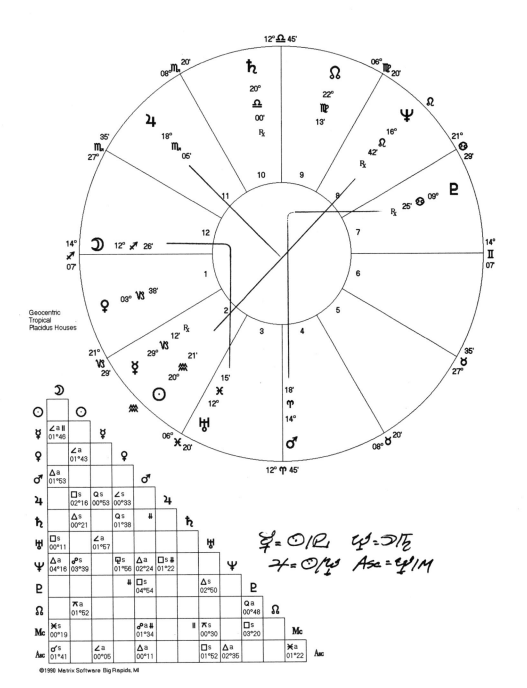

Geocentric
Tropical
Placidus Houses

©1990 Matrix Software Big Rapids, MI

Horoscope 55, Marion March
February 10, 1923, 3:46 A.M. CET
Nürnberg, Germany
11E04 — 49N27

Working with the natal horoscope and approximating Solar Arcs and watching the ephemeris for trigger transits, we can see the arc advance of Uranus to square with the Ascendant at two years of age; the arc of the Midheaven to opposition with Mars is also 2 degrees/years of age, with transiting Pluto squaring the Midheaven in mid-1925. This would be a first time period for inquiry in analysis to test the health profile.

Look at SA Midheaven=Saturn formed at 7½, *with transiting Pluto square natal Saturn*. This was a major time of life reorientation that could have had deep health repercussions, manifestation of anxieties, much as we have seen in our discussion of juvenile onset asthma.

We have a "feel" here, a sense of debilitation established astrologically. In consultation with the client—with Marion—we would search out activation of the matrix we think corresponds to her health debilitation. Determining the sensitivity of horoscope corroboration in her past would support the reliability of warning patterns in the future.

When the stroke occurred (Horoscope 55a), SA Neptune had advanced to tightening the square with natal Mercury. (Note SA Uranus at 23 Taurus; it had been square to natal Sun in August 1991.) There was no outstanding transit activity. The portrait of the stroke is weaker than we would expect. What do we learn from this?

Marion March has a powerful Mercury as we have deduced. Throughout her development with a debilitated health profile, that Mercury has become symbol of her health problems, her lung weakness (and her communication strength). The Mercury was being "attacked" by the Neptune arc, normally not a cause for any alarm; but for Marion, a stroke "happened."

But later, when Marion experienced lung failure (December 12, 1996), this Mercury by Solar Arc had come to 12 Aries 34, *exactly upon her fourth cusp, opposing her Midheaven*. SA Saturn was exactly conjunct her Venus, ruler of the Midheaven (i.e., two angles were implicated strongly). This is no astrological accident.

In McEvers' case the measurements for challenge to the system could have manifested in many different ways: in health breakdown of other parts of her body and/or professional ascendancy and/or a new home and/or much more, all adjusted to her age and life realities, of course. While there had been lifelong borderline high blood pressure but no noted cholesterol problem, her system was apparently strong. Something

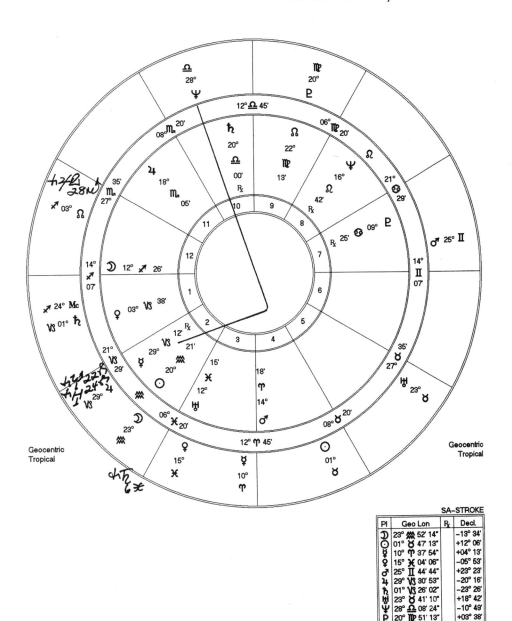

SA–STROKE

Pl	Geo Lon	Rx	Decl.
☽	23° ♒ 52' 14"		−13° 34'
☉	01° ♉ 47' 13"		+12° 06'
☿	10° ♈ 37' 54"		+04° 13'
♀	15° ♓ 04' 06"		−05° 53'
♂	25° ♊ 44' 44"		+23° 23'
♃	29° ♑ 30' 53"		−20° 16'
♄	01° ♑ 26' 02"		−23° 26'
♅	23° ♉ 41' 10"		+18° 42'
♆	28° ♎ 08' 24"		−10° 49'
♇	20° ♍ 51' 13"		+03° 38'

BIWHEEL

Horoscope 55a, Marion March

Inner Chart
February 10, 1923, 3:46 A.M. CET
Nürnberg, Germany
11E04 — 49N27

Outer Ring — Stroke
SA: December 15, 1994
Nuremberg, Germany
11E04 — 49N27

unknown "ordained" the stroke. Astrology before the fact could indeed anticipate *the challenge to the system* but, in this case and in Marion's, *not* specify this threat to life.

In Roosevelt's and March's cases, the body system for each had been debilitated for years before the cerebral hemorrhage and before the stroke and lung failure. For Roosevelt, the warning times were clear, but they were not clear for March. For Marion, however, *respect for the Mercury focal power in her horoscope* could indeed have lifted the potential reliability of the simple pattern that was present at her stroke.

But look at the questions we face: why did a stroke happen to healthy Joan McEvers? Why didn't Roosevelt succumb to pressures within his debilitated system *earlier*, say, early in 1942 when measurements were extremely dramatic? Why does Mercury become so isolatedly powerful for Marion March throughout her life? And earlier in this study: why did General Schwarzkopf's date-twin not develop any Plutonic disorder when he did? Why didn't everyone anywhere born on that same day develop physical problems?

Do overachievers (usually equated with Type A personalities) somehow get through things at their toughest, only to succumb out of schedule, if you will? Are we as *we think* we are?; do our minds help us transcend much of what is apparently due us? As in psychosomatic illness, does the brain somehow select where and when dysfunction will occur? Does Nature strategically select *who* succumbs?

Astrological signatures are not carved in stone; our cursory diagnostic abilities do go a good distance, but we must also know that they do come up short. However, astrological timing goes a long, long distance to afford people life-saving warning and referral, to catch breakdown *if* it is to occur, *before it does.*

The vagaries astrology must deal with impede our quest for the reliabilities promised in scientific method. That some other dimension comes into play in horoscope consultation is undeniable. It issues from the process of corroboration between client and astrologer: with every deductive step, the astrologer's path of surmise is adjusted, more carefully directed. Finally, the astrologer finds the destination *with* the client, and they arrive together. All that has been off the mark has been discarded; what remains is valid and important. In health matters, what remains is often critical.

This process is indeed similar to the enumeration and exploration of symptoms in a medical interview. Sometimes all the symptoms asked about are present consecutively, simultaneously; but sometimes seven are specified and three are confirmed. Those three lead to deeper questions, and finally the doctor sees the target...and so does the patient.

Gradually, as our study has gone through some fifty-five cases, we are finding that, as we approach the brain, the mind, our astrological correspondences begin to lose diagnostic specificity: we are now talking less about the condition of an organ and its dysfunction within the scheme of living and more about *consciousness,* the elusive awareness we have of life itself. The response to the brain by a *totality* of our body functions becomes our paramount focus; and that response is led by the mind, our initiation/response use of brain circuitry.

Please recall the earlier discussion of the brain and the problem with astrological rulership (see pages 39–40). Beyond the cases of Gershwin, Lewis, and Abernathy cited earlier, I have several cases of brain tumor. In not one was the Moon noticeably involved in natal predisposition or critical time development patterns. In one case in particular, a lady—an ex-fashion model—has been hospitalized for surgery thirty-two times in fifty-six years. The key health crises were a brain tumor when she was thirty-one and a mastectomy at fifty-one. In neither of these pivotal crises was the Moon clearly implicated.

But Pluto *was,* at *both* key times. And when I talk about all this with her, I find myself pursuing the textbook suggestions of weakness in her Pisces Moon, which is angular and well aspected, and contrasting that with her indomitable Aries Sun and Scorpio Ascendant. And suddenly, I am directed into the realm of Pluto as ruler of the Ascendant, to the Neptune opposition with her Venus, ruler of the 12th, and more.

I, the analyst, am reaching for significances, for meanings. This is what the geologist does inspecting exposed strata of the earth; so does the safety specialist inspecting a crash site; so does the doctor studying many medical tests. *Not everything is as important as we think it should be.* Conjecture must *cooperate with reality,* more than it must seek to explain it.

Horoscope 56, Male

Horoscope 56 is the horoscope of a male. The Sun-Moon blend promises that "the mental energies will work to identify the ideal, to understand impressions, and work with the intangible. There can be a martyr-like dedication to ideals, to the thoughts and feelings of others." *Uranus squares* this opposition axis and, at the Aries Point, makes these initial deductions extremely important, brings them "front and center" and intensifies them greatly. Jupiter also squares the Sun-Moon axis. We have the suggestion of an exacerbated mental-emotional construct.

Mars is square Venus, ruler of the 12th. Pluto is in sextile contact with Neptune and Mercury, bringing the two together into conjunction. Mercury rules the Ascendant.

The aspect arrangement links the rulers of the parental axis (4th–10th) and self-worth development (2nd), and relationships (7th) in a *cerebrally* tense construct. Additionally the need to think in a balanced, fair way is weakened by Neptune's reach to conjoin Mercury.

The midpoint pictures are very telling: Pluto=Neptune/Ascendant, "feelings of an oppressive environment, difficulty tuning in"; Pluto=Jupiter/Neptune, "self-projection out of hand, major adjustment of life circumstances"; Ascendant=Neptune/Midheaven, "tending to live in one's own foggy realm"; Jupiter=Saturn/Neptune, "very upset with the ways of the world."

We begin to feel a need to escape from tension.

At the time shown here, SA Pluto conjoined the Sun exactly, SA Mars opposed the Ascendant, and SA Uranus had just exactly conjoined Venus, ruler of the 12th. Transiting Pluto was exactly square its natal position, and transiting Saturn-Neptune were conjoined in 12 Capricorn exactly squaring the natal Neptune-Mercury conjunction. At this time, the man began to "hear voices," warning about and explaining a conspiracy against his family.

This man is gentle and well-mannered to a fault, appears to be very intelligent, but now lives with his voices in vagrancy and filth as a street person.

Discussions with this man *before* his break with society would certainly have revealed signs of disorientation. His suspicions and extreme sensitivity to slights and plots against him and his family by others, his secretive nature with this information, his exaggeration of all the

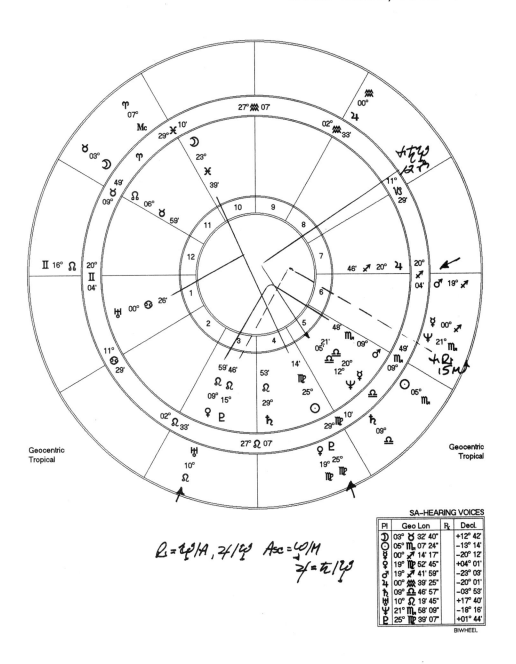

Horoscope 56, Male
Outer Ring — Hearing Voices
SA: February 5, 1989

problems, his blaming others for his plight, and his lack of circumspect humor or insight into the situation would have suggested paranoid personality disorder.

This man's imagined realities would easily play into his sensitivities to ideals, to his martyr-like potential to the way things are or should be. The time for his "hearing voices," the climax of his developmental change in life perspective—his escape from unfinished business in development—would have loomed large in his future, and the astrologer could have directed him to professional psychiatric help.

In this case, it is easy to expect some extraordinarily articulated Mercury problem. But at first study, we have a wide, simple conjunction of Mercury with Neptune. Then, we see that Mercury rules the Ascendant; that Neptune (and therefore Mercury) is involved with some recessive and confused midpoint pictures. But is this "enough" to put our man over the hill and out of the flow of society?

Note that Mercury is the dispositor of the Sun and Neptune is the dispositor of the Moon. This adds tremendously to Mercury's power focus here; indeed, to Mercury-Neptune's island of safety, sextile Venus (ruler of the 12th). Against whatever is symbolized in this man's reality by Saturn opposed Midheaven and the parental rulership grouping, this man's mind led him to serious, earnest, dedicated avoidance.

The accumulated problems this man has faced in life are his individualized *deficit-rating,* a concept that takes on great importance for the rest of our study; he lives with an accumulated deficit in development. We all do. The deficit comes to us genetically—the thread of diabetes running through family history, for example; the age of death, from the parents to their children, for another—and empirically, through our interaction with our families, their nurture of us, their modeling of behaviors for us, and eventually our contrast with them as we pursue individuation. This sense of accumulated deficit to one degree or another *begins to articulate the unseen, the unknown.*

Horoscope 57, Oscar Levant

Horoscope 57 is another horoscope that suggests the strong deficit that is developed in family life experience; the reality of the life that did indeed present mental aberrance...as well as phenomenal success and notoriety...to the world.

This is the horoscope of Oscar Levant whose musical talent (piano, composition) lifted him from the streets of New York City in his teens into the deepest of collaborative relationships with George Gershwin, into a concert career of his own that dominated the classical scene nationally, into a series of four-star movie appearances, the writing of many books, and TV stardom as a brilliant brain of facts and comedic one-liners; addiction to morphine, heart attacks, deep neurosis, commitment to sanitariums, all of which were parlayed into extraordinary public exposure for entertainment value. Levant was the very sick, celebrated, entertaining genius to the American people from about 1937 to 1972.[133]

Four dramatic measurement pictures are remarkable in this horoscope: Pluto conjunct the Midheaven, which almost always parallels some dimension of exhibitionism and public display; the Aries point configurations include eight midpoint combinations corroborating the Pluto Midheaven position; the Water Grand Trine—always a defense mechanism of emotional self-sufficiency—introduces a protection system that operates independently from the Sun-Moon blend (since the Grand Trine does not include the Sun or Moon), a split in the personality; and a peregrine Mercury, ruling the Ascendant and the Midheaven.[134]

Additionally, it is important to feel the Uranus conjunction with the Sun and the paradoxical opposition with Jupiter-Neptune: it is as if we have intensity blurred somehow, idiosyncratic development veiled or somehow complicated.

We note that the Sun rules the 12th and receives a quindecile from Pluto. Levant's obsession with public exposure threatens who he is; he is lured to it and fearful of it. Uranus is also quindecile Pluto, including the Midheaven; and Saturn, within the Water Grand Trine, is *quindecile the Ascendant.*

---

133 The literature records 11:45 p.m. as Levant's birthtime "from his birth certificate." But I think that the birth certificate is inaccurate. The time I present in this case, 11:27 p.m., alters the Midheaven and Ascendant from 27 Gemini 16 and 27 Virgo 37, respectively, to 23 Gemini 07 and 24 Virgo 02. Arcs and transits correlate life experiences far better with this earlier time.

134 Indeed, Mercury could be stretched to the 6-degree orb here to a square with Saturn; Levant's lifelong depression would corroborate it. But Levant's conspicuous brilliance, opinionation, and prolific communication skills, all converted to professional assets, suggest the outstanding, commanding, intense loneliness of peregrination.

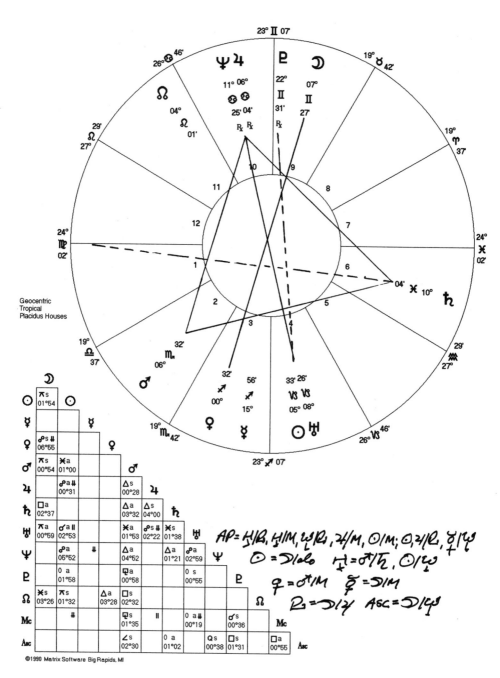

Horoscope 57, Oscar Levant
December 27, 1906, 11:27 P.M. EST
Pittsburgh, PA
79W59 — 40N26

There are very real warnings here: a highly developed publicly catapulted personality; a mind-set that runs wild, and a feeling of loss, of pain, or separateness.

Levant lived a life of sarcasm, at war with the world (Neptune retrograde rules the 7th). His brilliance became legend; his one-liners devastated everyone entertainingly, because they were wrapped in comedic delivery, both to help Levant discharge the thoughts and the public to manage them.

There is no doubt in astrology that Mercury references and Virgo references have a strong place in the syndrome of addiction, in neurosis. Levant was an obsessive compulsive neurotic; he himself quipped famously, "Rituals have taken the place of religion for me" and "I'm terrified of people, and they cooperate!"

What made Levant's horoscope go in this direction? There were other children born in Pittsburgh that day, near that same time; how many other problematic geniuses were there?

Genetically, reincarnationally, we do not yet know the legacy that defines, even selects individuality. But empirically, we do know much about the environment of deficit-potential in the early home, and this horoscope corroborates the painful early years in Oscar's development. Someone with a horoscope similar to Levant's would depart from Levant's identity development through genetic inheritance and other levels of early home-life developmental tensions, and other considerations not yet linked with the horoscope.

Pluto retrograde on the Midheaven, the enormous tension axis within the parental axis, Neptune's conjunction with the ruler of the 4th, and Mercury's peregrine state, ruling both the Midheaven and Ascendant, all suggest a highly tense family environment that would affect Oscar's development strongly, confusingly...dare we say psycho-neurologically?

It is known through biographical record of this most famous man, that Oscar was never, ever able to win his father's approval. Additionally, Oscar's mother inculcated feelings of deepest inferiority in him, making him a "mamma's boy" and having him sleep in a crib until he was eight years old (note the maternal/paternal tensions and, as well, Saturn square Moon, ruler of the 11th, the need for love; Mars square the Nodal axis).[135]

---

135 Any planet or point configurated by conjunction or square with the mean Lunar Nodal Axis, within 2-degree orb, almost invariably corresponds with an extraordinary influence of the mother in terms of the planet-need symbol involved. Mercury-Node, for example: the influence of the mother is of paramount importance in one's thinking process, mind set, etc. See Tyl, *Synthesis & Counseling in Astrology*, pages 49–64.

Uranus—prominent along with Mercury, as we have been discussing—is at the midpoint of Mars/Saturn promising intense drive, breaking loose from confinement, gaining independence through struggle, deep upset, confrontation with the life-death issue (challenging death?). The beginning of Oscar's rebellion was seen in his obstreperous behavior in school; his nascent genius emerged through his piano lessons, exposing him quickly as a prodigious talent.

Oscar's father died when he was fourteen and one half. His mother took him to New York City and left the fifteen-year old there, abandoned, with his talent, wits, and not much else. He found a way to play for Ignace Paderewski, the great Polish pianist and diplomat, in December 1922 (with transiting Pluto on his natal Neptune). Paderewski devalued the boy's efforts soundly, saying that "he had no soul." Here was a gigantic echo of the early homelife. Oscar was devastated for years. The deficit was growing.

When Levant met up with Gershwin the two became very close, but Levant bristled with frustration at being in George's shadow, being a scapegoat to George's egotistical upsets. This reaction was severe and permanent and haunted Levant throughout his life and appeared repeatedly in his one-liners, in his conversation, in the ad-libs that sparkled in his movies, in his television shows. References to the famous Gershwin were opening a window for Levant's insecurity and death wish.

Could astrology have seen this coming, about to develop, having already developed to one degree or another? Yes. But the *level* of musical talent, the *level* and circumstances of public outreach, the *level* of sickness would have to be clarified by Levant's reality. The horoscope *can* be fit to the individual's reality. It is that fit that facilitates astrology's *anticipation* of reality in the future.

Horoscope 58, David Helfgott

Horoscope 58 is the horoscope of David Helfgott, whose difficult early life and prodigious early talent were the focus of the award-winning film "Shine" (1996).[136]

The drama of the film and his life certainly is the mental breakdown David suffered, attributed to his relationship with an extraordinarily oppressive father. The tension of the parental axis rulers brings this clearly forward; squaring Saturn in the self-worth second. This is reiterated through the midpoint pictures that follow:

- Midheaven=AP=Sun/Saturn: the "lone wolf," lacking the feeling of success; isolation

- Neptune=Saturn/Ascendant: depressing and introverted life situations; tension about strange and obscure things

- Neptune=Pluto/Node: win at any cost

- Pluto=Neptune/Ascendant: feelings of an oppressive environment

- Venus=Sun/Midheaven: the arts, aesthetics, sociability

The organization of the horoscope emphasizes the Eastern hemisphere clearly, a defensive posture, guarding Ascendant sensibilities. And there we see Uranus peregrine: the extraordinary bid for individuation.

Going more deeply, we see Mars conjunct Venus, ruler of the 4th *and* the 12th. Venus is dispositor of both Sun and Moon: this blend of the Sun and Moon in Taurus promises behaviors that preserve security, that pursue the need to please, to keep things as they are or as they are supposed to be (the perfectionism dimension that was isolated and exploited by the father). These energies characteristically want and invite authority and leadership, protection and reinforcement. The father stepped right in on these needs.

A growth deficit that would be accumulated in the family environment was promised by the natal horoscope, as it is in so many horoscopes. But

---

136 Helfgott's birthtime circulated in the world is set for 8:28 A.M. GST. It is a rectified birthtime. In my study of the horoscope and the life, I discover that a shift in time to 8:28 A.M., altering the Midheaven from 27 Pisces 31 to 00 Aries 15 is extremely significant: it introduces the Aries Point to the Midheaven and, therefore, the cardinal-sign parental rulership axis articulated by the Mars-Venus conjunction, etc. Arcs and transits accompanying Helfgott's extraordinary vault back into public prominence work strongly with this cardinal-sign Midheaven axis. This time of 8:38 A.M., respectfully submitted, must indeed be evaluated seriously.

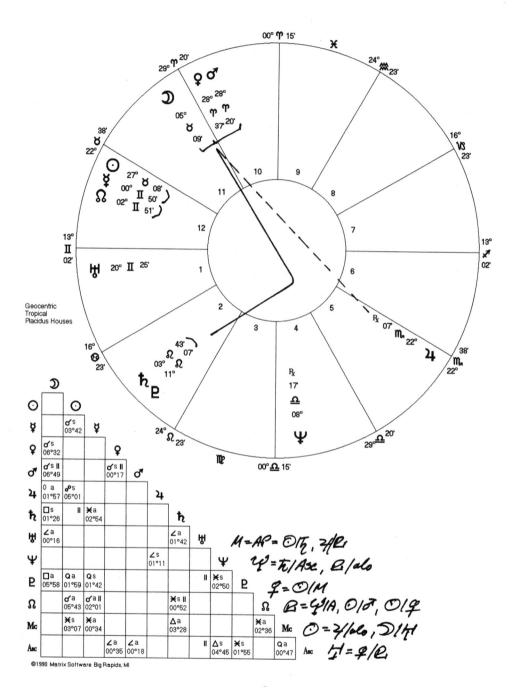

©1990 Matrix Software Big Rapids, MI

Horoscope 58, David Helfgott
May 19, 1947, 8:38 A.M. GST
Melbourne, Australia
144W58 — 37S49

the degree to which it would hurt young David's mental health can *not* be determined from the horoscope. Many, many variables come into play: the father's development within his own life as a persecuted Jew, his personal reactions to Second World War experiences, professional frustrations, needs served by music, gender identification and projection with and onto his son, denial/exploration of his son's Uranian press for individuation, the fight against David's defense mechanisms, their management of love issues together, David's mind's work to protect tortured sensibilities, especially with the intense need for relationship (Jupiter, ruler of the 7th, quindecile with the Moon).

All of these concerns are *beyond the planets.* These individualistically articulated concerns are what *bring the planets to life,* to David Helfgott's life; the planets then become guidelines to appreciate potential and development.

Mercury and Uranus have indeed come forward (recall page 206) as we study the brain, the mind, and the nervous center that articulate consciousness. Levant's Mercury was peregrine and ubiquitous; Helfgott's Uranus is peregrine and ubiquitous. These are important astrological statements; they are distinctively infrequent astrological occurrences.

Suicide

In our study, we have seen over and over again the activation of the angles of the horoscope in parallel with the onset or climax of critical illness. We have seen the ubiquity of Pluto, then Neptune and Saturn in the main, along with the startling quindecile aspect; and, at the same time, the key involvements of the outer planets in transit. Please look again at the Final Review of the Early Warning Patterns (page 170).

I have suggested that perhaps there is no specific rulership for the brain (page 40–41). Perhaps the horoscope *in its entirety* is the imprint of the brain, with each planet carrying into behavior a portion of that consciousness. We see suicide as the ultimate sense of futility experienced by the brain, a totality framed in the mind.

For example, we know that the Arc or Transit of Neptune over or square an angle of the horoscope corresponds most often to the elimination of ego definition, a "wipe-out" of some kind through drugs and/or alcohol, through delusion, through fantasy, through bewildering circumstance. This correspondence seems to occur more powerfully with the engagement of an angle than it does even in relation to the Sun or Moon.

We hear about the mind working against disease—the benefits of visualization and prayer that have indeed been clinically tested affirmatively—and then about the mind opening the body to the intrusion of disease, e.g., psychosomatic illness. And now, in our study of the brain, we are seeing the prominence of Mercury and the strong statements of Uranus, much like thought-center and thought-dispersion energy, respectively. When we say that "how we think is how we are," we are capturing this idea instinctively.

When we face suicide, we are confronting the ultimate critical illness, if you will. Psychoanalyst Edwin Shneidman, has studied suicide for some forty-seven years and is perhaps the world's most authoritative researcher of the subject. He has advanced the study of suicide far beyond the earliest pioneering work of Emile Durkheim, the French sociologist (1858–1917), who lay suicide innovatively in the lap of social systems and pressures. Dr. Shneidman presents suicide as "psychache," the result of holistic psychological pain rather than as the result of a specific psychological disease. The key to preventing suicide is not so much in the study of the structures of the brain or the study of social statistics about education, living style, demographics, etc. or even the study of mental diseases but more in the study, as directly as possible, of human emotions.

Shneidman sees lethality—suicidal death—as fulfillment of the idea to stop the psychache, to bring to an end the "complete" pain one is all too aware of. He argues for whole-person treatment rather than treatment of suicide as a disease that might be stimulating suicidal ideas: "We live our lives in pursuit of psychological needs. When an individual commits suicide, that person is trying to blot out psychological pain that stems from thwarted psychological needs 'vital' for that person."[137]

Suicide is now the third leading cause of death among American adolescents. In young adults, suicide is the second leading cause of death. The suicide rate among the young is rising rapidly; an estimated 500,000 teenagers *survive* suicide attempts each year, with many others—successes or failures—going uncounted because many attempted suicides are reported as accidents.[138]

---

137 Shneidman, page 18.
138 Mayo, page 135.

Early Warning

Shneidman has proved in clinical tests that *the occurrence of suicide can be detected ahead of time*. He asks then, "If suicide can be identified several years before it happens, does this mean that suicide is embedded in the life history? Are individuals star-crossed and unable to change their own fates? Is suicide in the character, 'bred in the bone'? Is one's life history immutable? To what extent is it malleable? Can things be done to prevent suicide?"[139]

Early warning astrological patterns for suicide are similar to early warning patterns for other critical illnesses, with perhaps intensified emphasis of angular "attack" and intensified interplay with accumulated psychological deficit (my term, being developed throughout this study), from the early homelife and the patterns that emerge in young development.

Shneidman's research points up that relationships with the father are more critical than relationships with the mother with reference to early warning patterns. These relationships, when negative, plant a seed of rejection (obvious or subtle) within the child's development. Astrology suspects (sees) this to one degree or another through the Saturn retrograde phenomenon, Saturn in demanding aspect with the Sun or Moon or Ascendant (or its ruler), almost invariably corroborated by developmental tension with one or both significators of the parental axis.[140]

Measures of success—objective measurement and self-measurement—are very important in the suicide profile. The trait-labels ascribed to the "most successful" (the dramatically less liable to commit suicide) are "ambitious, capable, competitive, contented, fair-minded, intelligent, outgoing, reasonable, secure, self-controlled, sincere, and sophisticated." The trait-labels ascribed to the "least successful" are "cautious, defensive, depressed, dissatisfied, frustrated, lonely, reserved, and vulnerable."

Early indications of "negatives" (say, before age twenty) are key identifiers of the potential suicide: alcoholism, suicide threats, homosexuality, conspicuous achievement failures, depression, neurasthenia (extraordinary, constant fatigue), marriage and divorce, and difficulty breathing (asthma, emphysema).

---

139 Shneidman, pages 83–84.
140 Please see Tyl, *Synthesis & Counseling in Astrology*, pages 35–48; 225–245.

Another key appears to be the support of one's spouse. Hostility, non-supportiveness, competitiveness, or domination in marital relationship exacerbates other deficit-significant dispositions.[141]

The commonalities of suicide include the thought-out desire to end unbearable psychological pain brought on by the lack of fulfillment of psychological needs; a sense of hopelessness and ambivalence; constricted perspective; and an extension of lifelong patterns of disorientation or futility, ways of coping with difficulties in life that are regularly (accumulatively) debilitating.

Shneidman offers many insights to these commonalities; here is one of them:

> ...there are some consistencies with how that individual has coped with previous setbacks. We must look to previous episodes of disturbance, dark times in that life, to assess the individual's capacity to endure psychological pain. We need to see whether or not there is a penchant for constriction and dichotomous thinking, a tendency to throw in the towel, for earlier paradigms of escape and egression.
>
> Information would lie in the details and nuances of *how* jobs were quit, how spouses were divorced, and how psychological pain was managed. This repetition of a tendency to capitulate, to flee, to blot it out, to escape is perhaps the most telling single clue to an ultimate suicide.[142]

We know people behave in individualized ways; they are consistent to the mold, so to speak, the individual mold. And that mold is reflected in the horoscope: the Sun-Moon blend, the dominant aspects, the hemisphere emphasis, rulership dynamics, and midpoint-point pictures. The needs are defined, and life becomes the process of working to fulfill those needs. Time development through Arcs and Transits marks the progress. It is extremely difficult for a human being to operate out of that mold, to behave "out of character." Humans rarely change their need focus and the behaviors to fulfill those needs.

At the center of his work, Shneidman presents an adaptation of psychological needs formulated in the 1930s by psychologist Henry A. Murray. Our astrology can reflect these needs well. For example, in my astrological work for twenty-five years, I have presented the reigning need of the Moon in Aries as "the need to be Number One." This

---

141 Shneidman, pages 86–88.
142 Shneidman, pages 135–136.

certainly fits Murray's "Dominance" need, to control, influence, and direct others.[143]

We have the reigning need of the Moon in Sagittarius as the need to have one's opinions respected; to be dramatically allied with the big picture. This need certainly fits Murray's need for "Understanding—to know answers, to know the hows and whys"; the reigning need of the Moon in Capricorn as the need to get things done to make things happen, to administer progress certainly reflects Murray's need for "Rejecting—to exclude, banish, jilt, or expel another person."[144]

There are many congruencies between what we know in astrology and what Shneidman presents from Murray: the needs for "Nurturance, Order, Counteraction, Affiliation, Abasement" certainly live through the Moon in Cancer, Taurus, Scorpio, Libra, Pisces, respectively. There is the need for "Defendance," which is caught up with vindicating the self against criticism or blame, clearly a need pronouncedly of Moon in Virgo.

While the Moon registers the reigning need, the chief embracing need of our life, using the Sun's sign-characteristic energy for fulfillment, the need concepts extend to the planets as well. (See page 8.) Everything works together to fulfill life, to define consciousness, to explain why we exist (or don't) in terms of life space (Ascendant) and life time (Midheaven). All this defines the two key continua of our existence.

Horoscope 59, Marilyn Monroe

Shneidman devised a point system to relate needs to individual lives, to objectify need-press to fulfillment. For example, for Marilyn Monroe (Horoscope 59, page 228), the highest ranking need focus (16) is given to "Exhibition—to excite, fascinate, amuse, entertain others." In astrological terms, this is a clear profile of Gemini needs. Monroe had Sun-Mercury conjunction in Gemini in the 10th, a peregrine island, if I may, making no other Ptolemaic aspect in the horoscope.[145]

---

143 In studying Shneidman's work, *The Suicidal Mind*, I identified on practically every page with his reference to individual needs and the drive we have to fulfill these needs. This approach was most comfortable for me in the alliance I have tried to forge between Psychological Need Theory and Astrology. It was then a delight rather than a surprise to learn that Shneidman and I both had studied with Dr. Henry A. Murray at Harvard, one of the great need-theorist innovators of 20th century psychology.

144 Please see full study of 144 Sun-Moon polarities in terms of energy and needs in Tyl, *Synthesis & Counseling in Astrology*, pages 65–102.

145 The strength of this conjunction is even more established by Mercury' position as final dispositor, dignified in its own sign and, of course, the Sun ruling the Ascendant.

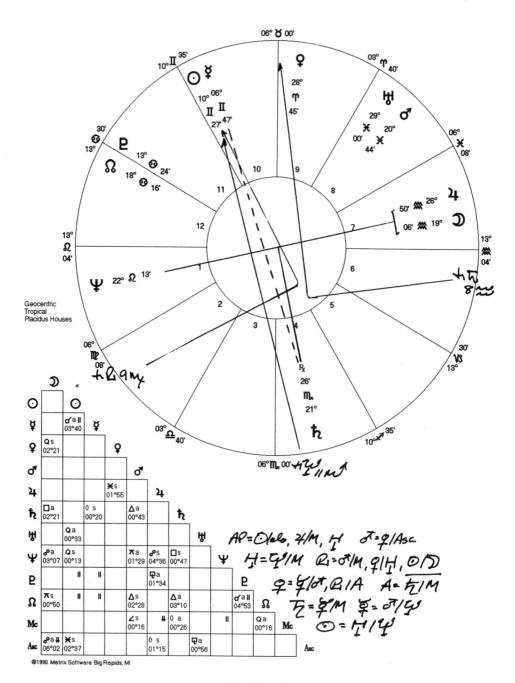

Horoscope 59, Marilyn Monroe
June 1, 1926, 9:30 A.M. PST
Los Angeles, CA
118W15 — 34N03

Her next highest ranked need focus was for "Succorance—to have one's needs gratified, to be loved (12)," which clearly is a Leo need complex, as we have here focused on her Leo Ascendant, opposed by the Moon in Aquarius in the 7th, with Jupiter making a quindecile with the Ascendant from the 7th.

The next highest need was for "Deference—to admire and support, praise, emulate a superior (10)," which clearly expresses a Piscean need focus. Monroe had Mars in Pisces (a subordinating position for Mars), weakly aspected. Mars also squared the midpoint of Venus/Ascendant, "using one's charm or sexiness to make something happen." Marilyn used this need for deference as a strategy in her life to gain love and acceptance, i.e., to help fulfill the succorance need (Leo) at the Ascendant. (See also, Case 65, page 241.)

The need for "Inviolacy—to protect the self and one's psychological space" clearly equates with Scorpio. In Monroe's ranking, this need was ranked a 4, near the bottom of the scale. Monroe's Saturn retrograde, in the parental 4th, isolated in the northern hemisphere, corroborating her traumatic relationship with her father (and other father figures) and much more difficulty, was square her Moon and *quindecile her Mercury*. The problems here consumed Marilyn's psyche, her mind; she was unable to protect herself; this need was constantly pressing for fulfillment, always frustrated.

Marilyn's Moon in Aquarius, using the Sun's Gemini energy, suggests a truly people-sensitive focus, a longing for intellectual study, for diversification, for communication, a public outreach for sure. This dominating need thrust was certainly undermined heavily by early-life experience; the deficit was building. In Murray's need list, Aquarius reflects the need for "Autonomy—to be independent and free; to shake off restraint (ranked at 5 points)." The deficit weight symbolized by Saturn retrograde square the Moon made fulfillment of this need life-consumingly difficult.

Shneidman distinguishes two kinds of psychological needs among the twenty isolated for study: those *modal* needs that characterize the "ongoing personality," the needs the person lives with; and those the individual focuses on when he or she is under pressure, suffering inner tension and being in mental pain. These latter needs are the needs that become intensified under duress: "these are the needs an individual is willing to *die for*, the *vital* needs."[146]

---

146 Shneidman, page 24.

When a person becomes suicidal, the inner focus shifts to these *vital* needs. Under life pressure, Marilyn focused on the needs of lower rank, those unfulfilled, those that formed life behaviors and, in their painfulness, were somehow put aside, into the background. The Saturn retrograde focus in Scorpio speaks eloquently here, a vital need thwarted in early life, weakening the system, raising its head in her marriages, and finally exhausting itself in complete loss, the ultimate deficit.

When Marilyn committed suicide on August 4, 1962, transiting Pluto was squaring her Sun, transiting Saturn was squaring her Midheaven, and transiting Neptune was squaring her Ascendant all at the same time. Her SA Midheaven was exactly conjunct her Sun.

Could this have been anticipated? Yes: the early warning signals from early life, the alcoholism, drug dependencies, relationship problems, and failures professionally, the public embarrassments, and more came to a peak with the earlier transit of Neptune across her fourth cusp and opposed her Midheaven. This astrological signal would have keyed into view the other angularly powerful transits soon to form simultaneously in her future. Combined with the life history, communicated threats of suicide, and the debilitated psychological need profile, the potential of suicide would have been all too clear. The angles of the horoscope dominate the portrait of disorientation and lethality.

Horoscope 60, Ernest Hemingway

Horoscope 60 belongs to Ernest Hemingway, who, on the crest of an extraordinary literary career, committed suicide on July 2, 1961, just nineteen days short of his sixty-second birthday.

Hemingway's horoscope is absolutely dominated by the opposition of Saturn retrograde and Pluto, and that axis is squared by Mars in Virgo, rising in the Ascendant: "fighting battles to keep life going; enormous undercurrent of frustration; a gun with a cork in its barrel."

With the Sun in Cancer and the Moon in Capricorn, a conflict is suggested between emotional energies and practical drives in life. The need here is to set oneself apart, to make things happen the way the ego must have it.

We see that there is great difficult suggested in the early homelife, identifying the father figure strongly (Saturn retrograde and its aspect configuration). There is the confusing and deeply intrusive relationship

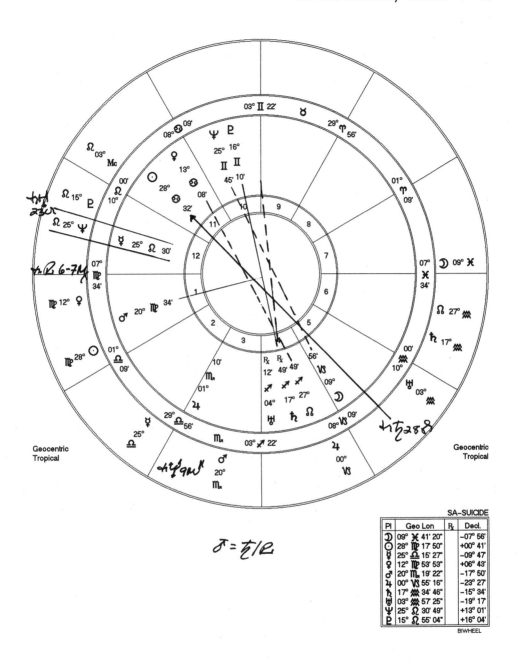

Horoscope 60, Ernest Hemingway

Inner Chart	Outer Ring — Suicide
July 21, 1899, 8:00 A.M. CST	SA: July 2, 1961
Oak Park, IL	
87W47 — 41N53	

between Neptune and the Moon, mapped by the quindecile between them. (This quindecile is also the potential inspiration indicator for his creativity.)[147]

The Moon-Neptune relationship is echoed by the Venus-Node quindecile: a second very strong emphasis of maternal concerns. The Moon is opposed Venus. The Moon rules the 11th, the House of love received, hoped for, needed, assumed.

- Hemingway's father was a doctor; he wanted Ernest to be a doctor too. Hemingway's mother wanted him to be a cellist. Young Ernest rebelled throughout his youth against the Victorian ways of his home and his parents. He boxed and played football, and ran away from home at age fifteen.

We must remind ourselves of the special attention to Mercury and Uranus emerging in our study of the brain and the totality of the life system. Hemingway's Mercury rules his Midheaven and his Ascendant, and his Uranus squares his Ascendant from the homelife-4th House.

Notice the defensive protection of planetary orientation toward the Ascendant, emphasizing the Eastern hemisphere. And lastly, note that the most difficult Saturn retrograde within the Pluto opposition axis is *quindecile the Midheaven:* this horoscope shows an enormous potential for developmental deficit and grief, for great trauma and an involvement with matters of death (Mars=Saturn/Pluto).

- Hemingway returned home after his rebellion at fifteen but then left home for good two years later. After repeated rejections by the U.S. Army, he wrangled his way into World War I as an ambulance driver in Italy. He was severely wounded on July 8, 1918, with 227 steel fragments entering his body.

- Over the years, Hemingway lived through his father's suicide by gunshot in 1928, a dozen operations on his knee, a skull fracture once, at least a dozen brain concussions, three auto accidents, two airplane crashes in two days, and gunshots through nine parts of his body; he had high blood pressure, an enlarged liver, and had received twenty-five electroshock therapies at the Mayo Clinic. In life and in his writing, he was obsessed with violent death.

---

147 This Moon-Neptune quindecile is an echo of that same relationship in the horoscope of Leonardo da Vinci (please see rectification study in Tyl, *Astrology of the Famed*). It is a keen focus on the mother figure as well as the potential for disorientation and inspiration.

Hemingway became the most celebrated writer of fiction in the world, dealing with themes of death and weak men warring against the world. Suddenly, in 1940, at the prime of his popularity, with SA Sun exactly on his Ascendant, Hemingway stopped writing, for ten years. Into that period, SA Mars squared the Sun, and SA Saturn, coming out of the opposition with Pluto, opposed his Sun, as SA Pluto was applying to conjoin the Sun!

When Hemingway shot himself in 1961, *SA Neptune was exactly conjoined with his natal Mercury,* ruler of Ascendant and Midheaven. Transiting Saturn was opposed the Sun and transiting Pluto was conjunct the Ascendant.

Could these exact measurements have been seen ahead of time? Yes, of course; we could have been especially alerted two years earlier by the important arc of the Moon conjoining the 7th cusp, opposing the Ascendant. and we would have seen that Hemingway was acutely vulnerable to mental breakdown with the accumulated life deficit established clearly throughout all his development. With the accumulation of these severe measurements, his mind could no longer cope with "things."

Symbolically, Hemingway's Moon in Capricorn had never got moving to fulfillment, in marriages or relationships of any kind (quindecile Neptune, ruler of the 7th); he could never carve his individual place in the world. Masked by the external war hero and adventurer image, weakness and confusion prevailed in Hemingway's inner environment and in the victim-heroes of his novels.

Horoscope 61, Judy Garland

Horoscope 61 (page 234) is a repeat of Judy Garland's horoscope (see page 25) showing the developed measurements to her drug overdose June 22, 1969. While there is no conspicuous angular "attack" (the exception, not the norm), there is a tremendous intensification of the problematic natal Mercury by the square from transiting Uranus, which simultaneously was exactly conjunct natal Saturn.

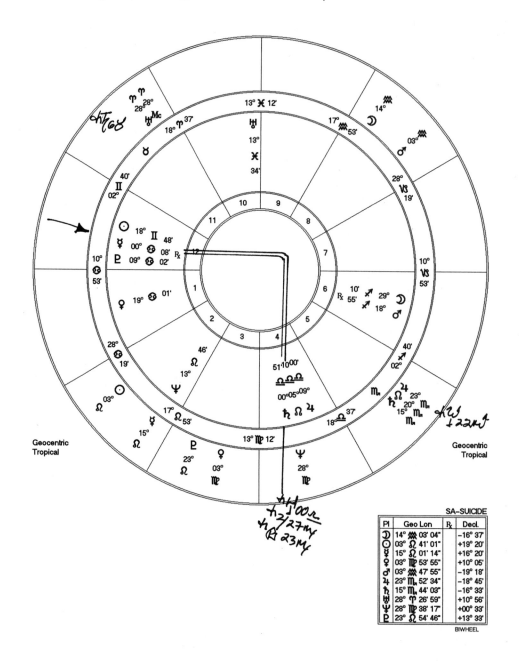

Pl	Geo Lon	℞	Decl.
☽	14° ♒ 03' 04"		−16° 37'
☉	03° ♌ 41' 01"		+19° 20'
☿	15° ♌ 01' 14"		+16° 20'
♀	03° ♍ 53' 55"		+10° 05'
♂	03° ♒ 47' 55"		−19° 18'
♃	23° ♏ 52' 34"		−18° 45'
♄	15° ♏ 44' 03"		−16° 33'
♅	28° ♈ 26' 59"		+10° 56'
♆	28° ♍ 38' 17"		+00° 33'
♇	23° ♌ 54' 46"		+13° 33'

SA–SUICIDE

BIWHEEL

Horoscope 61, Judy Garland

Inner Chart
June 10, 1922, 6:00 A.M. CST
Grand Rapids, MN
93W32 — 47N14

Outer Ring — Suicide
SA: June 22, 1969

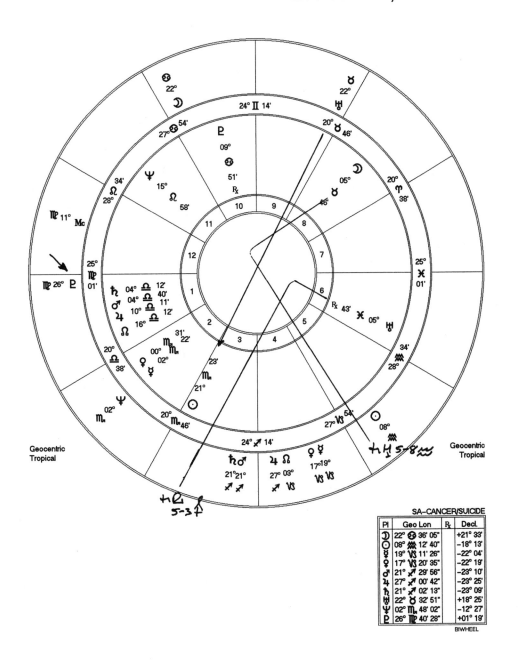

SA–CANCER/SUICIDE			
Pl	Geo Lon	℞	Decl.
☽	22° ♋ 36' 05"		+21° 33'
☉	08° ♒ 12' 40"		−18° 13'
☿	19° ♑ 11' 26"		−22° 04'
♀	17° ♑ 20' 35"		−22° 19'
♂	21° ♐ 29' 56"		−23° 10'
♃	27° ♐ 00' 42"		−23° 25'
♄	21° ♐ 02' 13"		−23° 09'
♅	22° ♉ 32' 51"		+18° 25'
♆	02° ♏ 48' 02"		−12° 27'
♇	26° ♍ 40' 28"		+01° 19'

BIWHEEL

Horoscope 62, Brian Keith

Inner Chart
November 14, 1921, 2:00 A.M. EST
Bayonne, NJ
74W07 — 40N40

Outer Ring — Cancer/Suicide
SA: June 23, 1997

Geocentric
Tropical

Geocentric
Tropical

Horoscope 62, Brian Keith

Horoscope 62 belongs to movie (eighty films) and television actor Brain Keith, who had cancer and who committed suicide on June 23, 1997.

At suicide, SA Pluto had come to his Ascendant, an extremely important time of life indeed. "Dramatic changes in perspective are possible. There can be identity transformation; taking command of things. It is a time of life milestone."

For Keith, this period if seen ahead of time *had* to suggest danger: arcing Pluto had come out of the 10th, out of its natal squares to Mars-Saturn and Jupiter rising in the Ascendant. At the same time SA Uranus was opposed the Sun.

Transiting Pluto was square natal Uranus, and transiting Uranus was square the Moon.

All of these measurements are threats *that arouse the natal configuration of Pluto,* its square with the cluster in the Ascendant. That Keith had severe physical debilitation with critical illness (cancer) at the same time as his suicide is clearly suggested within the patterns we have learned to analyze.

Horoscope 63, Michel Gauquelin

Astrologer-researcher Michel Gauquelin committed suicide May 21, 1991.

SA Neptune was conjunct his Mercury (having crossed his IC three and one-half years earlier), SA Saturn was exactly square his Sun, ruler of his Ascendant; SA Uranus was exactly opposed his Moon, ruler of his 12th. Additionally, transiting Neptune was opposed natal Pluto in the 12th. Transiting Pluto was applying to his Sun.

Natally, Gauquelin had the Aries Point=Mars/Saturn (1 degree 18 minutes orb), a difficult astrological signal, bringing life and death issues, extremism, the tragic or melodramatic view forward.

Saturn was opposite the Uranus/Neptune midpoint promising depression and loss of confidence. This natal Saturn conjoined Venus in the 5th and neither planet made any other Ptolemaic aspect in the horoscope. This focuses a need deficit in development within the emotions, the process of giving love, dealing with love issues. The Mars quindecile with Venus intensifies this deeply. The Sagittarian need here for understanding was undoubtedly difficult to fulfill for this brilliant statistician, astrologer researcher, when the need was involved with the world of emotions.

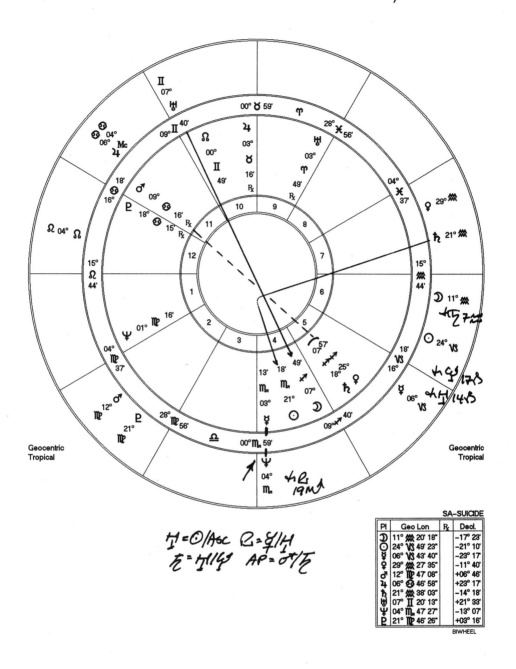

Horoscope 63, Michel Gauquelin

Inner Chart
Nov. 13, 1928, 10:15 P.M. GMT
Paris, France
02E20 — 48N52

Outer Ring — Suicide
SA: May 21, 1991

Horoscope 64, Adolf Hitler

Horoscope 64 belongs to Adolf Hitler, who committed suicide on April 30, 1945 in his underground bunker in Berlin as his world crumbled above him. His Moon-in-Capricorn need complex (to reject others for personal/national ascendancy) was mortally unfulfilled.

The natal square between Saturn and Mars-Venus is extremely critical here, with Venus retrograde ruling the Ascendant and the 12th House. This type of inter-relationship between Ascendant and the 12th House easily suggests being one's own worst enemy, to one degree or another; the undoing of one's lot in life. It is fascinating in Hitler's horoscope to find the Aries Point configured with the midpoint of Mars/Saturn and Venus/Saturn, the dispassionate confrontation with who lives/who dies issues.

Mercury is in a critical position here, conjunct the seventh cusp, conjoining the Sun and opposing the Ascendant. In Aries, this Mercury comes to signify the "Dominance" need. Mercury is also squaring the midpoint of Sun/Uranus: "quickness of mind; the spark of understanding; the harsh word; seeing things too analytically for comfort". And this image is complicated (modified) by Neptune=Moon/Mercury, "an active imagination, falsehood, delusion".

Uranus is peregrine in the 12th, again a measurement suggesting self-undoing, i.e., rebelling, asserting, pushing into nowhere, into limitation; working contextually with the Ascendant ruler, Venus, being retrograde and conjoined Mars.

When Hitler committed suicide, SA Pluto and Neptune had arced to square with his Ascendant, a colossally dangerous and debilitating measurement.[148]

SA Saturn was square his Moon. Transiting Neptune was applying to square his Moon.[149]

---

148 The conjunction of Pluto and Neptune was a major generational signature shared by enormous populations active in WWII, i.e., arcing within individual horoscopes to individual angles, etc. with extraordinary corroboration within a war-torn world.

149 This is a very seldom seen case where the Secondary Progressed Ascendant (see 4 Sagittarius) was significantly involved with a critical portrait: Hitler's SP Ascendant was at 4 Sagittarius exactly opposite his Pluto in the 8th House at the time of suicide.

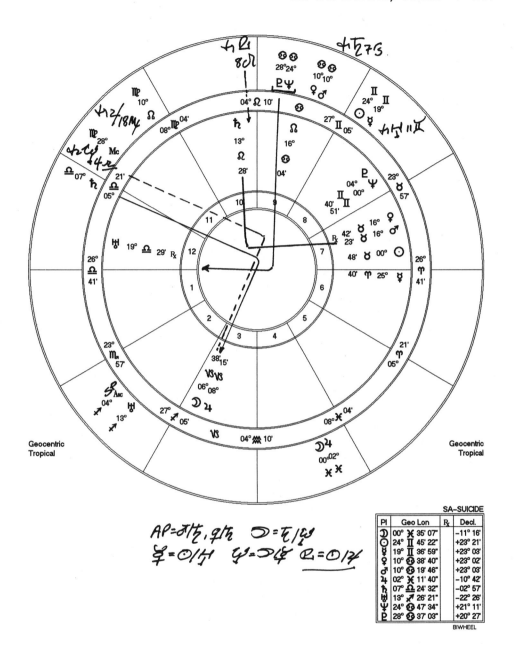

Horoscope 64, Adolph Hitler

Inner Chart	Outer Ring — Suicide
April 20, 1889, 6:30 P.M. LMT	SA: April 30, 1945
Braunau am Inn, Austria	
13E02 — 48N15	

Horoscope 65, Andrew Cunanan

Horoscope 65 shows Andrew Cunanan, who became a nationally pursued criminal after a string of murders and who committed suicide before capture on July 28, 1997.

The Sun-Moon blend here (Virgo-Taurus) is a statement of the importance of materialism to define identity, to establish security. Venus becomes extremely important as ruler of the Ascendant and dispositor of the commanding Saturn-Moon conjunction at the horizon. Here, Venus is square the Ascendant center, corroborating the theatrical beauty of the young man's person, adding a skein of charm, accentuating the importance of materialism.

This charm is reinforced by Neptune=Mars/Ascendant, linking the astrological components for charisma (see the Mars-Neptune relationship in Case 35, Marcello Mastroianni, page 135). This midpoint picture also suggests living "out of the mainstream."

An extension of this theme is immediately apparent with the midpoint picture of Mars=Venus/Ascendant (see also Case 59, Marilyn Monroe, page 228), "using one's charm or sexiness to make something happen."

The "something" here is fulfillment of the materialism needs, the strong bid for personal recognition (AP=Jupiter/Node, Midheaven= Moon/Uranus, Neptune=Uranus/Midheaven, Pluto trine the Midheaven, Sun sesquiquadrate the Midheaven).

Underneath all of this is a complex we do not understand easily: the Saturn retrograde phenomenon, Saturn ruler of the 10th conjunct the Moon, ruler of the 4th; the orientation of planets below the horizon (unfinished business in the early homelife); Neptune, ruler of the 12th, quindecile the Moon, a definite statement of potential self-undoing here. Concerns with both parents are indicated; the deficit brought into the powerful thrust for personal recognition. (Note the Sun and Mercury quindecile the North Node.)

Mars in Sagittarius (driving opinionation) is peregrine. This drive leads the bid for recognition and certainly plays into the colossal social-prominence need-thrust of the Jupiter-Mercury-Uranus conjunction in Libra.

Finally, we must assimilate somehow the Pluto=Neptune/Midheaven picture that promises "strange happenings on the job or in the home," a difficult picture.

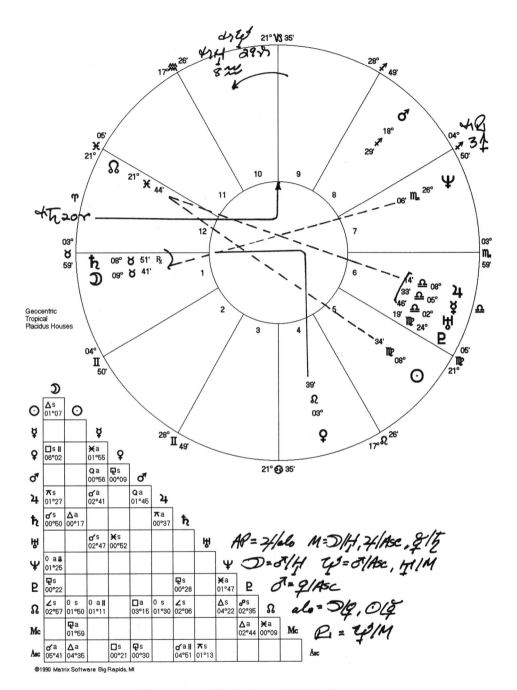

Horoscope 65, Andrew Phillip Cunanan
August 31, 1969, 9:41 P.M. PDT
National City, CA
117W06 — 32N41

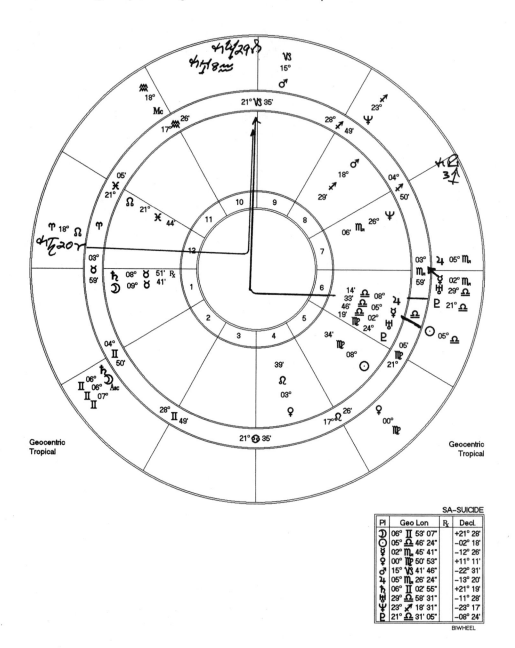

Geocentric
Tropical

Geocentric
Tropical

Pl	Geo Lon	Rx	Decl.
☽	06° ♊ 53' 07"		+21° 28'
☉	05° ♎ 46' 24"		–02° 18'
☿	02° ♏ 45' 41"		–12° 26'
♀	00° ♍ 50' 53"		+11° 11'
♂	15° ♑ 41' 46"		–22° 31'
♃	05° ♏ 26' 24"		–13° 20'
♄	06° ♊ 02' 55"		+21° 19'
♅	29° ♎ 58' 31"		–11° 28'
♆	23° ♐ 18' 31"		–23° 17'
♇	21° ♎ 31' 05"		–08° 24'

BIWHEEL

Horoscope 65a, Andrew Phillip Cunanan

Inner Chart
August 31, 1969, 9:41 P.M. PDT
National City, CA
117W06 — 32N41

Outer Ring — Suicide
SA: July 28, 1997

Cunanan's need thrust began to fail with the transit of Uranus and Neptune over his Midheaven in 1993–94, with transiting Pluto simultaneously on his 7th House Neptune, ruler of his 12th. At these times, Cunanan's social popularity crested and began to wane. Something strange happened (transiting Pluto conjunct Neptune) to Cunanan. We may never know what, but it had to do with the needs not being fulfilled, the need-for-love, self-worth/money anxieties (Uranus, ruler of the 11th, conjoins Mercury, ruler of the 2nd and the mental third).

At that time, the astrologer could not help but suggest that times would deteriorate, that Cunanan's lot in life would begin to fail dramatically: transiting Uranus would square the Ascendant in March 1996 and January 1997, usually suggesting relocation, traveling, changes, new goals, and then square the difficult Saturn-Moon placement exactly in July 1997 (See Horoscope 65a). At the same time, transiting Saturn would oppose natal *Mercury-Uranus* in May 1996 and January 1997 and go on to square his Midheaven in July-August 1997. And yet at the same time, SA Sun would be illuminating the *Mercury need complex* powerfully, exact in July 1997. *SA Pluto would be exactly square the Midheaven in July 1997.*

All these measurements show accumulating pressure, the threat of change, the breakdown of security, and the feelings of psychache that we can only infer were consuming Cunanan.

Suicide is not so much tied to the content of the need as it is to *the intensity of the frustration* of whatever need is basic in the functioning of that personality...and there are always more than one need involved. It is this frustration, the thwarting, the blocking, the incompleteness, the tension over the fulfilling of that need that causes the unbearable tension, the psychache.

In all these cases we have studied in this section—necessarily drawn from the histories of celebrated people to illustrate teaching insights dramatically—suicide was a way out, a way away from the pain of unfulfilled needs that had grown intolerable throughout the life.

The objective of critical illness—including suicide—is to take over the living organism, to destroy it, to remove it from the social position that occupies a place in the food chain, to allow for the new and healthy. It is a tactic in the thrust of Natural Selection. Condemnation to death is a condition of our birth.

Cells in our body are constantly tapping energy and new materials from outside themselves in order to keep going. They can continue to exist only at the expense of their environment. Paradoxically, cells have to keep changing in order to remain the same. Aging becomes a kind of "biological treachery," as older or broken down organisms are pushed aside for the stronger and the changing.

The upper limit of the human life span is constant around the globe. Why? Statistics tell us about "rates of living"; psychiatrists tell us of needs thwarted to one degree or another causing behavioral reaction, modification, and the subjective mind-sets of frustration, bewilderment, loneliness, and pain. Why are the limits on our life so many, so complex, so inscrutable? Why do we ourselves lower those limits through our living habits, through our fears, through our actions?

When genetic flaws surface in our life, it is part of this aging process toward death; it is past deaths remembered within our inheritance. When behavioral routines are set and broken, it is part of this aging process; it is the individuation curtailed, subjugated, abandoned. When the mind can no longer see ahead, when in aloneness and futility it forgets how to dream, it is part of this aging process as well.

Astrology is witness to the process, the subjective motives and the temporal measures, the relentless interaction between the inner environment and the outer. We stay alive and fight the process as best we can through alertness to what is happening, through warnings of what may come.

We are all together.

And we should all find some comfort, some dignity, and even a smile from the insight of Montaigne, *"If you know not how to die, do not trouble yourself. Nature will in a moment fully and sufficiently instruct you. She will do it precisely right for you; do not worry about it."*

3.

CLIENT COMMUNICATION: MAKING CREATIVE CONNECTIONS AND DELIVERING THE MESSAGE

The details of our study are compelling and conclusive to a high degree, but what we know about cursory diagnostics and the theory that supports early warning are not fool-proof. The methodology of their application is interpretive. They apply relevantly a majority of the times that they are used, but not every time.

Accumulated Developmental Deficit

The reliability of what we have studied increases with the age of the client and with the degree of genetic and developmental deficit accrued in the years of early growth and maturation. We must know that early difficulties in life open the door to earlier difficulties later. (Recall "Jones," page 71.) We must know that the inheritance of health and the inheritance of sickness are quite measurable circumstances. Dr. Shneidman observes: "When genes and fortune are bountiful and give a lucky individual a better brain, they also tend to give that person a better skeleton and a better heart."[150]

For the most part, the modern astrology consultation has finally departed from the jargon-ridden, confining declarations of an inscrutable

---

150 Schneidman, page 85.

wizard. Our psychological sensitivities and vastly improved teaching programs are producing astrologers who bring the consultation to the level of rich insight and meaningful client discussion, the sharing of the human condition within time and the projection of plans and potentials into the future. More than ever before, we are able to relate the horoscope and its guidelines to the life reality being lived by the client, rather than relating that life *to the horoscope,* confining it to what we know about astrology.

As we appreciate the reflection of the horoscope in the client's reality, the symbols of the horoscope focus at many different levels. To serve our study in this volume, we are analyzing those symbols on four levels:

- First, as the registration of the need patterns that spur development for every individual;

- Second, as the aspects of need-press and frustration that suggest accumulated developmental deficit;

- Third, as the symbols of the needs translated to the symbols of body organs and systems, with tension at one level translating to tension at another through the shared symbol;

- And fourth, as symbolic development within the extended time period of the aging process, predicting the occurrence potential of critical illness.

Horoscope 66, Female

Horoscope 66 is a private case, a lady. In the first look at this horoscope, let us assess the potential for developmental deficit through the family environment; we know this will relate to pressures upon the need fulfillment drives and translate to one degree or another into body weakness: the Moon is conjunct Neptune on the nodal axis (mother influence); the Sun (ruler of the parental 10th) and Mercury (ruler of the 11th) are squared by Pluto (a "blanket over a grenade," i.e. swamped by the home situation; Pluto rules the Ascendant); Uranus is peregrine (ruler of the parental 4th) promising rebellion, individuation with minimal support; Saturn in the 11th tells us of an extraordinary focus on the need for love.

Self-worth issues will predominate throughout development (Jupiter, ruler of the 2nd, is quindecile the Midheaven, linking them to the parental problems and seeking resolution through professional success). The hemisphere emphasis is Eastern (defensive) in orientation.

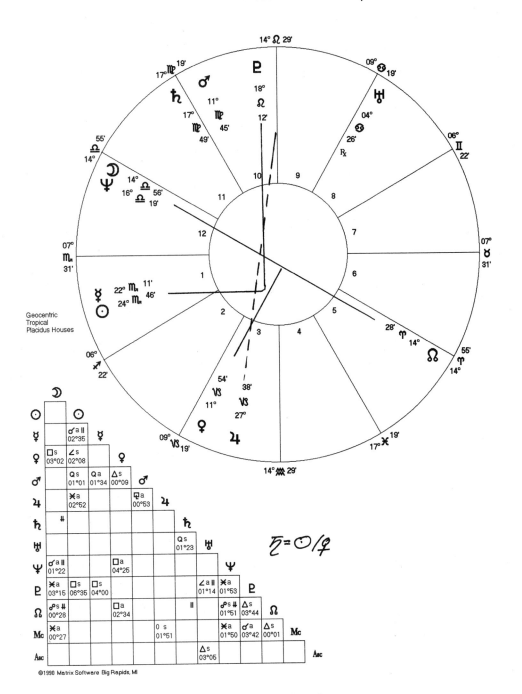

Horoscope 66, Female

My client has ardent life energies that press to be appreciated by everyone (reigning need of the Moon in Libra, supported by the Scorpio life energy). Her mother was "antagonistic, horrible...horrible, narcissistic." My client's father was very ill when she was born and was passive thereafter. There was extremely little attention and support given to her development. Frustrations accumulated.

With the significator of the 9th House (the Moon) under high developmental tension (conjunct Neptune in the 12th), we can expect that the education was interrupted.[151] The education was interrupted when transiting Neptune conjoined Sun-Mercury and transiting Saturn opposed Moon-Neptune. My client had a nervous breakdown. [In consultation, we learn what she understands today about that breakdown in the past. That understanding is vital for assessment of the horoscope as it reflects the client's reality past, present, *and* future.]

During the client discussion about development, the initial hypotheses were corroborated.

The translation of the tension structures into weak points in the physical body occurred when I began to discuss the transit of Pluto conjunct her Moon-Neptune conjunction in 1977–78, with transiting Saturn square her Sun at the same time (May–June 1978). My client had married and had had a child, five years earlier. At this time in 1978, her child was very ill with a congenital heart deformity and difficulties in the urinary tract. (We note Neptune's rulership of the 5th.)

In the period when transiting Uranus came to my client's Sun throughout 1980 and then when transiting Pluto came to her Ascendant in 1986, my client herself had many surgical difficulties: her feet ("both of them had to be redone"; Neptune within the complex, referring to Pisces, of course), her lower back, a breast tumor, constant gynecological difficulty, and the urinary tract and bladder.

My client's daughter had developed the same "Libra/Venus" weaknesses as *her* mother had been born with. My client revealed that her mother also had been very sick with "female difficulties."

---

151 This is an extremely important deduction in any horoscope born within the American culture, since education is put at such a premium, the credentials are essential for professional advancement, and the experience away from the home is vital to acculturation and the process of leaving home problems behind (if possible).

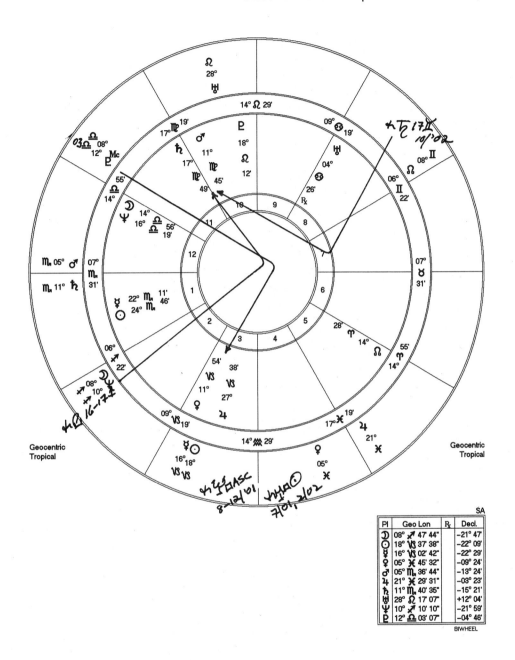

Horoscope 66a, Female
Outer Ring
SA: November 17, 2002

Everything fit together with genetic and need-frustration deficits. We saw them "coming" as it were, and we see them synthesized eloquently in the midpoint picture Saturn=Sun/Venus, Saturn related to the life-giving ruler of the 10th and Venus, ruler of the 12th.

Chart 66a shows the projection I made into the future beyond my client's Solar Arc chart for the client meeting, at which time SA Pluto was at 7 Libra 00. As we have done so many times in our study, I am looking ahead for major planetary contact that could possibly threaten the system. I saw immediately that SA Pluto would come to square with natal Venus, the significator of so many of my client's difficulties, her continuing problems with her urinary tract, the pressure in her bladder and the tissue destroyed on the walls her bladder by so many infections. The square to Venus would occur in 4½ to 5 degrees/years past the consultation date. I drew the Solar Arc chart for her birthday in 2002.

The 2002 chart shows the key transits that will be in effect at the same time: transiting Pluto square Saturn, transiting Saturn square Saturn, transiting Neptune square the Ascendant, and transiting Uranus square the Sun. The dating of the transits seem to focus on late 2001 and Spring 2002, i.e., *triggering the backdrop of SA Pluto square Venus*. While the date was some 4½ degrees/years into the future from the time of consultation, my client's apparently chronic health conditions warranted my discussing the future time with her, citing the warning times in between now and then, seen simply by watching transit development to this climactic time shown in Chart 66a.

Throughout the life study with my client, we had clearly concluded that her body tended to break down every time she faced a new challenge in personal growth. It broke down in college (and precipitous pressure about marrying). It broke down at her divorce. It broke down after big moves and professional changes. And there were more instances of the parallel occurrences. We agreed that the need for love is yet unrequited and that frustration, when she is isolated within the dynamics of change, undermines the body in many ways. She had stagnated in her development because *she instinctively avoided changes that would have advanced her development;* in other words, not changing at all was a *protection* because it stabilized predictable, reliable routinized behavior.

2001					
	MARS	JUPITER	SATURN	URANUS	NEPTUNE	PLUTO
MONTH	LONG	LONG	LONG	LONG	LONG	LONG
JAN	05 ♏	02 ♊	25 ♉	19 ♒	05 ♒	14 ♐
FEB	23	01	24	20	22	28
MAR	07 ♐	03	25	22	23	28
APR	21	08	28	23	23	28
MAY	28	13	01 ♊	25	23	27
JUN	26	20	05	25	23	26
JUL	18	17	09	24	22	26
AUG	16	04 ♋	12	23	22	25
SEP	26	10	14	22	21	25
OCT	13 ♑	15	15	21	21	26
NOV	03 ♒	16	14	21	21	27
DEC	27	14	12	21	22	28

2002					
	MARS	JUPITER	SATURN	URANUS	NEPTUNE	PLUTO
MONTH	LONG	LONG	LONG	LONG	LONG	LONG
JAN	17 ♓	11 ♋	09 ♊	22 ♒	07 ♒	16 ♐
FEB	09 ♈	07	08	24	09	17
MAR	00 ♉	06	08	26	10	18
APR	21	07	10	27	10	18
MAY	12 ♊	11	14	28	11	17
JUN	02 ♋	17	17	29	11	16
JUL	22	23	21	29	10	16
AUG	12 ♌	00 ♌	25	28	10	15
SEP	02 ♍	06	28	26	09	15
OCT	21	12	29	25	08	15
NOV	10 ♌	16	29	25	08	16
DEC	00 ♏	18 ♑	27	25	09	17

Understanding the potential of Uranus peregrine, we can introduce a corollary to the discussion: the more she breaks free, defines herself professionally, asserts herself, comes out into the world with an understanding of all of this, the more her body will be *refreshed*. And then, the emanation of her selfhood will attract different kinds of people.

Jane started to show timidity and doubt about this.

I asked, "What is Jane saying to herself?"[152]

Jane replied, "I'm not going to do this again."

---

152 I intentionally spoke in the third person singular to maintain objectification, avoiding the imbalancing "you."

"What is 'this'?"

"I get hooked up with men who are dishonest with me."

This very short exchange helped focus the problem in another way, upon the neglect and/or exploitation by others throughout her life. [Note that the problematic Venus, ruler of the 12th, also rules the relationship 7th.] But I was looking for that to change, for Jane to break out of the routine. I wanted so much to see the blanket lifted from Jane's development, to break her thinking (Mercury) away from the tension focus conjunct the Sun, squared by Pluto.

We see in Chart 66a that the Venus "target" here is ruler of the 7th. We can see that the Sun will have arced to a square with her Moon and the Nodal Axis (significator of relationships, meetings, etc.) four degree/ years *earlier* from this Chart's date in 2002. In other words, I was preparing my client for an important meeting, possibly leading to marriage, using another set of measurements all focusing one year after our time of consultation.

This case study shows very well the accumulation of developmental deficit in early life, the translation of symbols from the need-fulfillment level to the "medical" level, and the projection of those symbols back into the past for corroboration and then into the future for warning. There was hope that the need for love would gain some fulfillment; that developmental efforts would mature significantly, and that change might occur without physical breakdown. Warnings about potential freedom and success are part of the health profile as well.

Horoscope 67, Helen

Horoscope 67 is a lady involved with a metaphysical bookstore and export-import business (9th House considerations, of course). Before we get orientated to this horoscope, please look back now to Horoscope 2 (page 14). Both horoscopes have the Sun and Moon in Leo, with Pluto, and both are driven by Mars; both have a Scorpio Ascendant. Both have heart concerns; both have mother concerns of enormous importance (Horoscope 2: Nodal Axis conjunct the horizon, Mars square Nodal axis, Moon-Pluto conjunction, Mercury retrograde and without aspect in the 10th; Horoscope 67: Pluto on the Nodal Axis, Jupiter square it, one parental ruler stressed).

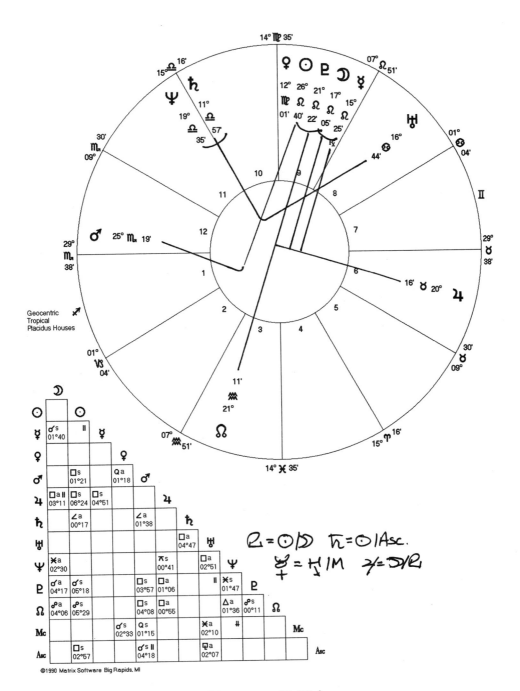

Horoscope 67, Helen

Horoscope 67, Helen, also shows Pluto=Sun/Moon, normally a tremendous liaison with power on one's own part or through relationship.

"You mean the power that *isn't* there; it was taken away by my mother."

Helen continued, "When I was a child, I never *felt* like a child. I never cried. I was an alien to my mother. She told me that I was too good to be true. My grandmother once said that I was the first person who had ever made *her* feel loved! And from that time on, I was my mother's enemy."

Helen started seeing a therapist when she was in the second grade.

With all of the tension focused in the 9th House, we can expect a complicated picture with regard to education: interruption, yet emphasis. Transiting Neptune came to Helen's Ascendant when she became eighteen. Helen ran away from everything, including college.

Helen studied *her* way and now owns and operates a substantial metaphysical bookstore. (Case 2 saw Constance espousing Scientology, writing a romance novel.)

Helen's heart-valve problems have developed from a genetic disorder (inherited deficit) called Ehlers Danlos Syndrome, a dysfunction of the blood and connective tissues (Neptune).

It is important to note the sense of inherited deficit here—both genetic *and* environmental: there is the blood disorder and there is the mother's difficulty with *her* mother, and there is the fact that Helen is a product of a mixed racial marriage and herself is married inter-racially. The repetition of circumstances in health and welfare concerns is omnipresent in life and in astrology.

Creative Connections

As analysts in astrology, we are constantly making creative connections, conjectures about the chain of events in life development and, here in our study, about the symbological interplay between behaviors to fulfill needs and the weak places in the physical body (often when those needs are frustrated). The client corroborates the creative connections; often the creative connections reveal significant insight—understanding, very much a part of healing—which often seems to hold at bay the manifestation of physical grief. In a sense, the right frame of mind seems to buy time. Health correlates more with success; illness correlates more with failure, frustration, loss, aloneness.

Horoscope 68, Marie

Horoscope 68 was the client I saw immediately after Helen, above (Case 67). Marie has the Sun-Moon blend in Capricorn-Aquarius: "Ambition in this blend finds fresh applications, probably through humanitarian or social service channels. There is a stability of purpose and performance that brings success. Innovation is the goal; significance is the prize." Marie is a psychologist Ph.D..

The beginning of our consultation was immediately addressed to the maternal influence during the development years (Moon-Mars opposition from Pluto, ruler of the Ascendant; parental ruler Neptune square the Sun, parental ruler Mercury squared by Saturn, opposed by Uranus).

> "Oh! My mother: she was HORRIBLE. She has ruined every Christmas for my whole life, and that's 46 of them! This past one, my husband and I saw it coming, and we sent her packing back home *before* Christmas arrived! It was the first time I ever stood up to her."

> "And how did your father interact with you in those early years? Was he passive, out of the picture?" [My reply appeared to be an abrupt non-sequitur, but I was looking for a pattern all too familiar in my experience.]

> Marie continued, "Yes, he was out of the picture; he was an alcoholic; he would leave the house for days at a time, my mother would send me out to find him.

> "You know, this past Christmas, in the confrontation with my mother [Marie returned to that subject to say more], we had a big tearful scene. I asked, I literally begged her, 'Mother please tell me you love me. I know you do, but please tell me!

> "And Mother said only, 'I'm *not* going to tell you I love you. NO, *I won't do that.*'"

> There was a moment of quiet, and I replied, "Can you imagine that your father had said as much, something like that, *to her*, 'Please tell me you love me', just as you did? Can you hear her turning *him* down? Did you ever hear that?

I had made a creative connection here: Marie was always sent off to bring the wandering drunk father home. Perhaps the mother identified Marie with the father. And now, with the father gone, the

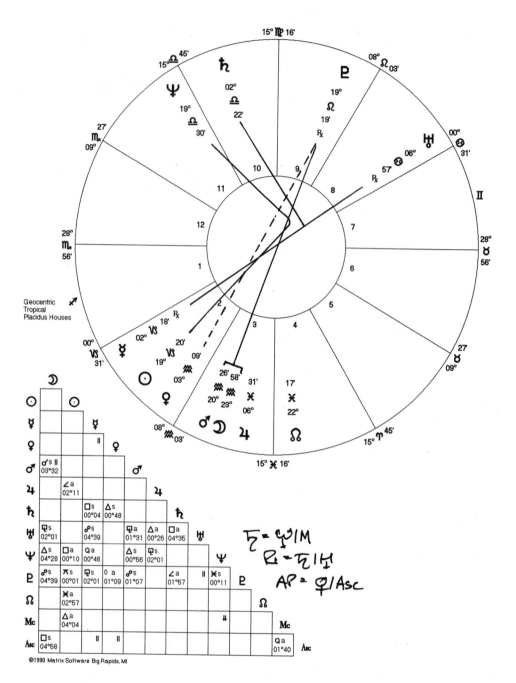

Horoscope 68, Marie

projection of the mother's tensions upon Marie was a substitute outlet (displacement).[153.]

In our conversation, Marie the daughter gave way to Marie the psychologist who understood the connection I had ventured. She agreed. She recalled times between her mother and father that pre-echoed the time she herself had had with her mother the last Christmas.

> "Rejecting your mother, Marie, was so hard to do, even in the very moment of the action—you had to beg your mother for love while asking her to go—it was triggering the suggestions in your horoscope that outline your obsession for love (Venus, ruler of the 11th is quindecile Pluto) and your fear of loss of any kind (Pluto=Saturn/Uranus)."

Marie replied, "You're exactly right; EXACTLY!"

Past difficulties in her development haunted everything in Marie's development (Saturn=Neptune/Midheaven). In her marriage, she withstood flagrant affairs conducted by her husband (when SA Neptune came to her Ascendant, "ego wipe-out," followed by transiting Saturn conjunct her Sun) and many other dissatisfactions in order to preserve her own home stability, not to fracture it for her own daughter.

The consultation developed some very important strengthening considerations and strategies to lighten these love-security shadows. Marie's profession was extremely successful and secure, using New Age innovations and alternative methods to supplement her psychology practice. We began to talk about health; I would take the symbols that had led our discussion so well psychodynamically *into the level of the body and its systems*..."I am not a medical doctor, but sometimes the horoscope speaks helpfully about the weak parts of the body, especially when it is under stress, emotional, vocational, etc."

Here is what we might have to discuss:

- The heart (Neptune square the Sun; Pluto powerful in its Leo opposition with Moon-Mars) and the eyes;

- The lower back (Neptune in Libra; Venus quindecile with Pluto); also the kidneys, bladder;

---

153 For a study of these classic defense mechanisms—projection and displacement and many others—please see *Synthesis & Counseling in Astrology,* pages 643–662.

- The nerves, knees, and breasts (Saturn square the Mercury-Uranus in Cancer axis and the Moon-Mars conjunction opposed by Pluto).

Marie has serious glaucoma as her father had had, but no heart complications of any kind; much lower back pain, highly excited nerves, but no breast problems (and she was indeed getting an annual mammogram as a precaution).

In this case, why were not more things wrong? This is a strange question, but it is a reasonable question, after all the cases we have explored! Marie did volunteer that she had a growing anxiety about deafness (Saturn), and had detected some hearing drop-off.

Inherited abnormalities may cause deafness. It may accompany hereditary nephritis (*kidney infection*), a kidney disorder that runs in families (note Venus rules kidneys, and Marie's Venus is quindecile Pluto).

Normally, almost a third of all people over the age of sixty-five have a noticeable hearing loss, but Marie was only forty-six!

We were cued by the client's reality; this would be an area to watch into the future. In the horoscope, the trine between Venus and Saturn relates the two symbols in an easy way; i.e., it is easy for the tensions of Venus (in quindecile with Pluto) to flow out into the depository of Saturn, square the Mercury-Uranus axis.

Might few things have gone wrong in the past because Marie was genetically strong and, in her studies, had gradually learned to understand the complex through which she was living? Might things be there problematically in times to come? The answer to both these questions is emphatically, Yes, and astrology is the reflective companion on the way. (Please refer to 2001 and 2002 Tables, page 251.)

For example, let's look ahead: *transiting Pluto will be square to Marie's Midheaven in 2001-02*, with *transiting Uranus opposed her Moon in 2001*, with *transiting Saturn square the Midheaven in October 2001* and May *2002. SA Saturn will be square the Moon in 2001*, at the same time. Further communication is planned between us into the future. I've noted this time period ahead in her file; warning will be shared appropriately.

Our psyche makes creative connections among occurrences in our life in order to protect us, to make sense of things. [Just as we dream in order to stay asleep, incorporating potential disturbances into thought content that stretches to be significant and, therefore, non-disruptive.) Sometimes those connections are overdone, or are invalid, or are flat-out an extension of our negative state of mind. (Sometimes the stimuli are too great for the mind, and we awaken.) For example, Jane's (Case 66, page 249) fear of linking up again with dishonest men could very well be a projection of her perception about her parents, that they were untrustworthy and not dependable to support her needs for love.[154]

Marie (Case 68, page 256) says she needs "others to depend on me so that I feel loved." This is the Venus rulership of the 7th and the 11th in the quindecile with Pluto. She saw none of that in her early home. She's a psychologist to help others with their problems, perhaps to solve her own at the same time. Perhaps that is also what keeps her with her unfaithful husband, helping him through his problems...he *did* come back to her.

It seems that bodily difficulty is somehow invited to appear in the places that symbolize our vulnerabilities from these kinds of developmental problems and need fulfillment shortfalls. It is not a hard and fast rule, of course, but it is a definite, empirically supported observation which we have seen demonstrated time after time throughout this study.

Horoscope 69, Jeffrey Green

Horoscope 69 is the horoscope of astrologer Jeffrey Green, international lecturer and author, and author of one of astrology's best-selling texts, *Pluto* (presently in two volumes).[155]

In the first view of this horoscope, we see the potential signature for diabetes: the Venus-Jupiter conjunction at the Ascendant, here intensified by the square from the Pluto-Saturn conjunction, Pluto ruling the Ascendant. Venus rules the 12th. There is no doubt about it. (See Diabetes, page 19.)

In Jeffrey's family, diabetes is inherited through the male side of the family, manifesting in every second generation in males between forty and forty-five years of age. Jeffrey is the second generation and would become diabetic. His father advised him of this when Jeffrey was thirty-two years

---

154 If this projection extends to the whole world, it can be dangerous, i.e., there is no one there to care for me, no one I can trust. Personal orientation is threatened.

155 Jeffrey uses the Prophyry House system in his work. His horoscope is presented here in the Placidian system. In all House systems except Equal House, the Midheaven and Ascendant are always the same. The internal Placidian House cusps in Green's horoscope vary only 4–5 degrees from the Prophyry; in this case no House placement of a planet or rulership reference is altered.

old (transiting Uranus was on his Ascendant and transiting Saturn was square his Sun, ruler of the Midheaven; SA Neptune was tightly square his Pluto, ruler of the Ascendant).

Warned by his father, Jeffrey began to combat the onset of diabetes with special herbs and diet control. Sure enough, in his forties, Jeffrey started to develop diabetes, was diagnosed as "borderline," but by continuing his combative measures, he has held the condition at bay.

At another level, this signature translates into *relationship difficulties* since Venus rules the 7th as well as the 12th. Green has written sensitively about these problems in his life.

Another key observation is that the Sun is conjunct the Nodal axis. This highly reliable measurement of maternal influence is an important dimension of this horoscope since the Sun rules the Midheaven, one arm of the parental axis, and the other planetary significator of the parental axis (Uranus) is opposed by Mars, and this axis is squared by the Moon, the vulnerable Moon in Pisces.

In the conversion of this axis into medical sensitivity, we have to be aware of the chest area, the internalized anxiety that can make vulnerable the Gemini region of the thorax. Additionally, with Mars in Sagittarius, we have another reference to the liver and pancreas, keyed first at the Ascendant by the Venus-*Jupiter* conjunction squared by Saturn-Pluto.

The Saturn retrograde is very strong here, conjoining the Ascendant ruler and issuing so strongly into the Ascendant. The father was somehow taken out of the picture early on in life; Jeffrey's upbringing was hampered by a breakdown of the son-father relationship; by an accumulated legacy of inferiority feelings from the early homelife.

Jeffrey writes about his early life poignantly, in the third person:[156]

> This is a case history of a man who was severely sexually and psychologi-cally abused by his mother. This abuse started right after birth; his first six months were spent black and blue, and this continued until he was placed in an orphanage at six years of age when his parents separated for a period of time [transiting Pluto conjunct the Midheaven]. After they got back together, they brought him home. The sexual abuse then stopped, but the psychological abuse continued.

These early trauma forced Jeffrey inward in defense, detaching him from the pain of the environment. "...Through living in his inner world,

---

156 See, Tyl, Ed. *How to Personalize the Outer Planets,* Llewellyn: 1992, pages 229–233 in Green's Chapter, "Trauma and the Outer Planets."

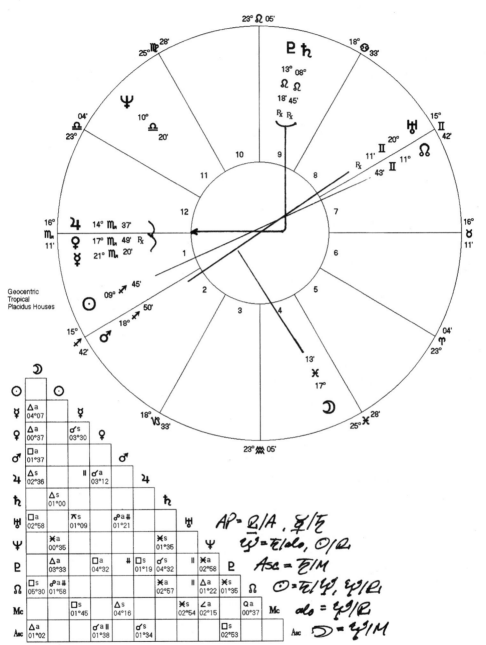

Horoscope 69, Jeffrey Green
December 2, 1946, 4:52 A.M. PST
Hollywood, CA
118W20 — 34N06

he [Jeffrey] became a loner as he grew up. Acutely shy and sensitive, he felt alienated...an extremely inferior self-image...[Jupiter rules the self-worth 2nd and is squared by Pluto; Mars in the 2nd is opposed by Uranus]. 'There must be something wrong with me.' "The potential for masochism embodied in the Piscean Moon was cultivated. This Moon opposes the midpoint of Neptune-Midheaven, suggesting "high sensitivity, being lost in one's own world."

> Jeffrey continues: "this masochistic emotional psychology, generated a reality of wanting to help others, to be of service to a larger whole, of never saying no....Even though he became very successful in his work role, inwardly he could not personally relate to his success or the acclaim heaped upon him because of messages that defined his wounded anima: there must be something wrong with me, I am nothing'."

We see this collision of worlds brought into the public through the contradiction of midpoint pictures configured with the Aries Point: AP=Pluto/Ascendant, "public personal power and persuasion ability"; and AP=Mercury/Saturn, "depressed externalization, wisdom through duress, maturation through depression, the sense of heavy responsibility."

Jeffrey's conventional education was interrupted (9th House condition, including the signification by the Moon) and yet he pursued with singular intensity his philosophical and spiritual development through initiation into shamanistic practices via the Navaho peyote tradition and by entering monasteries of an Eastern Tradition.

During his service in the Vietnam War, Jeffrey experienced extreme trauma that compounded the development deficit accumulated in his homelife. His entire health system is now debilitated with Agent Orange Syndrome, which lodges in the *liver* and affects the integrity of cells and tissues throughout the body. The astrology shows the difficult focus of Jupiter in Scorpio at the Ascendant, squared by Pluto; the life-revealed circumstances entered the body's system through that portal.

It is clear that genetic inheritance and early home development experience increase the deficit brought forward into life, thereby increasing the vulnerability to breakdown psychologically and physically. At the same time, *fighting pain and solving problems create our futures.* That's what self-empowerment is all about, that is the struggle we have been tracking throughout the studies in this book. It is no accident that Green's most celebrated work is titled *Pluto: the Evolutionary Journey of the Soul.*

The Search for Meaning

In our study, we have been translating symbols from the assessment of environmental conditioning in a person's life to the assessment of potential systemic and somatic breakdown within the developmental (aging) process. This translation of symbols calls attention to the interconnectedness of meanings that occur in the brain, gain articulation in the mind, and then touch body and spirit.

We have referred often to the breakdown of the body, of the body's system. That's how we see it: a breakdown of the inter-connectedness of efficiently functioning components that comprise the body. The corollary prevails throughout medicine, i.e., *that health is promoted by connected-ness.* This has been a working axiom since the time of Hippocrates and his ideas of balance throughout Nature.[157]

It is very important to understand the outreach of this concept of connectedness. It is more than one bodily system connected to another to another to another. There is a spectrum of connectedness from molecules to cells, to organs, to the whole body, to the species, and to life.

We can ask if the connectedness goes further...the whole body, to the species, to life, *to the cosmos?* And where does the mind—the seat of our consciousness and neurology (Mercury, Uranus particularly)—connect with everything? Does that connection occur between the organs and the whole body, and then does it go further? Is there a connection with the spirit?

The outreach of connectedness is hierarchical in structure: any effect anywhere in the chain will affect all other levels. We know that a mutation in the DNA can affect a person's social life, for example. (Think about that for a moment.) Conversely, losing your job can affect what happens in your heart and your biochemistry.

When interconnectedness breaks down, disease occurs: when there is break between blood/oxygen supply and the brain, we experience stroke and we face imminent death; when cells are cut off from their hormone regulators, we get tumors; when there is a break between the conscious

---

157 Almost all the ancient Greek thinkers pursued the idea of balance and harmony as essential to whole life. Heraclitus (c. 528 b.c.e.) worked with the world's balanced adjustment of opposing tendencies; his work was pursued later by Empedocles who introduced the Elements as the roots of things within the balance of all (strife separates, love unifies, i.e., breakdown and harmony); Pythagorean ideas worked to measure the maintenance of balance; Anaxagoras propounded the ideas of the microcosm/macrocosm, the infinite divisibility of matter. The presence of good defines evil; the presence of health defines illness.

and unconscious mind we get neurosis, psychosis; when we isolate ourselves from the group, we take on alienation, sociopathy; when the social group gets cut off from rest of the world or is set against another social group (i.e., interchange and communication have broken down), the result is strife, war, destruction. When the individual is cut off from the spiritual, there is a lack of meaning in life, a breakdown in orientation, the accumulation of psychache.

We have been trying to approach understanding of these questions throughout the studies in this book: time and time again, we have seen the pervasion of accumulated developmental deficit (including inheritance factors) opening the door to illness; illness occurring in one case but not in another case of very similar astrological organization at the same time within development; illness occurring under one signature for someone and in a different body region for someone else, under the same signature.

Somehow, within the interconnectedness throughout Nature, the body physical, the body mental, the body spiritual give "meanings" to disease, perhaps in support of a selection process. The astrologer sees the outlines of these connections and possibilities.

Professor Alastair J. Cunningham of the Ontario Cancer Institute at the University of Toronto/Canada also pursues these connections. He is taking daring steps into the concept of connectedness, dealing with mind and spirit. He sees that the model of the human must assimilate the languages of information, the powers of ideas, the effects of spiritual awareness. He sees a new world of adjunctive care for people with cancer or other chronic diseases, using psychological and spiritual techniques. He is conducting tests, already with impressive results, to establish the "meaning" of disease, to address potential cures beyond medicine. For him, information flows through the interconnectedness between and among all levels of the person.[158]

Cunningham *expects* informational therapies to influence physical disease. He works to strengthen connectedness through the awareness of needs and how to fulfill them. He points out how people with critical illness search to explain their illness, how most often they see the illness as a freak accident of their genes. They fight off feelings of being victimized

---

158 Many ideas contained in his paper, "Understanding the influence of psychological, social and spiritual levels of physical health: an informational approach" parallel the quest in our study. See *Kritik der medizinischen Vernunft* (A critical view of medical reasoning), a medical paper anthology edited by Schmidt and Steele; Kirchhheim Verlag: Mainz, Germany, 1994.

by fate, "Why was I singled out? Why does this terrible thing happen to my good child?"

At the height of the Freudian era in the 1950s and 1960s, psychoanalysts suggested strongly that disease is an expression of a conflict in the unconscious projected into the body: a person does not face up to a deep problem, so that person gets cancer instead. While this is not as prevailing a theory as it used to be, there is a great deal to this concept, but it is not a complete answer, nor one that is applicable broadly. It is just one important information level to understand critical illness.

Cunningham whose research has just come to my attention echoes many of the ideas developed in this book.

> He says, "The meaning of a fact, or a sensation, is its relationship to everything you've experienced in the past, isn't it? It means nothing in isolation. A person means nothing in isolation, really. I think cancer is the same, and cancer has a meaning—as does any event, in relation to everything else that's happening in that person's life, has happened, and will happen, both before and after, at all levels. If you say: That's going too far! If you say, No!, cancer has no meaning, then what I suggest you're saying is that your life has no meaning."

In parallel with this statement, I recall the scores of times in my lectures throughout a dozen countries when I received immediate understanding and corroboration of the thought, "You're never sick when you're successful." Somehow, that extreme conjecture strikes a chord. We *know* there is a lot to it. We know that, because we instinctively associate sickness with failure, with a psychological or spiritual state that is less than fine.

A male client of mine was diagnosed with a cancer two years ago, before I met him. He told me about the condition and its resolution on the telephone before our consultation together. In my preparation for the consultation, I could not easily find within a reasonable time frame an astrological focus of when the cancer could have all begun, i.e., the time when warning could have been given to him.

During the consultation, I asked him about a time quite a bit earlier (about five years) when his horoscope was definitely under tremendous challenge. At that time, he had undergone a divorce and a loss of his business, and he had "hit bottom." He had drunk heavily and was desperately lost. Was that the time that spawned his cancer? Was his cancer a redirection of a death wish from his crisis time? Needless to say, this observation stimulated a rich discussion during the consultation. When he left our time together, I remember his saying that he felt as if "tons of old business" had finally been dropped off, left behind. In other words, he felt healthy.

There are more and more texts being published that address mental causes (backgrounds) for physical illness and mental antidotes as well. One of these books shines particularly for me, filled as it is with extremely telling insights along the lines of our study in this chapter. For example, in reference to "heart attack," Louise L. Hay suggests in her book a probable cause as "Squeezing all the joy out of the heart in favor of money or position, etc." As a new thought pattern (a remedial or preventive suggestion), she suggests, "My heart beats to the rhythm of love." [Recall Case 46, page 172; Case 49, page 182. There are many cases where the absence of material security and the anguish about it end up making someone heart-sick, cause disruption in relationship or even prevent relationship.]

For "Prostate Problems," Hay suggests for probable cause the idea, "Mental fears weaken the masculinity. Giving up. Sexual pressure and guilt. Belief in aging." And for the new thought pattern, "I love and approve of myself. I accept my own power. I am forever young in spirit." I can confirm that, of the sixty-some cases of prostate cancer that I have studied and discussed the particulars of, the prevailing ideas among the men were embarrassment about the threat to masculine performance (not from prostate symptoms solely, but from feelings of inadequacy in relation to their wives, perhaps for years and years; and the desperate feeling of aging). We can ask if those feelings were there before the cancer occurred or after? How much is the prostate disease part of those thoughts and feelings?

For "Diabetes: Longing for what might have been. A great need to control. Deep sorrow. No sweetness left." And the new thought, "This moment is filled with joy. I now choose to experience the sweetness of today."

For "Depression: Anger you feel you do not have a right to have. Hopelessness." And the new thought: "I now go beyond other people's fears and limitations. I create my life."[159]

---

159 Hay. This remarkable little book was written in California, published in London, and given to me as a gift by a friend in Oslo. I thank Eva-Elisabeth very much for putting this book into my life.

All of this explorative work between the realms of mind and body, experience and vulnerability, living and aging is extremely significant. It is New Age discovery for the mind but it is the primal process of the human condition. We astrologers capture this connectedness when we study in our lives the accumulating deficit within development, within the aging process, the ebb and flow of need press and fulfillment, the focal points of parental interaction, self-worth conceptualization, interpretive mind-sets, giving and receiving love, cooperating and forming relationships, learning the values of others and the world we live in, making ends meet (a connective concept) through our profession, the projections of dreams, and the allure of rebirth in times to come.

Cancer specialist Dr. Cunningham is building highly sophisticated group tests about the connection between mind/information and body/cancer that will bear results over time, within the next two years. He cites the well-known Spiegel, Bloom, Yalom study (Lancet publications, 1989), in which randomly selected women with metastatic breast cancer were organized into a support group which met once a week for a year. There was a control group receiving standard care but not the support of the regular meetings. *Survival time was doubled by the therapy of the support group!*

No one knows what happened among the women to present such a dramatic result. We can suggest with Cunningham that more life time was available to the support group because of the interest in the "meanings" and information being developed among them, together. "Ultimately [it is] the discovery of meaning and trying to experience one's relationship to a larger order" that is the key.

Relationship to a larger order; extension of the interconnectedness beyond the body, the social order, beyond the ecosystem and biosphere, and into the spiritual existential order—these dimensions of consciousness strengthen the system and improve life. Did the women in the support group get outside of themselves, away from their anguish, by seeing the others in the group, appreciating the others and therefore themselves, living longer on the activities, sentiments, dreams, hopes, and wisdoms of others like them?

This is exactly the process conducted in the phenomenally successful Alcoholics Anonymous groups networked throughout the world. This is the model for support groups in connection with practically every serious illness we can name.[160]

The mind is pleased when significance is established. Even the wrong interpretation of information has therapeutic value since it exercises value judgment, just as night defines day, as noise defines silence. Pleasing the mind is relaxation; it is the alleviation of stress. Perception is clarified, identity is confirmed, life is appreciated.

These observations are fascinating points of light ahead of us. They start to define the framework to which we can tie the significance of the client consultation, the sharing of understanding through astrology.

In the consultation, we pursue connectedness among developmental life record, related ideas and meanings, and time periods of change. And above all perhaps, the consultation is a connectedness between two human beings sharing similar developmental need pressures, understandings, and fears. In the consultation, the client is no longer alone and neither is the astrologer. The consultation is a support group.

Communication of Warning

Our objective in this study of the astrology of critical illness is to take in through the horoscope an appreciation for the weaknesses of the body and its systems, to assess intensification of the potential for critical illness within the aging process, and to project a timing pattern when this potential might be dangerously focused. In short, we are working to spot weakness and give warning.

As yet, we can not be *precise* in spotting weakness or giving warning. We can not measure *precisely* accumulated genetic and developmental deficit within the aging process; and we can not assimilate *completely* the workings of the mind within all that is going on. We are dependent on case history corroboration to verify body weakness and the degree of manifestation of specific illness.

With that corroboration, we can time periods within life development that are to one degree or another periods of intensification, that present challenge to the body's systems, and, indeed, indicate possible danger to life.

---

160 And they are listed in many different directories in your city. A moment or two on the phone, or calling your local newspapers to locate the contacts, will put you in touch with the groups and their literature so that you can pass on helpful information to clients in need. It is helpful to ask several of the support groups if and when you may attend (they have closed meetings and also occasional open meetings) as an observer. You will learn a great deal.

With cursory diagnostic sophistication, with our appreciation of genetic and developmental deficit, and with our superlative awareness of patterns of time, we astrologers can give early warning that is valid and valuable. Astrology *can* help to save lives.

Consultation Syntax

Since our diagnostic timing abilities depend on case history corroboration for security, specific discussion of the health profile should take place at the end of the consultation, within the frame of projections and strategies into the near future, after the record of the past has been gathered and shared.[161]

Generally, a seventy-minute consultation might proceed as follows: the first fifteen to seventeen minutes devoted to the opening general statement of the what the horoscope suggests about the client's energies and needs; the key modifications and supports anticipated in development. Key to this opening discussion is the client's participation, his or her corroboration of events and themes of development, determination of levels of experiential intensity, and the value judgments of occurrences within life development.

A second period of about thirty-five minutes flows easily out of the first period with specific date references in the past grounding the experiences and value judgments being discussed developmentally. Here is were Solar Arcs and Transits (and the SP Moon) develop out of the radix and into life, relating to the angles of the horoscopes especially, to the Sun and the Moon, and into and out of key aspect pictures.

The astrologer is constantly making creative connections, refining discussions to manageable concepts, establishing corroboration within the client's life events and within the client's understanding for every major deduction.

The final fifteen minutes can introduce an extension of the past patterns into a projection of the client's plans for the immediate future, all matched with the time frames patterned by the astrologer before the consultation, in preparation for analysis. Health discussion can best be conducted in this concluding portion of the consultation.

---

161 Indeed, credentialed medical astrologers specializing in health concerns may devote the entire consultation to medical matters, gathering life record corroboration within the dynamic discussion they lead. Similarly, should the conventional astrological discussion become acutely focused on a time of illness when discussing past experiences and evaluations, further projections of the health profile—if they present themselves—could be include at that time.

Cursory Diagnostics

On every page in this study, we are making cursory diagnosis of the physical profile suggested in the horoscope. The entire first section of this book was developed in ever-increasingly detailed measurements, matched with the influence of genetic inheritance and developmental deficit in environmental experience.

We *know* with high probability the potential weak parts of the body and its systems, revealed through the natal horoscope, articulated by the aspect networks.

- The number of body references and the specific areas of weakness are tied to the astrological aspects of highest tension—the square, quindecile, conjunction, and opposition.

- The planets involved within the aspect structures (including key midpoint pictures) carry with them the archetypes developed diagnostically in relation to the signs the specific planets rule. High-tension contact between the planets is often enough to make tenable diagnosis, but highly emphasized placements by sign must be considered as well.

- In relation to signs that are especially pronounced in tension structures, the reflex inclusion of the opposite sign especially can also be a valid determinator.

The astrologer should be selective, working in the main with the references that are most dramatically articulated. *To try to be all-inclusive tends to dilute perception, squander authoritative insight, and waste the efficacy of warning.* When the list is too long, it is difficult to establish a hierarchy of real concern. Although the older the client, i.e., the farther along one is in the aging process, the more things there will be that will have surely gone wrong in the body; the list to be questioned will be longer. I normally find that one or two main weak places and two or three second-level concerns present themselves conclusively.

Review of the Past

Reviewing the past (and projecting the future) is best accomplished through Solar Arcs and outer planet transits, chiefly to conjunction and to square with the Angles, the Sun, the Moon, and the rulers of the angles. The first thirteen years or so—the crucially formative years of life—are easily seen within "rapport" arcs projected within the radix, one degree for one year, and then refined in measurement when needed (appreciating fast-arc/slow-arc considerations, making computer measurements for a specific year when the time is of key importance (see page 79). We have followed this process in practically every case presented in this study.

Analysis of past development takes the Sun-Moon blend (with the Moon symbolizing the reigning need of the identity, using the Sun's particular energy for fulfillment) through the aspect modifications shown in the birth horoscope—especially in relation to the networking of House rulerships—and applies hypotheses to the client's individual reality of development. Dating throughout the past quickly establishes not only the sensitivity of specific areas of the horoscope, but the specific *reaction record of the symbols within tension structures,* those symbols which will then be converted into guidelines for the health profile.

The chronology of development in life and the values determined by the client within that development give the astrologer *the sense of accumulating deficit within the client's aging process.* Extremely responsive spots—Angles, Sun or Moon, particular planetary positions—will emerge in the analysis and become more reliable for response in future contact situations. When these spots are articulated in the time period of the near future, strongly, according to guidelines established in this study (the Review, page 170, is extremely important; it should become instinctual for the astrologer), the patterning that supports early warning emerges.

Disclaimer

It is extremely important to point out—to caution—that **not every horoscope presents a time of challenge to the system at the time of consultation or, say, two years into the future.** Determining such a time is serious business—for Nature *and* for the astrologer; **it does not occur in every horoscope, in every consultation.**

Should a time present itself—as we have learned to see with so many case studies in this book—the astrologer, in service to the client, must be prepared to establish a warning.

Unless the astrologer is a medical doctor, the first step is to present a "disclaimer." This protects astrologer, astrology, and client. Here is what I recommend, already presented in several of the cases we have studied:

> I am not a medical doctor, but sometimes the horoscope speaks helpful-
> ly about the weak parts of the body, especially when it is under stress,
> emotional, vocational, etc.. Has there ever been detected by stethoscope
> or electrocardiogram a congenital heart anomaly? And secondly, is there
> back pain, pain in your spine? [Drawn from Horoscope 2, page 14.]

I have presented the first twenty-seven words of this paragraph
verbatim in thousands of horoscope consultations. It is professional and
very useful: it helps the client understand the question as a "research
question" rather than as a critique of his or her life condition; it further
establishes the holistic perspective of the astrologer; and it brings in
another value level to the consultation, which may not have been
expected by the client.

In this example, referring to the heart (see page 16 and 171), the
specificity of the question is veiled somewhat and given extra clinical
objectivity by the use of the words "congenital" (*born with*) and
"anomaly" (*an unknown*).

In relation to this specific question about the heart, it is shocking how
often one learns that the client has *never* had an electrocardiogram
examination. [And the reports of doctors not hearing accurately through
the stethoscope are many indeed.]

In relation to the regular checkup every woman should have—an
annual mammogram examination for breast cancer, a Pap Test for
cervical cancer,[162] for example, it is shocking how often one learns that
the client has never been tested, national advertising campaigns about the
importance of being tested not withstanding.

In relation to the regular checkup every male over forty should have
for Prostate Cancer (the effortless PSA blood test, see page 92), it is
shocking how few men have been tested.

In relation to the potential of the other most prevalent forms of cancer
and death—lungs and colon—it is shocking how few men and women
have regular chest xrays and stool analysis (especially after age fifty).

The point is that the astrologer must make sure that **the client is seeing
a doctor regularly for a medical checkup.** This recommendation
should be made with a tone of voice that is commonsensical and insistent.

---

162 The Pap test (after researcher Papanicolaou) is simple and painless and is used to detect cervical
cancer, a disease that occurs more often in women older than forty years, and is useful also in
detecting precancerous conditions.

I share this exchange about the health profile with every client I see, whether or not the client's horoscope shows a pattern of challenge in the near future. This allows me to practice diagnostic perception, to learn more about the client, and to compile research. It also allows a record to be made that may be very important when the client consults me again in the future.

Key Phrases

The actual "early warning" as we have been referring to it in this study is contained in a simple two-part exchange with the client, an exchange with enormous potential significance [Note also a variation, page 174]:

1. *When was the last time you had a physical checkup?*

   This question should be asked matter-of-factly, at the same word-speed established in conversation with the client up to that point, with no concern or emotional involvement on the part of the astrologer. How would you ask your neighbor, your brother or sister, your spouse the same question? Ask your client in the same natural manner.

2. If the client can not remember or recalls that it was some years before, the astrologer should insist gracefully that a physical checkup be arranged, especially when someone has recently relocated to the area, i.e., in order to establish a relationship and a record base with a local physician.

   If there is a pattern forming that will challenge the system soon in the time ahead, the astrologer can say,

   "Well, it is very important for all of us to have regular physical checkups. In this day and age, early warning almost invariably promises a cure, should anything be going wrong. There is a challenge here, possibly to the [prostate, to the kidneys...etc.] suggested in the horoscope—and it may have to do with the major changes we have been discussing. You really should get everything checked out. That's the way to be in tip top shape for the time ahead."

Notice some subtle key word groups here: "for all of us" unites the astrologer with the client, and the two with everyone else, instead of isolating the client in a position of insecurity or fear. "Early warning almost invariably promises a cure" is optimism at the beginning of any possible ordeal; it champions the suggestion the astrologer is giving; the suggestion is explained in the best terms possible...a cure.

A possible link is indicated between the warning and another big event—challenge—in the client's life, one that was surely already discussed. It could be a pending divorce, the conclusion of a divorce, the changing of jobs, difficulty with a child, selling a home, caring for one's parent(s). Tieing things together adds to the *reasonability of being in the best of shape, being strong to do the job.*

"To be in tip-top shape" is a desirable state. This is not deniable. This way of presenting the concern is far better than suggesting "to get something fixed" or simply "checked out."

Many, many people resist seeing a doctor until it is too late, as we have discussed. In these cases, aspects of denial are operating; there is the fear that certain mortal conditions *might* be detected; there is the fear of *other* conditions being discovered (that are thought to be "different than" critical illness) like alcoholism, venereal disease (even college professors may have Herpes), impotency, obesity, depression.

It is important that we be persuasive rather than matter-of-fact about "selling" the medical checkup. The way presented above is subtle, natural and effective.

3. If the client replies that he or she has had a full physical within the past six months, we must ask, "*Was everything alright?*", and this part of the question should be stronger in voicing, with firm eye contact, and it should be pushed for a full answer.

For example, recently, in a recent consultation, "Betty" had *transiting Pluto* about to square her *Ascendant* at the same time as *SA Pluto* was conjunct her *Moon*. There were other measurements, but this was strong enough, as we have learned and seen many, many times in this study. The situation was immediately upon us.

I asked Betty, "*When was the last time you had a physical checkup?*"

She replied that she had indeed just had one.

"*Was everything all right?*" I asked strongly.

She replied with great relief that everything was fine. There had been a small lump in her breast, and it was all checked out. There was nothing to worry about.

I recall vividly asking Betty again about the negative diagnosis, very strongly, searching her eyes, listening to the tone of her voice for ways I could measure the sureness of her response. I was waiting for a feeling of corroboration through my senses more than through our conversation.

I felt reluctantly satisfied when she insisted that all was well. I did not want to interrupt her composure. I made a decision to go on to other things to conclude the consultation.

For some reason, the thought of that exchange stayed with me for a long time. It was settled four and one-half months later when I received a card from Betty: "Dear Noel, Sorry you haven't heard from me sooner. Temporary setback. Breast cancer; chemotherapy with radiation to follow."

The doctor had made a wrong diagnosis. Astrology's warning had been clear. Believing my client's evaluation and relief, I had not stuck to my guns.

This happens all too frequently: the client is given a clean bill of health by a doctor, and misdiagnosis is discovered, sometimes too late.[163] When the astrological warning pattern is so pronounced and the sensitive points involved are well corroborated in the client's history, we must re-communicate with simple earnestness with our client: *"I'm happy that the diagnosis was negative, but, George, I think we really need to be sure, to be really sure. May I prevail upon you to get a second opinion; we would both rest even easier!"*

That is a powerful thought to place into the client's consciousness, but it is a thought of great caring and uncomfortably high validity.

In this particular instance, I did stick to my guns, as it were; I prevailed because of a technical observation: in George's recent physical examination (age fifty-two), he had not asked for the PSA prostate examination, thinking the digital rectal examination of the prostate would suffice. I explained that, in the digital examination, the physician can "feel" only perhaps forty to fifty percent of the prostate; that was the technicality. I told him, we were only half-way sure [meanwhile the astrology was dramatically unsettling].

---

163 At present, I have two clients involved with suits against doctors. I have seen repeatedly written case summaries from doctors that are packed with errors: medication amounts mistakenly presented by a factor of 5; conditions of the patient's sister (a different name) that had come up in conversation (medical history) were attributed falsely to my client!

In my own last physical checkup, I listened to a doctor tell me that I had the beginning of cataracts. I immediately went to an eye-specialist, went through every test there is, and was told everything was perfect.

The person is often being left behind by the general internist; diagnostic technique is faltering except in the hands of the micro-specialist.

George decided to get the PSA test; very easy, in and out of the office, only the nurse was involved.

George's PSA came back "a little high," and his doctor said it was high-normal and not to worry about it. I continued to stick to my guns, and I prevailed again with George. He went to a urologist who, although he told George initially that the probability of his having a cancer in the prostate was about 1 in 5, did urge George to have a biopsy. A cancer was discovered, and George was operated on three weeks later.

These situations can be very emotional for the astrologer: we empathize so with the client's anxiety, we are together in the time of warning and alarm—we invite it by using the first person plural "we" instead of isolating the client with the pronoun "you"—and yet, we must be poised, apparently non-emotional, yet supportive and guiding.

Our personal anxiety in identification with our client's situation is compounded by the unsureness we feel with our diagnostic tool, our astrology; it does not have the reliability of scientific method; it is still very much an interpretative art form. We have an ambivalence about the situation of critical illness, wanting the problem not to be there and yet wanting the astrology to be vindicated in the probable saving of life.[164]

Certain phrases can be very helpful to the astrologer and to the client in reaction to the early warning suggestion to get a medical checkup. If the client answers the initial question about the medical checkup, *"What do you see there? Do I have a big problem?"* I recommend replying,

> "Maybe not, I don't know—I'm not a medical doctor remember; **but we have a way in astrology to watch out for difficulty in the future**. I want you to be in tip-top condition, so I recommend strongly that you...."

The word groups here are very sensitive: "Maybe not" opts for the healthy outcome, but still leaves room for the problem. "We have a way in astrology, to watch out for difficulty in the future" is a very effective double phrase: it preserves objectivity by talking about astrology rather than the client's person, and the act of "watching out" for difficulty is vigilance that is welcomed rather than suspected. The calm reply to the nervous question says so much, yet it is comfortable.[165]

---

164 The astrologer must save his or her emotional response for private times. Many times in the writing of these cases, in reliving many of the private ones, I have gone through the tears and worry yet again. I have talked about this response, the pressure to be externally poised while internally wracked with empathy, with doctors. They have it too. It's human.

165 "We have a way in astrology" has a magical touch to it; it is one of my favorite and most effective ways of couching difficult insights with the client.

Inquiry about Death

In response to the simple question, "When was the last time you had a physical checkup?", or, after discussing the agreement to go for a checkup, the client may say bluntly, *"Do you see that I'm going to die or something?"*

The astrologer must be ready to answer instantly, without a moment of apparent deliberation:

> "Of course not! That's not what astrology does. We're talking about living long and well, as well as we can. Regular medical checkups are important to that process. Now, when will you make that appointment?"

The point here is for the astrologer not to enter into a discussion about death. There is simply nothing to say, from the astrologer's point of view, and the client's death is certainly not the focal point of astrological consultation. The client's blunt inquiry simply betrays his or her anxiety, perhaps an inner awareness that something is wrong, which has not been shared with the astrologer in that moment. In this day of modern medicine, the distance between diagnosis and death, for the most part, is longer and more hopeful than it ever has been before in history. Life has also become so variegated that experiences even during and beyond critical illness still have significant meaning and importance.

So, there is another strong, settling answer to the death question: "There's nothing about terminality here; that's not what astrology is all about. But warnings about stress, about illness, *are* possible. You know? The positive things ahead of you are the best medicine there is! Add a medical checkup to that—which is only reasonable—and you'll be in fine shape!"[166]

Notice throughout this discussion, from the very beginning with the initial question about medical checkup, the frightening word "cancer" is not mentioned until medical diagnosis has confirmed its presence. The word carries with it a horrible threat.

---

166 Within their maturation process, all astrologers must work out the references to death ascribed to the 8th House (and to the 4th). I have tried to help with that process in the literature—to avoid drama, alarm, and irresponsibility—by changing the reference from "death" to "matters of death." This allows discussion of managing matters of someone else's death (including abortion). This is almost always what is suggested by death references in the horoscope. There is the freedom a death of someone else can bring to the client's life; the dealing with inheritance factors, sustaining the survivor(s), and many more concerns.

As much as we are intrigued with the specificity that might be possible in predicting one's death, it simply is not yet in our astrological consciousness. There are predictions of death (usually after the fact) that do bring many measurements together in significant surmise, like age, genetic inheritance, ill health challenge. And that is what we are talking about in our study.

You can talk about a heart condition or a lung condition, even in the midst of a coughing attack, of weight problems, even in the midst of obesity or excessive weight loss (which are clear symptoms of different illnesses) and not encounter alarm or resistance, for the most part. But to talk about cancer, the word "cancer" itself carries a social taboo with it. To speak about this disease privately with someone is somehow out of the grasp of the astrologer, of anyone but a medical specialist.[167]

We must remember always: we are not making medical diagnosis (unless we are physicians with diagnostic support); we are not healing physical illness (unless we are physicians with healing resources). We are astrologers talking about time. We must not complicate or overextend that very special strength we have.

The client is as word and concept-sensitive as we. The client respects the authority of the astrologer that has been established throughout the consultation. The client is waiting for leadership that is sensible and reliable. A discussion of symptoms in relation to self-checking certainly is helpful—and every astrologer must be knowledgeable about the symptoms of major illnesses—but approaching convicted diagnosis is out-of-bounds for the astrologer, except for the medically credentialed specialist.

While we may know a great deal in terms of probability of a condition, astrologers should avoid stating specific diagnosis. We need not share with the client all that we may suspect. The objective is to direct the client to a medical checkup. If we were to go further without the proper credentials and technique—and without the client's expectation—there is the risk of severely intruding on the client's balance of self-awareness. Fear and depression can be aroused that, themselves, can precipitate a negative life condition.

---

167 I have observed doctors for some twenty years, listening to their words, their way with patients—even in television dramas and documentary reports that are sanctioned by medical authority—and learning the circumlocution of speech that eases confrontation with drastic real-

With Whom to Communicate

Astrological insight with regard to the timing patterns of critical illness can challenge our professional responsibilities and our ethical concern.

Horoscope 70, Roland

I have just received an inquiry from a client I have served for some five years. My work with this lady, now sixty-two years old, has been extremely successful; astrology has definitely enriched her life and planning; she respects strongly what astrology can do.

My client, "Margaret," had been in a relationship with a man for about four years. During the last year of that relationship, things started to sour as SA Saturn made a square to her natal Pluto, ruler of her 12th House and her Ascendant, SA Neptune=Sun/Moon (relationship), and transiting Neptune opposed the natal Pluto at the same time. It was all too easy to project a dismal end to her relationship and quite an empty time for her with regard to relationships, for about ten months, when she would then show SA Sun=Venus/Mars and transiting Uranus would oppose her Venus, ruler of the 7th.

Margaret truly suffered during this break of the relationship. At her age, she was fearful of time, of finding another relationship that would support her in many ways for the rest of her life. Her health suffered at the same time, though not "critically" (Pluto rules her 12th as well as her Ascendant) with colon concerns and glaucoma (Neptune=Sun/Moon).

This month, the "new" measurements became exact, and the Uranus transit opposed Venus, the ruler of her 7th indeed corresponded with her meeting a "fabulous" man, with whom attraction and rapport were instant. Margaret called me several times with news about the relationship as it built during the first new weeks together. There were many points of relationship between her horoscope and what we knew of his, and everything seemed to be in fine shape.

Another call came from Margaret: She and "Roland" had been at a tennis party and then at a bridge evening with another couple. Talking about all sorts of things, the other couple volunteered happy news about the man's recovery from prostate cancer, how playing tennis was now no longer difficult with the chemotherapy behind him, etc.

Later Margaret and Roland were preparing for their first intimacy, when Roland calmly shared the information that he too had prostate cancer, and was still fighting the battle.

This was a difficult set of conversations for Margaret. She had a lot of questions, and a lot of anxiety. She called me for help.

I gave her as much orientation I could to the subject of prostate cancer. She gave me Roland's birth date and place (the time was unavailable at this time in their relationship). I cast Roland's horoscope, which you see here as Case 70; at this time, he is sixty-three.

As soon as I saw the Sun-Pluto natal conjunction, I felt that the Solarscope might be a valid portrait as far as it could go for Roland's development and his present and future condition.

There was only one square in the Solarscope (Mercury square Jupiter) and no opposition (the Moon is unreliable in a Solarscope because of the 12-degree range possible for its position). However, there were *three* clear quindeciles: first, Saturn-retrograde and Neptune cues us to a probable early development deficit with regard to Roland's relationship (or lack of it) with his father (the Saturn retrograde phenomenon) and the potential for this area of unfinished business to haunt Roland's life. There is every suggestion that he would have to work extremely hard to prove himself in relationships (Saturn ruling the Solar 7th), to work against the modeling (or no modelling)that was provided for him between his father and mother, in his early development. Neptune in the Solar 2nd, with the Moon possibly related to Neptune and/or Saturn suggests a focus of self-worth anxiety that corroborates the Saturn-Neptune quindecile. Note that the Sun in the Solarscope rules the self-worth 2nd and is conjoined with Pluto, the "blanket over the grenade." The scenario of development begins to fit together into a pattern with which I have become all too familiar over the years of study and consultations.

The second quindecile is between Pluto and the Node: here is quite a powerful point of intensity with regard to the mother. With Pluto's rulership of the Solar 5th, we can start to see real problems of giving and receiving love born out of Roland's relationships in the early home and played out in Roland's relationships in later life.

There is the measurement Node=Saturn/Pluto ("suffering shared with others"). Roland works as a social-work professional; personally, is he sharing his own plight with Margaret, one lone person to another, to

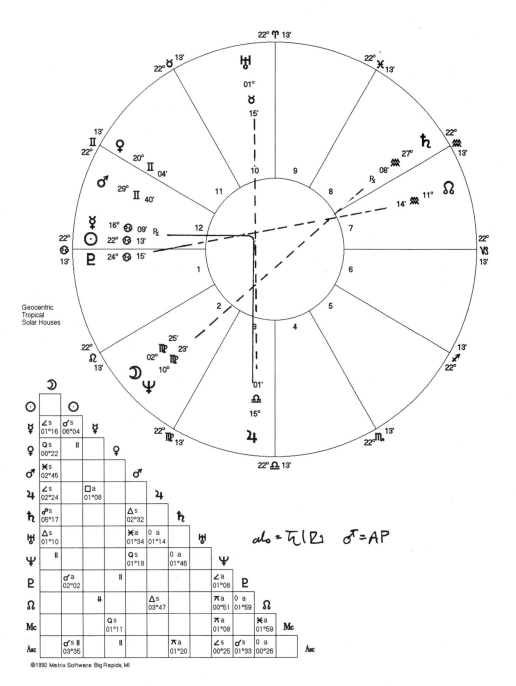

Solarscope 70, Roland ☉

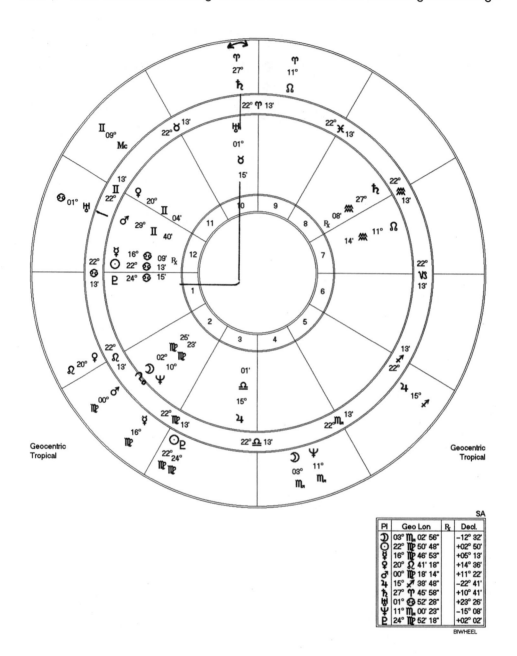

Solarscope 70a, Roland ☉
Outer Ring
SA: July 15, 1997

Pl	Geo Lon	℞	Decl.
☽	03° ♏ 02' 56"		-12° 32'
☉	22° ♍ 50' 48"		+02° 50'
☿	16° ♍ 46' 53"		+05° 13'
♀	20° ♌ 41' 18"		+14° 36'
♂	00° ♍ 18' 14"		+11° 22'
♃	15° ♐ 38' 48"		-22° 41'
♄	27° ♈ 45' 58"		+10° 41'
♅	01° ♋ 52' 28"		+23° 26'
♆	11° ♏ 00' 23"		-15° 08'
♇	24° ♍ 52' 18"		+02° 02'

SA

BIWHEEL

"tough" it through his anxiety together? Is Margaret to perform a maternal function for him?

The third quindecile is between Jupiter and Uranus, an echo of his social work professionalism (Uranus in the Solar 10th, ruling the 8th, others' values, with Jupiter ruling the 6th, the work environment, etc.). Was this his passion for physical fitness (Jupiter-Uranus contact usually), the breakdown of all this from his cancer, the compulsion to be the winner in the struggle?

The Node-Ascendant quindecile, a fourth one!, is a reiteration of the mother influence.

Gradually, a scenario was organizing itself to portray a fascinatingly articulate, wise, caring, athletic, but frightened man who had met up with my client, Margaret.

Chart 70a shows the Solar Arcs to Roland's birthdate this year. Within the guidelines of what we have learned in our study, this chart is extremely revealing. Note that SA Saturn had just separated from the square with natal Pluto in conjunction with the Sun.

When SA Saturn had been exactly square Pluto (3 degrees 30' "ago," i.e., three and one-half years), *was that the time when the Cancer had been detected, diagnosed, operated on?*

I checked the "Quick-Glance Transit Tables (page 284)" and immediately saw that three and one-half years earlier in 1994, with SA Saturn=Pluto, the following focusing transits occurred:

- Tr. Pluto was square natal Saturn in January, May, and November 1994;

- Tr. Neptune was opposed the Sun, February, July, and December 1994;

- Tr. Uranus was opposed Pluto and the Sun, January-April and august-December 1994;

- Tr. Saturn was opposed Neptune in May, 1994.

Clearly, the apex time for these measurements was March–April, 1994. This *had* to have been the time of critical illness, the time *that could have been anticipated much earlier.* Would earlier warning have made the operation easier, perhaps dictated a different technique than a partial prostectomy, fended off the complex problems Roland was having

	MARS	JUPITER	SATURN	URANUS	NEPTUNE	PLUTO
1994						
MONTH	LONG	LONG	LONG	LONG	LONG	LONG
JAN	09 ♑	10 ♏	27 ♒	20 ♑	21 ♑	27 ♏
FEB	03 ♒	13	00 ♓	23	22	28
MAR	25	15	04	25	23	28
APR	19 ♓	13	07	26	23	28
MAY	13 ♈	10	10	26	23	27
JUN	06 ♉	06	13	26	23	26
JUL	28	05	12	26	22	26
AUG	19 ♊	06	11	24	22	25
SEP	10 ♋	10	09	23	21	25
OCT	28	15	07	22	21	26
NOV	14 ♌	22	06	23	21	27
DEC	27	28	06	24	22	28

	MARS	JUPITER	SATURN	URANUS	NEPTUNE	PLUTO
1998						
MONTH	LONG	LONG	LONG	LONG	LONG	LONG
JAN	11 ♒	27 ♒	14 ♈	07 ♒	29 ♑	07 ♐
FEB	05 ♓	29	15	09	00 ♒	08
MAR	27	06 ♓	18	10	01	08
APR	21 ♈	13	22	12	02	08
MAY	13 ♉	20	26	13	02	07
JUN	06 ♊	25	29	13	02	07
JUL	26	28	02 ♉	13	01	06
AUG	17 ♋	28	03	11	01	05
SEP	07 ♌	25	03	10	00	05
OCT	27	21	02	09	29 ♑	06
NOV	15 ♍	18	00	09	00 ♒	07
DEC	03 ♎	19	28	10	00	08

post-operatively now, with a PSA that was rising once again, with fatigue and sexual concerns as well, as Margaret was asking me about.

Indeed, Margaret corroborated the general character sketch I was drawing of Roland, and she then learned from Roland that, indeed, there had been a "second" cancer operation in the Spring of 1994, but also in mid-1990 as well, at initial diagnosis of his prostate cancer (when transiting Saturn was exactly opposite natal Sun-Pluto!). The astrology was right on target.

Margaret asked about his prognosis. I reminded her, formally, that I was not a medical doctor but that, since the astrology of Roland's diagnosis had been accurate from his untimed horoscope, I could suggest a pressure point on the weakened place in Roland's body (in his horoscope, the Sun-Pluto conjunction) in the near future. The Transit Table for 1998 revealed that transiting Saturn would square his natal Sun-Pluto conjunction in April 1998 at the same time as transiting Neptune would square his Uranus, ruler of the 8th. This could be a critical time.

Ethical Concerns

But then, in my discussion with Margaret, the difficulties of that information presented themselves. Would Margaret stay with this gentleman with whom she shared such a powerful attraction and rapport through the travail he was feeling presently and perhaps facing in the time ahead? Had the cancer indeed "come back" active and strong? Had there been metastasis? Should she then not commit further, since Roland would surely have sexual difficulty (already showing in their relationship), and a sexual relationship was very important to Margaret?

Had Roland been seeking out someone to help him through this time, to make him feel supported and loved? Had all of that worked out into a fragile balance that was now jeopardized by the reality of a possible end?

Was the information through astrology going to be used by Margaret as a red flag, a warning *not* to continue the relationship? Would her ending the relationship be a shock to the early trust formed between the two of them? Would Roland be crucially set back, set apart, left alone? Would Margaret have to rationalize her abandoning the situation and live with those effects for much time ahead? Would Margaret have to reconcile her sense of sacrificing something of herself and her dreams to the relationship, taking on *his* care, *his* sorrow, and worse?

If I the astrologer had said nothing about this, i.e., not given warning about the time ahead, would things have taken their own course as they might have been supposed to take? Would all of this come down to a test of character for those involved?

There are no easy answers here. The issues are complicated because I gave the information—that things could very probably get worse in the Spring of 1998—to a *third party*, to Margaret instead of to Roland. I do not know Roland; Margaret is my client. I responded to her joy in meeting Roland, her caring for him, but she and I began to fear the repercussions of the difficult news.

If *Roland* had telephoned me—"Mr. Tyl, I understand from Margaret that astrology might help me understand my condition and its development. May we talk about this?"—and I had given *him* the information, it would have been up to him entirely to determine whether and what he would tell Margaret. In other words, his decision would leave me out of it; my feelings as the bearer of the news would be spared, if you will.

I think there is a parallel here with the situation we face when parents ask us to do the horoscope of their newborn or very young child. The child has barely formed any mode of self-expression, has not made selective judgments in its process of learning, had not made any mistakes, and certainly has not comprehended at the conscious level the goings on within the household group. What will corroborate the astrologer's deductions? What if the child has a very demanding horoscope in consideration of developmental deficit in the early homelife, say, a serious Saturn retrograde placement echoed by rulership dynamics, and more?

In this situation, the astrologer is pressed to be exquisitely graceful with observations. Whatever is said may be adjusted and used within the parents' own matrix of expectations and dreams for the child rather than in their support of the child and its particular needs and energies, let alone within the time structure shared by them all!

We can suggest that the father learn early on a bonding with the child through touch and attention and, eventually strong, loving leadership. But what if we see that that can be undermined by the mother's exploitation of the child for her own satisfactions, her own unfinished business with *her* father, now acted out in her relationship with her husband? The child is in the middle—and so is the astrologer.

Each astrologer learns to negotiate this very difficult traffic pattern. I turned down scores of such young-child commissions early in my career until I felt I had studied the difficulties of the situation as thoroughly as I could and that my technique had matured.

Another parallel is the issue the astrologer faces in giving analytical information about an employee or prospective employee to an employer. The employer is the client; the astrologer is operating as a management consultant. What the astrologer says may indeed affect the future of the employee on the job or applying for a job position.

Of course, within our professionalism—our skill, circumspection, sensitivity, experience, fairness—we have every responsibility and right to serve our client and make analytical reports to be helpful. Being an astrologer does not disqualify us from the management consultant position; quite the contrary, the matured astrologer is a formidable consultant. And the matured astrologer knows how to counsel for the best for the client as well as for the best for the employee. As in every consultancy in the spectrum of professions, it is not that one is a consultant that is at issue but the job the consultant does.

I had one commission from an internationally famous industrial firm to analyze the potentials and the tenure projection of two very highly placed management executives, both males, both married. The astro-profiles were sharply etched and conclusive in the terms the client (employer) had given me for its needs: character, ambition, energies for advancement, people management sensitivity, money management skills, creativity, communication skills, openness to further education, marriage stability, trustworthiness, projections of tenure in the new job, and much more. Then I was asked the question, "Which one of these men was a homosexual? Or were both of them homosexual?"

The question that was asked *presumed* that one (or both) of the men was a homosexual. I quietly and firmly refused to answer this question for this industrial client. In this day and age, the question of sexual preference, like the question of race or religion, should play no part in job performance, and certainly not in the equal opportunity job market process.

This requested information about sexual preference is very much like an inquiry about critical illness. For example, "Will this employee be critically ill in the near future?" Obviously there are concerns of job performance and job tenure and much more within the purview of this question, but we must recognize when such inquiry invades personal privacy.

Additionally, we must know that, when it comes to the question of critical illness, the question is *in the province of the medical examination and case history taken by the doctors studying the employee.* They are the health experts; the astrologer is not.

Indeed, a challenge to the developmental system, as we have seen so vividly so often, which can manifest in many ways, can manifest in a health crisis. The probability has much to do with accumulated genetic and developmental deficit and the current health status of the individual.

The point is strategically sensitive but dramatically simple: in one-on-one consultation with a client, the objective is to make sure the client is receiving regular, comprehensive medical checkup. The intensity with which we press that objective is in relation to the early warning patterns we see in the horoscope.

In consultation with an employer, as we have been discussing, we must simply recognize that the "subject"—the employee—is to be tested for the determination of critical illness by the empoloyer's *medical* authority, not by the astrologer's assessment.

With astrology's strength as an early warning detector for the onset of critical illness, it will not surprise me that eventually astrologers will be contacted by actuarial departments of insurance departments asking us about early warning formulae that could be related to applicants for health insurance. The information of astrology can then be exploited to deny individuals the protection of health insurance. The business strategy of corporations could defeat the benefits of astrology's service to individuals. This invasion of personal privacy can stigmatize the client's life record.

Our answer must be that the objective of the astrology is to bring the individual to the medical checkup, not to the suspicion of the insurance company. After all, we must remember that the insurance company does indeed insist on a medical checkup before giving an applicant insurance coverage. The insurance company has *already* brought the individual to the checkup; astrology need not be involved.

Medicine and Astrology: How Close Are We?

In the 1950s and '60s, medicine went through a growth crisis. The extraordinary discoveries made by Freud and his creation of psychoanalysis had given medicine a new challenge: understand that there is more to the human being than flesh, bones, muscles, nerves, and fluids, that there is a world called the unconscious that dictates in significant measure the development of the entire human being, including health. The work of Jung, Adler, Maslow, Murray and many others extended human sensibility into connectedness with ethereal inspiration and primal needs. Medicine was forced to talk to the patient and to listen to the patient, to evaluate and appreciate *beingness* in addition to existence.

As the concept-movement of holistic medicine grew, medicine in its traditional biological orientation had to open its laboratory doors to the sociologist, the cultural anthropologist, and the psychologist, to ambition, memory, dreams, love, and religion. The concept of disease changed.

With the increase of technology adapted from the war effort to medical diagnostics and treatments, there was a parallel shift of doctor/ patient interaction from the patient's home, from the doctor's home-like setting (often actually in the doctor's own home), to the new hospital center. Now, another adjustment followed so that the hospital became humanized; it had to take on the trappings of home, the setting that showed less formality, and this allowed for a return of intimacy between doctor and patient, a greater communication, understanding and trust between the two. The "total" patient had earned a new respect.

That was a half-century ago. During the past fifty years, there has been an explosion of technology and research, to the point that medical science has become so vast and so centralized that no general practitioner can master it all. The era of the specialist has been born, and so has a convoluted bureaucracy to manage all the business details. The present day doctor is now a tightly focused genius in relation to his or her specialty but has relatively narrow vision with regard to holistic concerns.

Specialization has caused fragmentation in the medical world. And this fragmentation has pulled the doctor away from holistic concerns that initially changed medicine fifty to sixty years ago. Dr. Ingrid Naiman, the leading medical astrologer in the world today, lives in both worlds. Her view of the situation is that "modern medicine has become so vast and specialized that the parts seem ever more separated from the whole to which they belong. This fragmentation as well as the emphasis on the scientific to the exclusion of the philosophical has led to a situation in which the illness often seems quite unrelated to the person who is sick and suffering."

Astrology has much to offer Medicine. In the discussions I have had with doctors and surgeons for the research in preparing this book, I have made some presentations that were to show what astrology can do. I would begin matter-of-factly, "Doctor, we in astrology can inspect, say, 100 horoscopes spread out on that table over there—spend perhaps three seconds with each, or simply have a computer-selection order given if all the data is on disc—and identify those patients who have a diabetic family history. We can do that with about eighty-five percent accuracy. That could be so helpful to doctors. And there is so much more we can do."

The response I have gotten beyond the perfunctory appreciation was mostly silence. It may have been courtesy; perhaps I was wasting their time. Perhaps they felt, "So what? I can just ask them the question in my office." My presentation was authoritative and dignified for sure; they had to believe what I was saying. The research I showed some of them did attract a respectful silence and a kind of shock on their face. One doctor did say, "Do you know how many people this book of yours will upset?"

What would frighten the establishment?

When I explained this book, this study, the response I had gotten from lectures before support groups, I realized I was backing the doctors into a corner. They had no way to respond; they had never heard these things before. It was like introducing a piano to a culture that knows only drums; they did not know how to use it, what to make of it.

Indeed, the doctor can inspect some 100 electrocardiogram records and quickly identify cardiac abnormality from among them. The doctor can inspect blood test results and quickly identify any number of patients with specific illness potentials. Astrology is not competing.

The point is that, at the easily accessible level (inexpensive, easy to use, permanently reliable), Astrology and Medicine have powerful diagnostic tools. Astrology can suspect illness and physical breakdown; Medicine can make the concrete determination.

But Astrology can go deeper, farther, more dynamically into the contributing causes of disease initially than Medicine can. In a matter of a few seconds, astrological patterns can suggest levels of developmental deficit within the early homelife (Saturn retrograde, Nodal axis, Solar-Lunar aspects, and rulership network dynamics), how those levels attract and increase the potentials of specific illnesses, and, above all, determine the time structure of the development of critical illness.

Naiman continues, "Astrology, with its unique emphasis on the individual, offers the hope of restoring focus on the person who is ill and the meaning of that individual's process in life. In skillful hands, the essential energetic and dynamic nature of astrology promises to reveal the origins of imbalance and the key to pschospiritual as well as physical well-being."

This is the ultimate thrust of this study of mine, this book: we are appreciating the client's development within the aging process and we are giving every encouragement of early warning against the critical illnesses we can expect, when their occurrence is suggested. At the same time, we are bringing more of the human condition to Medicine than Medicine initially appreciates. We are making an offering to the future of Medicine.

The coming together of Medicine and Astrology depends on the rededication of Medicine to holism, to the interconnectedness of the human concerns, to the outreach of mind and spirit. It depends on the rededication of Astrology to advanced education, to specialized education toward credentialization.

There *are* medical doctors, psychiatrists, psychologists (and practitioners in other disciplines, of course) who *are* listening, who *have* opened the laboratory to alternative studies. More and more "alternative medicine" subjects are appearing on the programs of medical conventions. Ingrid Naiman is working with the University of Natural Medicine in Santa Fe, New Mexico to institute a medical astrology curriculum with five academic degrees now available. The University integrates Allopathic, Western Medicine, and Natural, Holistic Medicine in its accredited programs, supported by an international network of clinics.

To open more doors, to extend our world of Astrology ever more to Medicine, we must serve our clients creatively and responsibly with the assessment of illness potential and the timing that is essential for early warning. We must offer to work with doctors, to complement their diagnostic skills; we must share our results with the medical community. We generalists must complement our holistic strengths with specialized refinements, those especially linked with considerations of time.

Every day in our work, through the astrology of critical illness, when the predisposition is established and the timing pattern is determined, the warning must be given. As we appreciate and support fulfillment of the individual, we astrologers must know that, with knowledge, responsibility, and with grace, we are indeed able to help save lives.

A Post Script, Please

Two days after completion of this book, I received a letter from a client with whom I had consulted six weeks before at an astrological seminar in Vancouver, B.C. The letter ties together all we have studied, and I thank my client for her permission to share her words with you:

> Dear Noel...When I met individually with you in Vancouver, for a reading of my natal chart, you asked me during the reading if doctors had ever discovered a possible congenital heart condition. I didn't really pay much attention to what you said, but, following the reading, I was seeing my doctor in Vancouver for my yearly physical testing, etc., and, this year for the first time, he ordered an electrocardiogram and, just as you had pinpointed, there is indeed something irregular with my EKG.
>
> My doctor was quite distressed, as there is a history of heart condition in my family, and he wanted me to change my plane ticket back to Montreal. But I managed to have an EKG stress test before I left, and so I was able to return to home.
>
> I have changed my diet, increased my exercise routine, and will see a doctor in Montreal and follow up on this...I am reading books about how the heart functions and how to maintain a healthy heart.

This is what our study has been about—early warning—and it is an example of the analytical and consultation work that you can now incorporate in your astrological service to others.

Working Together

When you communicate effectively with a client about the importance of medical checkup in the light of a time of pressure and possible critical illness, **would you please share it with me?** [Noel Tyl, 17005 Player Court, Fountain Hills, AZ 85268-5721.]

Send me the horoscope drawing in the style of our study, with your abbreviated analysis, the counsel you shared, and whatever transpired with your client thereafter. In this way, we can continue our research together, and I can support your work

Thank you for sharing this intense study with me and for the good work you will continue to do with your clients.

BIBLIOGRAPHY

Bostwick, David G., M.D., MacLennan and Larson. *Prostate Cancer.* New York: Random House, for the American Cancer Society, 1996.

Carper, Jean. *Stop Aging Now!* New York: HarperCollins, 1995.

Chessick, Richard D., M.D., Ph.D. *The Technique & Practice of Listening in Intensive Psychotherapy.* Northvale, NJ: Jason Aronson Inc., 1992.

Clark, William R. *Sex & The Origins of Death.* New York: Oxford University Press, 1996.

Cohen, John and Clark, John H. *Medicine, Mind, and Man.* San Francisco: W. H. Freeman and Company, 1979.

Gosden, Roger. *Cheating Time—Science, Sex, and Aging.* New York: W. H. Freeman and Company, 1996.

Haggard, Howard W. *The Doctor in History.* New York: Barnes & Noble, 1996.

Hay, Louise. *Heal Your Body—The Mental Causes for Physical Illness.* London: Eden Grove Editions, 1989.

Hartmann, Franz, M.D. *Paracelsus: Life and Prophecies.* Blauvelt, NY: Rudolf Steiner Publications, 1973.

Jaco, E. Gartly, Ed. *Patients, Physicians and Illness*. Glencoe, Illinois: The Free Press, 1958.

Klein, Donald F., M.D. and Wender, Paul H., M.D. *Understanding Depression*. New York: Oxford University Press, 1993.

Majno, Guido, M.D. *The Healing Hand—Man and Wound in the Ancient World*. Cambridge, MA: Harvard University Press, 1991 Edition.

MAYO Clinic. *Mayo Clinic Family Health Book*. New York: William Morrow & Company, 1996.

Podell, Richard N., M.D. *When Your Doctor Doesn't Know Best*. New York: Simon & Schuster, 1995.

Rosenfeld, Isadore, M.D. *Modern Prevention—The New Medicine*. New York: Bantam Books, 1991 Edition.

Russell, Bertrand. *Wisdom of the West*. New York: Doubleday, 1959.

Shneidman, Edwin S. *The Suicidal Mind*. New York: Oxford University Press, 1996.

Smith, Adam. *The Body*. New York: Viking Penguin, 1986.

Stoddart, Anna M. *The Life of Paracelsus*. Mansfield, Notts, UK: Ascella Press, 1911, modern edition.

Tobyn, Graeme. *Culpeper's Medicine—A Practice of Western Holistic Medicine*. Rockport, MA: Element Books, 1997.

Trefil, James. *The Edge of the Unknown*. Boston: Houghton Mifflin Company, 1996.

Wallerstein, Robert S., M.D. *The Talking Cures*. New Haven, CN: Yale University Press, 1995.

Astrology Texts

Cornell, H. L., M.D. *Encyclopaedia of Medical Astrology*. St. Paul, MN: Llewellyn, third edition 1972.

Hammerslough, B. F. "AIDS": an Astro-Medical Perspective," in Tyl, Ed. *Sexuality in the Horoscope*. St. Paul, MN: Llewellyn Publications, 1994.

Jansky, Robert C. *Modern Medical Astrology*. Venice, CA: Astro-Analytics, 1974.

Lehman, Dr. J. Lee, Ph.D. *The Book of Rulerships—Keywords from Classical Astrology.* West Chester, PA: Whitford Press, 1992.

Naiman, Ingrid, M.D. *The Astrology of Healing/Cancer.* Santa Fe: Seventh Ray Press, 1993 Edition.

————. *The Astrology of Healing/The Elements: Symptoms of Disease.* Santa Fe, NM: Seventh Ray Press, 1989 Edition.

Munkasey, Michael. *The Astrological Thesaurus: House Keywords.* St. Paul, MN: Llewellyn, 1992.

Nauman, Eileen. *Medical Astrology.* Cottonwood, AZ: Blue Turtle Publishing, 1993 Edition.

Tyl, Noel. *Synthesis & Counseling in Astrology—The Professional Manual.* St. Paul, MN: Llewellyn, 1994.

————. *Prediction in Astrology.* St. Paul, MN: Llewellyn, 1991.

INDEX

A

Abernathy, Ralph, 40
Abortion, 42
Adrenaline, 19, 176
Aging, 69, 72, 183
Air Family rulerships, 21
Alcoholics Anonymous, 267
Alexander the Great, 3
Anabolic steroids, 50
Angles of the horoscope, 73, 123, 158, 171, 201, 269, 271
Anorexia, 60
Anus, 42
Aquarius rulerships, 22
Arabian influence in medical astrology, 4
Aries Point, 24, 77, 133, 146, 214
Aries Point with Mars/Saturn, 236, 238
Aries Point with Mercury/Saturn, 262
Aries Point with Pluto/Ascendant, 262
Aries rulerships, 17
Aristotle, 2
Arthritis, rheumatoid, 39
Ascendant, 43

Ascendant ruler peregrine, 118
Ascendant with Neptune/Midheaven, 214
Ascendant with Saturn/Pluto, 33, 197
Ascendant with Sun/Saturn, 204
Aspect routings, 58
Asthma, 27
Astrology and insurance companies, 288

B

Back, 10, 21, 66
Bacteria, 116
Bile, 18, 45, 50
Blood, 42, 116, 132
Blood and the kidneys, 129
Blood pressure, 56, 66
Body, orientation to weaknesses, 8, 31
Bone Cancer, 125
Bones, 50, 127
Brain, 39, 40, 223
Brain, need for oxygen, 200
Breakdown, 263
Breast cancer, 90, 93, 145

Breasts, 39
Brynner, Yul, 197
Buchwald, Art, 34
Bulimia, 60

C

Calcium, 6, 22, 50
Cancer, 89
Cancer of the skin, 53
Cancer rulerships, 39
Cancer, the Dark World of, 75
Cell division, 88, 101
Cell division and Jupiter, 88
Cells, 244
Cerebrovascular disease, 200
Cerebral hemorrhage, 203
Child's horoscope, difficulties
    interpreting, 286
Cholesterol, 45, 201
Colon, 42, 64, 128
Colon Cancer, 94, 109, 113, 128
Communication of Warning, 268
Connectedness, 291
Connectedness and health, 263
Consciousness, 41
Consultation syntax, 269
Cornell, Dr. H. L., 6, 10, 139
Crenna, Richard, 142
Cunanan, Andrew, 240-243
Cunningham, Alastair J., 264
Cystic Fibrosis, 206

D

Date-twins for medical analysis,
    107
Deafness, 258
Death, inquiry about, 277
Death rate from breast cancer, 145
Death rate from heart attack, 175
Death rate from prostate cancer, 93
Death rate from stroke, 200
Deficit accumulation in life, 71,

216, 220, 245
Deficit, psychological, 225
Depression, 21, 36, 134, 266
Depression, Mercury with Saturn,
    24
Developmental tension,
    astrological, 9
Developmental tensions and
    aging, 73
Diabetes, 18, 19, 64, 74, 86, 179,
    183, 266, 289
Diagnostics, cursory, 270
Diet concerns, 17
Diet, parasites, 18
Disclaimer, 271
Disease, understanding in ancient
    Greece, 2
Disease, understanding in ancient
    times, 2
Disease, understanding in China, 5
Disease, understanding in Roman
    times, 3
Doubling rate of tumors, 140
Dual Rulerships, 60
Dylan, Bob, 178

E

Earth Element missing in
    articulation, 23
Earth Family, 50
Eating disorders, 60
Eclipse activity, 203
Endometriosis, 43
Epinephrine (adrenaline), 19, 176
Erection of the penis and prostate
    condition, 94
Ethical concerns, 285
Eyes, 62, 68, 73

F

Fallopian tubes, 21, 66
Father relationship and suicide, 225
Fire Family rulerships, 17
Ford, Betty, 146
Freud, Sigmund, 9, 288
Frustration, 243

G

Galen, 3
Gall Bladder, 50
Garland, Judy, 23, 233
Gauquelin, Michel, 236
Gemini rulerships, 22, 167
Gershwin, George, 217
Glaucoma, 62, 64
Gompertz, Benjamin, 70
Gosden, Roger, 70, 71
Grand Trine, 217
Green, Jeffrey, 259

H

Hamilton, Scott, 101, 206
Hearing voices, 214
Heart, 14, 40, 53, 64, 73, 171
Heart attack, 174, 179, 181, 185, 266
Heart attack, without Sun involvement, 143
Heart, functional description, 15
Heart valves, rheumatoid inflammation, 191
Helfgott, David, 221
Hemingway, Ernest, 230–233
Hemorrhoids, 42
Hepburn, Audrey, 109
Hippocrates, 2
Hitler, Adolf, 238
Holism, 288
Holistic view of illness, 8
Hormones, 71

Hyperthyroidism, 142
Hypoglycemia, 19
Hypoglycemia, reactive, 19

I

Infection, 116
Insulin, 18, 19
Iron, 52
Ischemia, 200

J

Jacobs, Jayj, 179
Jones, Hardin, 71
Jupiter, special considerations, 134
Jupiter with Saturn, 58
Jupiter with Saturn/Neptune, 214

K

Keith, Brian, 236
Kidney cancer, 129
Kidneys, 10, 66, 129
King, Larry, 181
Knees, 50, 56, 68, 77, 81

L

Leo rulerships, 10, 14
Leukemia, 49, 120
Levant, Oscar, 217
Libra rulerships, 10, 14, 21, 32
Life spans, 69
Liver, 17, 18, 45, 64, 68, 97, 116
Liver, managing cholesterol, 45
Lower back, 31
Lung Cancer, 49, 140, 197
Lungs, 22, 30, 68
Lymph system, 90

M

March, Marion, 208
Mars and adrenaline, 176
Mars and anxiety, 17
Mars as co-ruler of Scorpio, 42
Mars retrograde, 31
Mars rulerships, 17
Mars with Neptune, 34, 133, 240
Mars with Saturn and Pluto, 230
Mars with the Sun, vitality, 10
Mars with Uranus, 59
Mars with Venus/Ascendant, 229, 240
Masochism, 262
Mastroianni, Marcello, 133
Mayo, Charles, 74
McEvers, Joan, 201, 208
Medical checkup, 272
Melanoma, 53, 64, 90
Menstruation, 71
Mental causes for physical illness, 265, 266
Mercury and nerves, 22
Mercury and Uranus, importance in brain/mind, 223
Mercury rulerships, 60
Mercury with Saturn, 23
Mercury with Sun/Pluto, 208
Mercury with Sun/Uranus, 238
Metastasis, 89, 90, 92, 101, 106, 140-141, 186
Midheaven with Moon/Pluto, 34
Midheaven with Sun/Neptune, 36
Midheaven with Sun/Saturn, 36
Midpoint structures, 24
Migraine headaches, 21
Mind, 208
Mind, and disease, 29
MiXXe, AdZe, 104
Monroe, Marilyn, 227
Montaigne, Michel, 244
Moon with Neptune/Midheaven, 262
Moon with Pluto, 152, 255

Moon with Sun/Neptune and gynecological problems, 165
Murray, Henry A., 226
Muscles, 50
Mutual reception, 208

N

Naiman, Ingrid, 7, 17, 23, 39, 167, 186, 289, 290, 291
Natural Selection, 240
Nauman, Eileen, 8, 22
Needs, psychological, 8, 224, 226
Negatives, in relation to suicide, 225
Negus, Joan, 129
Neptune and the blood, 122
Neptune, arc or transit involving an Angle, 80, 81, 86, 95, 106, 130, 133, 149, 165, 167, 192, 204, 230, 250, 254, 257
Neptune rulerships, 42, 116
Neptune with Mercury/Saturn, 49
Neptune with Moon/Mercury, 238
Neptune with Sun/Moon, 279
Nervous habits, 22
Neurosis, 219
Nodal Axis and mother influence, 219
Node with Saturn/Pluto, 280
Nutrition, 50

O

Oriental planet, 26, 34
Osteoarthritis, 56
Osteoporosis, 127
Ovaries, 41, 43

P

Pancreas, 18
Paracelsus, 1
Paranoid personality disorder, 216
Patterns of Warning, 113, 151, 170
Peregrination, 18, 30, 31, 33, 49, 88, 104, 118, 133, 134, 217, 221
Pill, birth control, 71
Pisces rulerships, 42
Pluto and prostate cancer, 93
Pluto, arc or transit involving an Angle, 80, 118, 158, 194, 203, 210, 233, 236, 238, 243, 248, 258, 274
Pluto rulerships, 42
Pluto with Moon/Node, 185
Pluto with Neptune/Ascendant, 214
Pluto with Neptune/Midheaven, 240
Poliomyelitis, 31, 204
Pregnancy, ectopic, 66
Prostate cancer, 280
Prostate gland, 6, 42, 77, 86, 93, 183
Prostate problems, 266
PSA, prostate-specific antigen test, 82, 90
Psychoanalysis/psychotherapy, 42
Psychosomatic illness, 224

Q

Quincunx, 45
Quindecile, 30, 50, 59, 75, 92, 109, 111, 113, 116, 123, 125, 129, 133, 183, 280
Quindecile, explanation, 9

R

Reflex action among signs, 10, 21, 39
Resistance from client, 274
Respiratory tract, 167
Review of the past, 270
Reviews of Early Warning Patterning, 115, 170
Rheumatic Fever, 191, 192
Roosevelt, Franklin Delano, 31, 204
Roosevelt, Theodore, 27
Rostenkowski, Daniel D., 95
Rulerships, confusion, 6, 10, 21

S

Sagan, Carl, 125
Sagittarius rulerships, 18
Saturn with Moon/Mercury, 34
Saturn with Neptune/Midheaven, 257
Saturn with Neptune/Pluto, 34, 134
Saturn with Pluto, 52
Saturn with Sun/Moon, 36
Schwarzenegger, Arnold, 50
Schwarzkopf, Norman, 75, 107
Scorpio rulerships, 41
Scorpio weaknesses, 43
Semisquare, Solar Arc, 139
Shneidman, Edwin, 224, 245
Sinuses, 167
Skeleton, 127
Skin, 50
Solar Arcs, Review Section, 79
Solarscope discussion, 165
Solarscopes, 82, 280
Spine, 10, 13, 14, 21, 31
Spouse support and suicide, 226
Stomach, 30, 123
Stomach Cancer, 123
Stomach, nervous, 39

Streptococcal bacteria, 191
Stress and Reactive Hypoglycemia, 19
Stroke, 40, 200
Success, measures in relation to suicide, 225
Sugar, 19
Suicide, 223
Sulfur, 50
Sun with Mars, vitality, 10, 38
Sun with Mars/Saturn, 34, 49, 161, 171
Sun with Pluto, 30, 280
Support groups, 267, 268

T

Teeth, 50
Tensions and aging, 73
Testicular cancer, 101
Therapies, high-tech, 22
Thrombosis, 200
Thyroid, 71, 142, 149
Tumor, 130
Tumor growth, 140
Tumor, spread factors, 140
Type A/Type B personalities and coronary disease, 175

U

Ulcers of the stomach, 30
Unconscious, 265
Untimed births, 82, 84

V

Venereal disease, 42
Venus rulerships, 60
Viruses, 116, 204
Vitality, 10, 38

W

Wallace, Mike, 36
Warning, early, 90, 140
Warning Patterns, 75, 151
Water Family rulerships, 39
Weakness of the body, orientation, 8, 31

Your deductive skill as an astrologer rests on the base of your technique—how you bring together all you know about astrology into a concept of life that is meaningful to your client ...

"By any standards this is one of the most exciting and demanding works that natal astrologers are likely to meet. Demanding, because it 'calls for us to be creative with what we know,' and it is impossible not to get drawn into the weight of experience and knowledge that underlies every page....It is a great book from a great astrologer at the height of his maturity, and it simply pulsates with power. This is professional astrology of the highest calibre ....To read him is to read state of the art astrology. Yes, he does make us proud of where we stand as astrologers at the end of the millennium."

—Paul Newman
The Astrological Journal, London

• **Technique Supports Talent**   • **Tyl Supports You!**

SYNTHESIS & COUNSELING IN ASTROLOGY
The Professional Manual
by Noel Tyl

An articulate, creative, triple cross-referenced work, 1000-pages powerful, presenting techniques for psychodynamic analysis of the horoscope to enrich your skill and support your talent. Essential!

One of the keys to the successful practice of astrology is the art of synthesis, the capacity to take the disparate parts of our knowledge and combine them into a coherent whole. Many times, the parts may be contradictory (the relationship between Mars and Saturn, for example), but the art of synthesis manages the unification of opposites. Now Noel Tyl presents ways that astrological measurements—through creative synthesis—can be used to counsel individuals effectively. Discussion of these complex topics is grounded in concrete examples and in-depth analyses of 122 horoscopes, celebrities, politicians, and private clients.

Noel Tyl is the man who brought psycho-dynamic sensitivity into astrology 25 years ago. He has led the movement to bring the insights and techniques of modern psychology securely into astrological practice. Through his many books and lectures, Noel Tyl has had enormous influence upon the development of an entire generation of astrologers. *Synthesis & Counseling* is a masterpiece of modern astrology.

Tyl's objective in providing this vitally important material is to present the technique he has innovated and practiced over his distinguished career to provide the best possible resource to astrologers. In these nearly 1,000 pages, he has succeeded in creating a landmark text that has become a classic reference for professional astrologers. No professional astrologer's library should be without this incredible book.

Synthesis & Counseling In Astrology: The Professional Manual
1-56718-734-X, 924 pp., 7 x 10, 115 charts, softcover $29.95

PREDICTIONS FOR A
NEW MILLENNIUM

Noel Tyl

He predicted the exact dates of the Gulf War and the fall of the Soviet Union. Now Noel Tyl foresees key events, with 58 predictions about the dramatic political, economic, and social changes that will occur between now and the year 2012. *Predictions for a New Millennium* prepares us to see beyond the crisis of the moment to understand world changes strategically. Here are just a few of the momentous events that we will witness as we enter the 21st century: assassination of another U.S. president … China abandons communism … Saddam Hussein toppled from power … Hitler revival in Germany. The new millennium is a pivotal time in our history. How will these events affect the economy, the world powers … how will they affect you? The answers are here.

1-56718-737-4, 304 pp., 6 x 9, maps, graphs, index, softcover   **$14.95**

PREDICTION IN ASTROLOGY

Noel Tyl

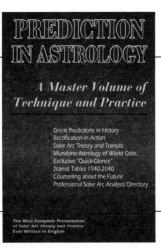

PREDICTION IN ASTROLOGY

A Master Volume of Technique and Practice

Great Predictions in History
Rectification in Action
Solar Arc Theory and Transits
Mundane Astrology of World Crisis
Exclusive "Quick-Glance"
Transit Tables 1940-2040
Counseling about the Future
Professional Solar Arc Analysis Directory

The Most Complete Presentation
of Solar Arc Theory and Practice
Ever Written in English

No matter how much you know about astrology already, no matter how much experience you've had to date, you'll be fascinated by *Prediction in Astrology,* and you'll grow as an astrologer. Using Solar Arc theory and methods he describes in this book, the author was able to accurately predict the Gulf War, including the actual date it would begin and the timetable of tactics, two months before it began. He also predicted the overturning of Communist rule in the Eastern bloc nations nine months in advance of its actual occurrence.

Tyl teaches through example. You learn by doing astrology, not just thinking about it. Tyl introduces Solar Arc theory in terms of "rapport" measurements, which you begin to do immediately, without paper, pencil, or computer, dials, or wheels. Just with your eyes! You will never look at a horoscope the same way again!

Tyl, in his well-known, very special way, also gets personal. He presents 30 Aphorisms, the keenest of maxims, the most practical of techniques, to create predictions from any horoscope. And as if this were not enough, Tyl then presents 20 Aphorisms for Counseling. Look for Tyl's "Quick-Glance" Transit Table, 1940-2040, to which you can refer more quickly than a computer. The busy astrologer will use this Appendix every day for many years to come.

0-87542-814-2, 360 pp., 6 x 9, softcover   **$17.95**

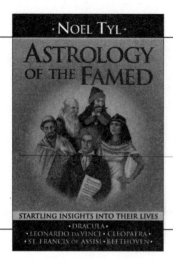

ASTROLOGY
OF THE FAMED
Startling Insights into
Their Lives

Edited by Noel Tyl

The lives of Cleopatra, Dracula, St. Francis of Assisi, Beethoven, and Leonardo da Vinci take on exciting new dimensions in this work by master astrologer Noel Tyl. History buffs and astrologers alike will be amazed at how he merges the technique of rectification with the adventure, genius, and drama of five of the most unique and provocative lives in all of history.

Astrologers use rectification when the birth date or time is not known accurately. They work backward and allow life events to determine the time of birth. To determine the birth year, date, and time for Cleopatra, for example, Tyl transplanted himself back to 69 B.C. and walked through her footsteps to translate her actions into a horoscope that symbolizes her life's events and her character.

And there is so much more to this book than rectification. There is good solid history and analysis of the personalities. Tyl then uses astrology to color in their motivations and mind-sets over the black-on-white historical facts.

1–56718–735–8, 384 pp., 6 x 9, softcover   **$19.95**

COMMUNICATING
THE HOROSCOPE

Edited by Noel Tyl

Help your clients reach personal fulfillment through thoughtful counseling! Each person's unique point of view is a badge of identification alerting you to what you should listen for in their consultation. The horoscope is a portrait of each person's perspective that the successful consultant will use to communicate and counsel clients more effectively.

Communicating the Horoscope presents the viewpoints of nine contributing astrologers on factors crucial to a client's successful analysis:

- One's Point of View: So Close to the Sun – Noel Tyl
- The Magic of the Consultation Moment – Christian Borup
- Creative Listening and Empathy – Haloli Q. Richter
- A Communication Model for Astrologers – Diana Stone
- Solving Problems: Key Questions to Ask Yourself and the Client – Donna Cunningham
- When the Client Avoids the Issue – Karen M. Hamaker-Zondag
- Bottom-Line Astrology – Susie Cox
- Telling Stories to Make Your Point – Jeff Jawer
- Working with Measurement, Memory and Myth – Wendy Ashley

ISBN: 1-56718-866-4, 256 pp., 6 x 9, charts, softcover $12.00

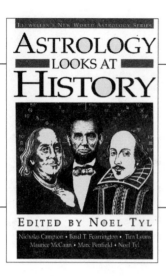

ASTROLOGY
LOOKS AT HISTORY

Noel Tyl

This book shows astrology performing at its very best through rectification (working backwards to determine someone's correct birthtime), capturing in astrological terms the fascinating lives of geniuses who have touched the development of the arts, sciences, and government in Western history. *Astrology Looks at History* reveals the details of personal development in the lives of 10 notables.

- Astrology times Nelson Mandela's past and future – Noel Tyl
- What do the Creation of the World, the horoscope of astrology and Jack the Ripper have in common? – Nicholas Campion
- Scholars are one day off on Shakespeare's birth; astrology closes the case … and establishes that he was murdered! – Maurice McCann
- Why such a powerful man named Machiavelli was so withdrawn, reclusive, and realistic – Basil T. Fearrington
- Astrology studies with keen historical grounding the many times lightning struck in the life of Benjamin Franklin – Tim Lyons
- Historical detail about Slavery, Jamestown, and Lincoln reveals a country in the making – Marc Penfield

1-56718-868-0, 464 pp., 6 x 9, 92 charts, softcover **$17.95**

Designed and typeset by Connie Hill
in Galliard and Futura typefaces.

Printed by Viking Press of Banta Corporation
Eden Prairie, Minnesota

minardi Salon